Yellow Smoke

Yellow Smoke

The Future of Land Warfare
for America's Military

Major General Robert H. Scales Jr.
(U.S. Army, Retired)

ROWMAN & LITTLEFIELD PUBLISHERS, INC.
Lanham • Boulder • New York • Oxford

ROWMAN & LITTLEFIELD PUBLISHERS, INC.

Published in the United States of America
by Rowman & Littlefield Publishers, Inc.
A Member of the Rowman & Littlefield Publishing Group
4720 Boston Way, Lanham, Maryland 20706
www.rowmanlittlefield.com

P.O. Box 317, Oxford OX2 9RU, United Kingdom

British Library Cataloguing in Publication Information Available

Library of Congress Cataloging-in-Publication Data

Scales, Robert H., 1944–
  Yellow smoke : the future of land warfare for America's military /
Robert H. Scales, Jr.
      p. cm.
Includes bibliographical references and index.
  ISBN 0-7425-1773-X (cloth : alk. paper)
  1. United States.—Armed Forces. 2. Military doctrine—United States.
3. World politics—21st century. I. Title.
  UA23 .S29497 2003
  355.02'0973—dc21

                                                    2002151037

Printed in the United States of America

♾™ The paper used in this publication meets the minimum requirements of
American National Standard for Information Sciences—Permanence of Paper
for Printed Library Materials, ANSI/NISO Z39.48-1992.

Every age has its own kind of war, its own limiting conditions, and its own preconceptions.

—Carl von Clausewitz

Contents

Preface: "Yellow Smoke"

*D*uring the fateful battles around Ap Bia Mountain in Vietnam—"Hamburger Hill" in soldier's parlance—I commanded a field artillery battery with the 101st Airborne. Over months of combat, the brigade that my battery supported came up with a curious way of recognizing those officers lucky enough to complete a tour in the vertical position. As a symbolic last gesture, a departing officer would toss a yellow-smoke grenade out of the helicopter as it lifted him away from the field and climbed above the jungle toward base camp and home. In October 1969, I said goodbye to my men as they stood on the pad at Firebase Bayonet, only a few miles from the Demilitarized Zone. Unfortunately, I had the bad judgment to hitch my last ride aboard the battalion commander's Huey. He was only a week into the job and had yet to internalize the lore of my brigade. He gave me one of those incredulous, unknowing looks as I began to unwrap the tape that held the spoon tight to the body of the "yellow smoke" I had been harboring in anticipation of just this moment. To this day, I regret having refrained and wonder what my haggard, hollow-eyed veterans thought as they witnessed a liftoff without the traditional gesture.

I consider this book a yellow smoke trailing my departure from active service, and I have looked forward to tossing it for some time. Unlike my previous works, it is a personal perspective, not a history. By intention, footnotes are few. Most of the views expressed are my own—or at least a distillation of thoughts, ideas, and concepts gathered personally from long association with a very special group of extraordinary colleagues. The full list of these intellectual fellow travelers is far too long to recount in detail here; a few, however, deserve special mention. My greatest debt is to the officers I recruited for the Army After Next project (AAN) between the fall of 1995 and the summer of 1997. I must make special mention of and offer sincere thanks to Colonel

(Ret.) Robert Killebrew, who served as my deputy and "soul mate" during the formative period of the AAN project. Colonel (Ret.) Michael Starry and Mr. Louis Napoleon were equally involved in the creation of the project. I owe the most to General (Ret.) William Hartzog. If our past divergences of view continue today, I know he will not agree with much of what I say here. Yet he has always been an officer who has gone the extra mile to encourage the diverse views of others and their public expression.

I owe an equal debt to a group of thinkers, both soldiers and civilians, who have sharpened and often shaped my perspective on future war. First among these is Colonel (Ret.) Richard Sinnreich—in my opinion the most gifted writer and thinker on future war. Brigadier General (Ret.) Huba Wass de Czege quite literally wrote the book on maneuver at the operational level of war; the fruits of many years of discussion between us on the subject are reflected in these pages. I was also privileged to learn the complexities of the Marine Corps vision of future war from Lieutenant General (Ret.) Paul Van Riper, one of the most insightful and keenest intellectuals ever to wear the Globe and Anchor.

During my time as Commandant of the Army War College, Professor Williamson Murray, formerly of Ohio State University, donated a year of his time to teaching me the lesson that the future course of military transformation is firmly rooted in the past. In the company of Len Fullencamp and Colonel Mike Methaney, Professor Murray also helped me to found another remarkable organization, the Advanced Strategic Art Program. The ASAP initiative was intended to be an honors seminar composed of the most brilliant and motivated students in each Army War College class. If the students of subsequent ASAP seminars prove to be as outstanding (and as intellectually unforgiving) as this first group, the concept will stand the test of time. These students, along with others—among them Colonels Dan Bolger and Dave Lamm—will see their values and vision reflected in the following pages.

I owe a special debt to Generals Donn Starry and Paul Gorman, who were the soul of the Army's last successful period of institutional transformation following Vietnam; they devoted their time and wisdom to sharpening and guiding our later efforts to replicate in some small measure the great creative leap ahead in the art of war that was AirLand Battle.

I must also thank General (Retired) Gordon R. Sullivan, President of the Association of the U. S. Army, and Colonel Scott R. Feil, Executive Director of the Program on the Role of American Military Power, for enthusiastically and generously supporting my effort to write and edit this volume.

The central thesis of this work maintains that America's new age of warfare began long before the fall of the Berlin Wall and the collapse of the Soviet

Union. Starting with Korea, this country found itself perched on the cusp of a new era of "limited" wars—wars fought for limited ends with equally limited means, the most limited of which was the latitude given to combat leaders to expend soldiers' lives. Practical experience gleaned in every active conflict since Korea has provided pieces for a puzzle which, when assembled, will clarify America's strategic direction and lead to the codification of a new and uniquely American way of fighting limited wars.

I had just finished an analysis of the war in Kosovo, the intended last piece of the limited war puzzle, when the fanatical followers of Osama bin Laden drove three pirated airliners into the Twin Towers of the World Trade Center and the Pentagon. The subsequent campaign to destroy the criminal forces responsible for killing so many innocent people not only overwhelmingly demonstrated the competence of American arms but also added another confirming piece to the thesis presented in this work: a perspective on ground warfare that argues for the creation of a balanced firepower and maneuver strike force, projected and employed principally in the air and capable of fighting and winning against ruthless and adaptive enemies of the sort this country will face in the new era of firepower-intensive, limited wars. This new force will exploit the advantages of superior knowledge and speed to collapse an enemy's centers of gravity before that enemy is able to disperse, hide, and "go to ground" in an effort to lessen the overwhelming killing power of American precision weaponry.

The nineteenth-century German military philosopher and theorist Carl von Clausewitz was the first to offer a holistic explanation of the character of human conflict. The thesis of his classic work, *On War*, states simply that "war is an act of force to compel our enemy to do our will." The object of war is to compel, and the means to achieve that end is force. While the specific means, the actual application of force, may change with the introduction of new technologies, the fundamental nature of war, Clausewitz argues, is immutable. War is not just about killing. It is the sanctioned use of violence to achieve a legitimate political objective. Wars cannot be divorced from political authority. Wars always take place within certain political, cultural, technological, economic, and geostrategic contexts. It would be disingenuous, therefore, for anyone to attempt to offer a convincing view of how wars will be fought in the future without attempting to anticipate the conditions—the "who, what, why, and where" of future conflict—as a necessary prologue to the "how." The first several chapters of this book therefore will attempt to describe generally what type of world our military forces will encounter as they attempt to compel a determined enemy to do our will on a battlefield of the future.

This is not to say that America must not give attention to lesser conflicts that involve engagements below the threshold of physical violence—even those conflicts arising in regions of the world of little strategic importance to the United States. Humanitarian efforts to lessen suffering and curtail regional unrest are both necessary and well within the capabilities of our military forces today. The longer and the more effectively the United States can keep conflicts simmering below the boiling point by engaging its military in lesser conflicts, the less likely it is that its power will have to be employed in an active role against an opponent who seeks to do serious harm. But American policy makers must be careful not to allow the necessary attention paid to lesser threats to weaken the ability of the United States to fight serious wars against competent opponents. The record of recent history clearly shows that the U.S. Army does peacekeeping, peace enforcement, and other such constabulary missions very well. No one who has visited our troops recently in the Sinai, Bosnia, Haiti, or Kosovo comes home with anything but praise for how well they perform.

Decades of practical experience demonstrate convincingly that the U.S. Army is good at peacekeeping because troops properly trained to fight full-scale war always perform well in less demanding contingencies. However, experience with the performance of troops thrown into combat in Korea, after years of constabulary service in Japan, suggests that the reverse does not apply. Very painful experience in the Korean War also amply reinforces the truth that, in this new age of limited warfare, the conduct of shooting wars is what the United States most often does least well.

There is a fortunate convergence between the concepts for fighting a serious war in the future that is discussed in this book and the suitability of these concepts for engaging in non-shooting constabulary missions such as peacekeeping. The abilities to command indirectly and to operate independently for long periods on dispersed battlefields located in distant and hostile regions are qualities that will be in demand in *both* stability operations and shooting wars. The case made here for the importance of high-performing small units carefully selected, trained, and bonded together to fight the close battle will also produce units superbly prepared to perform well in lesser conflicts. Likewise, the need for greater strategic, operational, and tactical mobility and agility—as well as the ability to see the battlefield with greater clarity and to strike with greater discretion and precision—will all be essential for the higher end of the peace enforcement mission.

The focus of this book is on land forces: the U.S. Army and the U.S. Marine Corps. The other four dimensions of war—air, sea, space, and information—are as integral to the thesis of the book, however, as they are to the conduct of war. Warfare on land is inexorably tied to and interdependent with the services that operate in other dimensions. While other services can speak about fighting wars exclusively in their own domains, the Army and the Marine Corps cannot. Land combat can be prosecuted only as part of a collective effort sustained principally by the firepower, transport, intelligence, communications, and logistics provided by air and naval forces. Therefore, while this is a book about landpower, much of it is concerned with how the currents of change will alter the way land forces must interrelate with the other elements of military power in order to maintain the dominance of American arms on a future joint battlefield.

Thus the purpose of this book is to look into the future to the depth of about half a generation in an effort to anticipate how changes in geopolitics, technology, and the domestic political scene will alter the character of shooting wars. Michael Howard, the military historian and theorist, once wrote that the object of studying the nature of war is not to get the future exactly right, but to avoid getting it exactly wrong. Howard understood what all soldiers know to be true: Those who proclaim to be able to anticipate the future course of war with scientific exactitude are doomed to be exactly wrong. With deference to Howard's wisdom, my hope is not to get it exactly right, but to avoid getting it terribly wrong. I will try to paint a picture of the future that is as clear as I can make it and as supportable as the evidence available today allows. My first task will be to describe and clarify the nature and character of the limited war environment that the U.S. Army will face in coming decades. I will then identify some lessons and insights from the laboratory of our recent experience with limited wars to demonstrate how the past can tell us a great deal about the future.

• 1 •

The Emergence
of an American Style of War

*E*very great power, over its respective span of influence, eventually evolves a style of war derived and personalized from the unique strategic and cultural circumstances that brought the country to greatness. In Alexander the Great's time, the phalanx of pike-wielding hoplites gave him a steady, reliable foundation of infantry around which to maneuver his cavalry with great confidence and decision. For nearly five hundred years, the flexible, facile legion provided the Romans with the ideal instrument for defeating a wide variety of enemies in many varied circumstances of climate and terrain. Napoleon perfected the division and corps structures as a means for creating a similarly flexible force from the masses of citizens soldiers drafted into his national army. The regimental system allowed the British Army to maintain dominance of a vast empire economically by using a mix of British and indigenous units stationed at home and overseas. The Germans achieved a stunning series of victories early in the Second World War by creating a balanced force of aerial and mechanized formations capable of breaking free of the tyranny of trench warfare to strike deep into the enemy's rear.

This particular view of history has a contemporary corollary. After the Second World War, a new "American age" of warfare began to emerge—completely unique and clearly distinguishable from the military systems of past great powers. The distinctive character of warfare in the American age emerged from the strategic and theoretical clutter of the great industrial-age total wars of the first half of the twentieth century. The searing experience of two global conflicts and the threat of a thermonuclear reprise served to fixate the attention of three generations of American military thinkers on preparing to fight another great war against another great power on the familiar battlefields of Europe. Too riveted a gaze on the European battlefield caused "cold

1

warriors" to overlook the less familiar but more relevant real war experience in less favorable environments and climates.

Only in the past decade have the post–Second World War, limited-war experiences in Asia and the Middle East come to be recognized as the incubators of a new and uniquely American style of war suited to winning smaller conflicts against lesser enemies for less than vital strategic ends. Limited wars fought for limited ends demand that the means offered to fight these conflicts be limited in proportion. First in Korea, later painfully in subsequent conflicts from Vietnam to the Gulf War, and most recently in Kosovo and Afghanistan, American military leaders deliberately modified their fighting methods to accommodate the imperative that wars must be won at "limited cost"—a cost measured principally in terms of the lives of their soldiers.

The most dramatic manifestation of this new imperative was the gradual appearance of an American warfighting doctrine that sought to trade firepower for manpower. During the early years of this transformation to a new style of firepower-intensive warfare, progress was painfully slow. In Korea and Vietnam, the American firepower system initially proved to be unresponsive, inefficient, and slow to change, giving the enemy time to adapt tactics to obviate its killing effects faster than the Americans could build up and perfect a system for delivering it. Toward the end of the Korean and Vietnamese conflicts, the enemy managed to reach a point of stasis where his ability to seek cover, disperse, hide, and deceive balanced American ability to find, track, and pile on explosive killing power.

After Vietnam, the fortuitous development of revolutionary information and precision technologies gave the U.S. military a means to overcome past inefficiencies and, in the process, radically alter the balance between protection and killing power in favor of the latter. The adaptation of laser technology, and later of global positioning technologies, to delivering killing power, principally from the air, increased by two orders of magnitude the probability of an air-delivered munition killing a target. The new American way of war was born of the premise that technology could kill the enemy faster than the enemy could find the means to offset this overwhelming advantage in information and precision. It should come as no surprise, therefore, that the services responsible for delivering aerial killing power, the U.S. Air Force and the U.S. Navy, would be the first to perfect and codify a firepower-centered doctrine tailored specifically for fighting limited wars. Both services eventually accepted the concession that, in this new type of war, aerial combat would be directed almost exclusively against ground rather than air and sea targets.

While the air services have had the luxury of leveraging firsthand experience to evolve a satisfactory doctrine for attacking ground targets, the ground services continue to struggle to divine a fighting method that adequately accommodates the realities of this new era of firepower-centered warfare. Fifty years of war experience from Korea to Afghanistan have, however, begun to yield a wealth of evidence and insights that will allow the emergence of a ground warfare corollary to the proven doctrine for the employment of air forces in this new era of limited wars. The evidence that I present to make the argument for a new ground warfare doctrine is derived partly from a study of recent limited wars and in part from my own experiences gained while both observing and participating in the U.S. Army's efforts to come to grips with the new realities that are beginning to alter the way American ground forces fight.

EYEWITNESS TO TRANSFORMATION

For the past decade, I have had the privilege of spending most of my time as a general officer in assignments that allowed, at times even demanded, that I reflect, write, and speak on the subject of the art and strategy of future warfare. I have also had the great fortune to be involved in shaping, and to participate in, most of the U.S. Army's post–Cold War efforts to transform itself from an industrial-age to an information-age army. Some of the details and observations of my experience in this period of transformation serve as a metaphor and a catalyst useful for understanding the character of the challenges confronting the U.S. Army as it continues along this difficult path to transformation.

For my first assignment as a general, I was selected to put together a team of very talented officers to research and write the U.S. Army's official history of the Gulf War, *Certain Victory*. The Gulf War happened to fall between two epochs: the fading machine age and the newly emerging information age. Consequently, the conflict had about it the characteristics of both periods. In our study, we found evidence to suggest that European machine-age methods of war were still relevant and effective. The campaign began with a massive, methodical buildup of logistical infrastructure reminiscent of the American staging operations in the United Kingdom prior to D-Day in the Second World War. The buildup was followed by an enormous aerial firepower onslaught intended to weaken the will of Iraq's leadership and the war-making capability of its military—also reminiscent of the effort by British and American airpower to isolate the beachhead prior to the Allied amphibious landings in Normandy. The Gulf conflict culminated with a mechanized war of movement reminiscent of the great tank battles of the Eastern front in the Second World War.

We also found evidence in our study that new information technologies had substantially altered the character of the Gulf War. Laser-guided weapons had made an appearance in Vietnam and proved to be extremely effective at striking fixed objects, such as bridges and buildings. But the enormously greater success of these weapons, when matched with space-based sensors, seemed to us to be a certain indicator that we were entering nothing less than a new precision age in warfare. We could see then that the time was not far off when precision technology would permit us to strike any target on the surface of the earth with greater than one-meter accuracy.

We learned new lessons about the value of operational and tactical speed on the battlefield. The U.S. Army pioneered the use of aerial maneuver using helicopter-borne infantry in Vietnam. The dramatically more impressive performance of a new generation of helicopters and air assault doctrine took the Vietnam-era concepts to a new level of effectiveness in the Gulf. In Vietnam, the 101st Airborne Division could move a battalion only a few miles into enemy territory and sustain it for only a short time. In the Gulf War, that same division moved multiple brigades hundreds of miles behind enemy lines and was prepared to sustain them for weeks if necessary. A Vietnam-era airmobile unit could fight effectively only against a lightly armed dismounted foe. A Gulf War air assault unit, thanks to the availability of attack helicopters firing laser-guided precision weapons, possessed some capability to destroy modern armored vehicles. Unfortunately, once deposited on the ground, heliborne units lacked the ground mobility, protection, and logistical staying power to take on large armored formations in open warfare.

The subsequent escape of most of the Iraqi Republican Guard back into Iraq at the end of the campaign reinforced a classic lesson of land warfare: To be assured of a decisive effect—that is, the total disintegration of the enemy—the attacker should possess a significant advantage in speed of maneuver over the defender. If the relative speeds are the same, the defender can avoid collapse and defeat by disengaging and running away. During the ground phase of the campaign, aerial interdiction was helpful in delaying withdrawal and in causing some damage, but without a force blocking its path, the Republican Guard was free to continue to seek sanctuary inside Iraq.

In the course of our study, we asked ourselves what the consequences would have been had aerial maneuver units such as the 101st Airborne (with its quantum advantage in operational speed offered by the helicopter) also possessed the ability to fight armored formations on equal terms. Would we not then have been able to lift the division deep across the Basra-to-Baghdad highway and to destroy the Guard as it attempted to escape?

I left the Desert Storm Study Project with a certain sense of unease. I was uncomfortable with the stridency and authority of some of our conclusions. Not only were we at times hasty with our opinions, but we believed that lessons derived from any war fought against a less competent enemy must always remain suspect. Everything seemed to work too well in the Gulf. It was as if the experience of a pre-season scrimmage with a college team were sufficient to prepare an NFL team for the Superbowl. We suspected that perhaps the size and strategic importance of the Gulf War, coming so quickly after the U.S. victory in Panama, may have eclipsed in the public eye a smaller war that was perhaps a more relevant analog of the nature of wars to come. Had we allowed our experience in Panama to drift into the shadows of contemporary analysis too quickly after Saddam Hussein became the centerpiece of our attention? We were not sure.

Between the fall of 1995 and the summer of 1997, I led a remarkable organization charged by the U.S. Army Chief of Staff to delve into the very distant future in order to postulate the course of warfare. This Army After Next (AAN) investigation has stimulated a rich intellectual debate within the defense community. It differed considerably in scope, period, methodology, and focus from similar future-gazing efforts by the U.S. Army and other services. We chose a far more distant perch, the years 2020–30, so as to move comfortably beyond the acrimony usually associated with debates over existing or near-term programs and budgets.

Our study of history seemed to confirm that every revolution in the nature of warfare—whether political, economic, or military—unfolds in evolutionary steps. Generally at least half a generation, about 15 years, is required for vision and ideas to mature into secure and irreversible change. It likewise takes about that long to "grow" a battalion commander or platoon sergeant— or to develop, test, and field major systems. It may take even longer to truly alter the institutional culture sufficiently to internalize revolutionary change. General William DePuy (when he was commander of Training and Doctrine Command, the Army's principal agent of change) once said prophetically, "Change doesn't occur until fifty-one percent of the officer corps believes in it." The post–Desert Storm U.S. Army found itself very much a fellow traveler in a grander societal revolution. Global institutions and cultures were busy shifting from the industrial age to the information age. The Army had a foot firmly planted in both. Materiel and structures developed in the era of the recent past had to be either modified or replaced to prepare for conflict in the information age. Thus a focus comfortably beyond 2010 would give us the perspective necessary to forecast what new structures and materiel the Army will need in the next major wartime encounter.

Initially, AAN studies and gaming focused on the strategic level of war. This proved to be an enormous cultural shift for a service that takes great pride in having brought about a renaissance in the art of war at the operational level with the development of AirLand Battle doctrine during the waning days of the Cold War. But the secure strategic anchors of the Cold War as manifested by the great global war plans had been wrenched from their moorings by the time the Berlin Wall fell. To our minds, the post–Cold War Army needed to reset its strategic moorings and derive a clear understanding of its strategic relevance to America's future national policy before it could reasonably be expected to devise a new operational method for fighting on land.

We committed ourselves to testing our hypotheses about the future in a rigorous synthetic environment of force-on-force, computer-driven, free-play wargames. These were very elaborate and complex affairs conducted at the Army War College and elsewhere; they often involved hundreds of players, gamers, and observers, as well as some of the most sophisticated gaming and simulation models and facilities available in the world. We made sure that our "virtual" enemy was competent and credible. We selected the most diabolical and imaginative enemy leaders we could imagine. They were free to engage us using any style of war consistent with the culture, means, and national strategic ends of the contending state. Often our AAN battle force did not do well against such competent opposition, but the experience convinced us that we were pursuing a meaningful course whenever we beat him "clean and fair."

Each exercise would be followed by a period of validation and reassessment conducted by a cadre of scientists and operational artists charged with refining our hypotheses and developing a new set of structural and doctrinal parameters for the next yearly gaming cycle. The process of validation and assessment was iterative and dialectical. We began the gaming virtually unconstrained. For instance, during the first wargame, we assumed that in 2030 we would have the capability to deploy a close-combat battle force consisting of about 5,000 soldiers directly from the continental United States into a distant (and usually primitive) theater of war ready to fight immediately upon arrival. While such a capability fit the requirements of our national strategy, scientists in our group determined that such a capability was neither affordable nor technically practicable by 2030. Therefore, for the next iteration of games, we were obliged to alter our strategic projection scheme by inserting an intermediate staging base within operational reach of the battle area.

Technical changes demanded doctrinal changes. Adding an intermediate base slowed the rate of closure. But it also opened the prospect of exposing the base to the enemy's weapons of mass destruction delivered by long-range cruise and ballistic missiles. These changes in premise demanded substantial changes to our postulated doctrine and caused us to search out other technical solutions to accommodate these new variables in our warfighting equation. After several more experimental iterations, we developed an operational concept along with structural and materiel requirements to allow this new style of war to be successfully prosecuted on some future battlefield. We concluded that successful operational maneuver from a staging base to the area of operations required the use of an aerial vehicle capable of transporting ground forces to distances of up to about 600 miles.

Recent history, particularly in Afghanistan, seems to have validated our conclusions. Reliance on intermediate staging bases in Uzbekistan and offshore aboard aircraft carriers as well as the time-distance factors and the number of troops deployed inside operational areas in Afghanistan proved to be virtually identical to those we had postulated for campaigns in similar regions of the world during our AAN simulations.

Another remarkable confluence of game and actual war experience occurred when we sought during the AAN games to find the best technological solution to the perplexing problem of "dwell time." We discovered that our virtual enemies in 2030 would seek to avoid the killing power of American precision munitions by dispersing their forces and by constantly moving about the battlefield. Our efforts to defeat these tactics using contemporary firepower systems and methods proved frustratingly ineffective. The problem was time. So much time was consumed processing target information, deciding how to engage the target, and then waiting for the weapon to arrive from some distant platform that an agile enemy had plenty of time to perform his mission and disperse. Our scientific advisors concluded that the only practical solution to the problem was to station the launch platforms directly over the target and directly under the immediate control of close-combat forces in contact with the enemy. We postulated that such an environment would be too hazardous for manned aircraft in 2030, so we placed precision weapons aboard large unmanned aircraft stationed miles overhead—some in the stratosphere, some in space. The image of high-flying B-52s launching precision weapons at Taliban positions at the command of Special Forces soldiers in contact reminded us that the technologies that separate these two solutions to the "dwell time" problem might have been decades apart, but the problem and its conceptual solution were virtually identical.

From the moment we began our study, we were struck by the degree to which U.S. experience in the Gulf War had come to monopolize thought about the future course of warfare. To be sure, practical firsthand experience exerts a powerful influence on the leadership of any profession—particularly if that experience brings with it the self-congratulatory fulfillment of success in battle. Throughout the history of warfare, armies that have viewed themselves as successful in the contemporary practice of war have tended to be very reluctant to pay much attention to the experience of others, or to put much credence in the abstract notions of military theory. In peacetime, the practical present tends to trump the theoretical future even when cataclysmic shifts in conditions make the experience of the practical present irrelevant or obsolete.

Arrogance also played a role in sustaining U.S. myopia. Americans had a propensity then (and still do to some degree) to assume that the possession of overwhelming military power carries with it a monopoly on wisdom. How quickly had so many within the defense community who had not witnessed Vietnam firsthand forgotten that relative physical strength and technological sophistication have little to do with the ability of a state, or state-like power, to understand and anticipate changes in the art of war. While directing the AAN project, I traveled overseas frequently with the mission of sampling opinions about the future with as many foreign militaries as our budget would allow. I concentrated principally on the periphery of the shell of topography that circumscribes the outline of Asia, the Middle East, and Western Europe—where I knew I would find the most intellectually active group of soldiers from armies likely to be either allies or competitors in the future.

Secure on their own turf, the officers I met were remarkably candid and eager to exchange ideas and express opinions. Collectively, they all shared a remarkably consistent and realistic view of the strengths and weaknesses of U.S. military power. They were uniformly impressed with the technological prowess demonstrated by the United States during the Gulf War. The media images of "smart bombs" systematically taking apart the main forces of the Iraqi war machine left a perhaps more indelible mark on their armies than they did on ours. Yet these senior officers and academics were also quick to pick up on what they perceived as weaknesses in the American military method. They remarked almost universally on our sensitivity to casualties—a sensitivity that further intensified after the killing of eighteen Rangers prompted our withdrawal from Somalia.

One very senior official from a large Southwest Asian country expressed the sentiment of many of his peers when he commented that we Americans have about us a curious passive-aggressive nature. He noted that we are a nation slow to anger and reluctant to become involved in the affairs of others. Our general ambivalence often gives regional aggressors the impression that they can pursue their own intentions without interference from us, or that they can threaten our welfare from afar without fearing serious retaliation. All too often, however, our ambivalence is taken for neglect, and the result at times has been serious strategic miscalculation on both sides. We suddenly reverse ourselves and, fueled with outrage, are prone to intervene in some distant theater with unexpected vengeance at inopportune times and for seemingly illogical reasons. To this officer, it seemed that we break through this "strategic glass ceiling" only when the confluence of public outrage meets the perception that a terrible injustice has been done. The greatest strategic blunder when confronting the United States in the future, he concluded, would be to violate American territory with acts of violence. Getting blamed for a terrorist attack on the homeland would be the surest way to bring on this so-called Pearl Harbor effect. The wisdom of our military peers haunted me years later as I watched the terrorists of Osama bin Laden sheltered by the sham rulers of Afghanistan attack the heart of America.

In the spring of 1997, I spent some time observing the U.S. Army's Advanced Warfighting Experiment (AWE) then being conducted at the National Training Center in California. The AWE was the Army's first effort to use a live simulation to gain some insights into how the information revolution would influence the conduct of land warfare at the tactical level. The process of changing how an army fights usually begins with the development of theories that postulate how external variables such as technology and changes in geostrategic conditions will influence the nature of warfare. This theoretical first phase in the creative process, while often controversial, is usually devoid of political and practical obstruction; this is because mere writing and public debate do not threaten weapons-development programs or the sanctity of established structures and institutions. Moreover, thinking about war is cheap. Serious institutional and political resistance to change does not begin to solidify until ideas and concepts are translated into some form of tangible action, such as experimentation with real forces. Thus the experimental phase of the change process is the one most likely to end with frustration, failure, and the pursuit of false prophets.

The AWE was not the first occasion that Western militaries have had to deal with the challenges of experimentation during periods of seismic shifts in the technology of war. During the period between the two world wars, France, Britain, Russia, and Germany accepted the fact that mechanization would in some way affect the course of warfare. In the late 1920s and the early 1930s, they all conducted field experiments to determine the influence that mechanization would have on the course of war. Credit for much of the early theoretical development of mechanized warfare belongs to British military theorists such as B. H. Liddell Hart and J. F. C. Fuller. A few farseeing reformers in the British military hierarchy were willing to accept some of the tenets of mechanized warfare put forward in the popular press by Liddell Hart and Fuller. But the practical concerns of an army focused on fighting limited wars within the British empire, combined with the inherent conservatism of the Imperial General Staff, created just enough resistance to stifle and eventually crush efforts at legitimate reform.

The death of doctrinal reform in Great Britain occurred on the maneuver ground at Salisbury Plain. Political interference and the reaction of an often hostile media allowed the results of the experiments with armored forces to be interpreted in light of the preconceptions and biases of conservative military and civilian leaders. All the lessons were there to be seen. The British Army and its supporters in Parliament and the media simply chose not to see them.

Similarly, the doctrine of the "methodical battle"—inherited from experience in the trenches of the First World War—was so deeply imbedded in the psyche of the French Army that experiments with armored formations failed to convince it that mechanization would fundamentally change the nature of land warfare. In one of the great, tragic ironies of modern military history, the French Army—the largest, richest, and most respected army during the period between the two world wars—spent its energy and its wealth on an obsolete concept of war kept alive and perpetuated by firsthand experience inherited from a past war that technology had long since rendered irrelevant.

The principal variable evaluated in the AWE exercises was "dominant situational awareness." An otherwise traditional armored brigade was "digitized" with an assortment of off-the-shelf computers and sensors and then linked via a tactical internet to create the field version of a local area network. The tactical intent was to allow every soldier in the formation to know his location and that of his buddies exactly, as well as to have a fairly precise picture of the position of the enemy. Soldiers could be in constant contact with each other and know the commander's decisions and orders in real time. The Army's senior leadership accepted the hypothesis that "situational awareness" would alter the shape and nature of the battlefield and thus have a profound influence on the course of future warfare. In past wars, the size of a combat formation was determined principally by the need to maintain cohesion and control. The closer soldiers were together, the easier they were to order about the battlefield. Virtual contact via the Internet allowed these physical connections to be severed and the maneuver to be shaped solely by tactical considerations.

A decided advantage in knowledge allowed the brigade formation to open up and spread out. Distances between individual fighting elements were limited only by the range limits of individual weapons. Freed from the need to maintain visual contact, the digitized brigade footprint expanded by a factor of four or more. As the brigade dispersed to those distances, commanders saw immediately that the shape and form of maneuver was changing. Linear formations began to break apart, and close combat became less structural and more organic in appearance. The ability to see the enemy from greater distances allowed the more clever commanders to engage the enemy at greater distances. The close fight was becoming less close. We could see that situational awareness clearly gave to precision warfare what it lacked most: the ability to sense, identify, and locate targets with precision equal to that of the precision of the weapons.

The field experiments conducted at Ft. Irwin validated on the ground the phenomenon that we had observed virtually during a series of computerized Army After Next (AAN) wargames conducted at Ft. Leavenworth in the fall of the previous year. These experiments sought to measure empirically the effect of information dominance and situational awareness on the dynamics of combat at the tactical level. The AAN team built a free-play, force-on-force simulation that varied the amount and quality of battlefield information given to each of the contending sides.

While the results were very tentative and the methods used relatively crude, we did observe some remarkable consistencies of action and behavior that seemed to confirm the conclusion that, as the relative differential in knowledge increases between opposing forces, the battlefield behavior of both changes considerably. During the games, the side with a marginal information advantage of about two to one maneuvered with greater confidence and managed to anticipate the enemy's movements effectively, placing them consistently "inside the decision cycle" of the side with the information deficit. Yet the pattern of maneuver and the geometry and densities of forces on the battlefield remained doctrinally correct and consistent with patterns of maneuver similar to those practiced during Desert Storm in the Gulf War. However, when the information advantage increased by a factor of four or better, the velocities of maneuver increased arithmetically, and formations began to spread out and disperse to the point where familiar linear battlefield geometry disappeared. Freed from the need to fight in lines, the game players consistently swept tactical units across vast distances without regard to fronts or flanks. As a consequence, the tempo of battle accelerated considerably. Engagements that normally took days to culminate were over in hours. As time compressed, the size of the battlefield expanded—in some cases as much as an order of magnitude or more over conventional mechanized warfare.

During the AWE, we discovered that young X-generation soldiers raised in a world of computer games trusted the icons and believed what they saw on the screen. Many of their seniors were not so comfortable. Those of us who spent our professional lives learning to fight linear warfare thought in linear terms and followed linear, sequential processes of command. Younger officers in the command posts often grew frustrated with their superiors, who demanded eyes-on verification of enemy activity discovered by remote sensors. The younger officers preferred to act immediately on what the screen was telling them; their commanders, in contrast, preferred to act by following staff processes which, when completed, often produced excellent plans to accommodate situations that no longer existed.

The near-perfect connectivity offered by the tactical Internet proved to be too great a temptation for those commanders inclined to micro-manage the battle. The ability to loiter virtually over the battlefield became an information-age corollary to the Vietnam-era battalion commanders who could not resist the temptation to circle over every platoon in contact and direct the firefight from 3,000 feet. Some observers thought that perfect connectivity might make over-control a virtue rather than a vice. The experience of the AWE taught the opposite lesson. Able to see everything moving in real time on a display panel, commanders with micro-managerial instincts found that they could intercede directly in all their subordinates' decisions. But, even when aided by exceptional access to information, such commanders inevitably failed; this was so simply because they were unable to appreciate that close combat is too chaotic, fast-moving, and unpredictable to be managed by a single hand.

War is quantum, not Newtonian, physics. As soon as a micro-manager intervenes to alter conditions in one small piece of the battlefield, his decision changes the conditions in all other areas under his influence. Too many things happen too quickly to allow a commander to over-centralize. While he may be able to see the battle with great clarity, he will inevitably lose control as he finds himself bombarded with detail and consumed with the task of making an endless series of decisions concerning tactical and administrative minutiae. The enemy may see and know less, but, unencumbered with detail, may well be able to make the critical decisions that will alter the course of battle faster than his overburdened opponent. Perfect situational awareness is no good to a commander if he does not trust his subordinates to act on his intent in order to make the multitude of spontaneous adjustments necessary to ensure that each piece of the clockwork mechanism of the battlefield is synchronized and in harmony with the others. A commander of the future blessed with the advantage of superior situational awareness is much like a conductor blessed with perfect pitch and the ability to play every instrument in the orchestra.

A popular anecdote, perhaps apocryphal, told to me by a few of the junior officers who participated in one AWE rotation illustrates the point and highlights the greater challenge of fighting in the information age. Early in the battle, the operations display in the command center clearly showed the enemy force turning in column and swinging south toward the brigade's southern or left flank. Delighted with the obvious advantage and smelling victory, the young staff officers eagerly ushered the brigade commander in to see for himself. Their hearts sank when the commander ordered out his ground scouts to verify the sighting and put his staff to work to come up with scripted alternatives to respond. The outcome was predictable: The enemy spotted the scouts, realized that his maneuver was compromised by the real-time sensor feeds, and changed his attack to the opposite flank. Meanwhile, watching in horror as the enemy changed directions, the brigade staff continued to drill on three alternatives perfectly suited to win a battle on a flank no longer threatened.

The story highlights the truism that the most serious challenge of information-age warfare involves *people*, not technology. The advantage of dominant situational awareness gives commanders the perfect instrument to lead indirectly—to command effectively from a distance. But indirect leadership requires the ability to think in real time and influence the battle by intent rather than directly by touch. Soldiers are trained today to lead directly. We reward the "action officer" who deals with the certainty of daily life in the Army. He is the one who gets things done, the "can do, go to" guy we have all come to rely on to fix immediate problems and keep the organization operating efficiently. Increasingly, however, our experience in recent wars and exercises tells us that we need indirect leadership skills at lower and lower levels if we are to get the most from a battlefield dominated by information. Indirect leaders are as educated in the art of war at the strategic and operational levels as they are trained in processes and rules at the tactical level. Time dedicated to understanding the higher orders of conflict inculcates mental agility and the ability to be creative as well as technically competent. A well-read and -educated leader will be better prepared to deal with the uncertainty and chaos of combat.

We did find commanders who thrived during the AWE. They seemed to know intuitively how to adapt and improvise in the heat of battle. They demonstrated a refreshing style of indirect leadership that fit this new style of distributed, non-linear warfare perfectly. In very short order, these very exceptional officers became comfortable with what they saw on the digital displays. They developed the ability to deal with complex information by mentally filtering out detail and focusing on the keys, the electronic hints, that told them what the enemy was intending to do rather than focusing on what he had already done.

The problem was that we were unable intuitively to predict who these leaders were before they proved themselves during the AWE. Most of the traditional indicators of performance seemed to fail us. Smart, charismatic, efficient, physically fit leaders were not necessarily those who proved able to deal with the complexities of modern battle. Only exposure to the simulated battlefield environment of the AWE allowed us to identify those with the "right stuff" of information-age warfare. But experiments are expensive and not intended to be platforms for identifying and acculturating leaders to the new realities of the information battlefield. Learning to fight by fighting has been an unfortunate characteristic of many previous American wars. In the future, the American people will not tolerate using the experience of real combat to weed out bad leaders. Nor will they tolerate expending soldiers' lives to educate the better ones in the art of indirect leadership. The challenge, then, is to select those leaders best qualified to lead indirectly and then educate them properly before the real test of war begins.

Reactions to the AWE were interesting. Some, particularly those in the media, saw only what looked to be another overly expensive National Training Center exercise in which the digitized force lost as many engagements as it won. Others saw beyond the issue of "who won" and realized that the AWE substantially proved the hypothesis that the information revolution had begun to usher in a new age of warfare. Among my AAN colleagues, the "what ifs" came forth in abundance. But one observation in particular captured our attention: Consistently, the pace of ground movement by mechanized forces was not fast enough to fully exploit the speed of decision making offered by dominant situational awareness. What if, they asked, the speed and agility of decision making and precision of observation that we witnessed in digitized units could be matched with a concomitant increase in the speed and agility of movement about the battlefield, perhaps by air rather than by ground?

In the spring of 1999, General Wesley Clark invited me to observe the Kosovo campaign from his headquarters in Belgium. It was a time when NATO was engrossed in the process of deciding whether or not to release ground forces for an invasion of Serbia and Kosovo. From that experience, I learned firsthand that, in spite of the advantages offered by the sciences to modern war, once the dogs of war are unleashed and the shooting begins in earnest, conflicts tend to follow unpredictable courses. As Clausewitz warned many times, wars are contests between two active, willing opponents both of whom expect to win.[1] Thus an action by one side to gain advantage precipitates a response by the opponent to counter it. Once begun, war, with its neatly crafted plans and comforting expectations, quickly devolves into a series of stratagems and counter-stratagems by both sides as each seeks to retain advantage on the battlefield long enough to gain a decisive end by collapsing the enemy's will to resist.

Despite its video-game image, NATO's campaign against the Serbs proved to be no exception to the classic Clausewitz construct. The Serbs sought to overcome a tremendous materiel and technological disadvantage by capitalizing on their own strengths: their ability to gain operational objectives quickly and then disperse in order to avoid the inevitable aerial assault they knew would follow. They trusted that patience, tenacity, guile, and the ability to sequester ground forces throughout the countryside would give them the interval needed to wait out the resolve of the NATO coalition. The plan did not work. In the end, the political will of the NATO coalition proved to be stronger. But the skill and perseverance of the Serbian Army in the face of an overwhelming onslaught by a thousand or more NATO aircraft armed with precision weapons presents us with a compelling demonstration of a thinking, creative, and adaptive opponent who can foil the best-prepared plans of a superior opponent simply by capitalizing on his own inherent strengths while minimizing those of the opposition.

For the last fifty years, the militaries of the Western powers, and particularly of the United States, have been remarkably consistent in how they have chosen to go to war. They have inherited the ability to translate technological innovation, industrial capacity, and national wealth into effective battlefield advantage. In this new era of limited wars, however, America's measured commitment to fight for limited ends automatically imposes a limit on the means available to achieve those ends. The lives of soldiers have become our most precious resource, and we increasingly seek to develop a method of war that will replace manpower expenditures with an ever-multiplying expenditure of firepower.

As I witnessed in Kosovo, however, and as I learned firsthand from the wisdom of officers of foreign armies, our future enemies are watching. They understand the American preoccupation with firepower. Therefore we should not be surprised when we encounter a future opponent who has learned how to nullify our firepower advantage. We have consistently been slow to perceive the growing effectiveness of the opposition in part because of a characteristic Western arrogance: the presumption that, to be a challenge, non-Western militaries must either symmetrically challenge us or mimic Western ways of war. Consequently, the growing skill among non-Western militaries at countering our firepower-centered method of war has remained shrouded in the shadows of unfamiliar military cultures. In part due to the cultural schism that divides the world's advanced industrial democracies from the other four-fifths of the planet, U.S. military analysts have missed much of the discourse and experimentation taking place in non-Western military institutions.

As threads of historical continuity move the story of combat actions in limited wars away from Korea and Vietnam and closer to Kosovo and Afghanistan, we will begin to see the outline of a style of firepower-intensive warfare whose character and pattern is becoming increasingly and distinctly American. The recent media images of American bombers discharging precision-guided missiles against a primitive enemy huddling in bunker complexes far below serve to illustrate the truism that continued American success in future limited wars will depend in large measure on the ability of American ingenuity, inventiveness, and industrial capacity to offset a determined enemy's efforts to reduce or eliminate our firepower advantage by exploiting his own advantages of mass, will, and the ability to adapt on the battlefield.

America will remain dependent on its ability to continue to develop the technical means for substituting killing power for manpower. But the conduct of war still remains as much art as science. Therefore the challenge for the future will be to ensure that we seek to understand how patterns of warfare will themselves be altered by technology even as we seek to exploit the advantages that technical advances in the science of war will offer in the decades to come.

NOTE

1. Carl von Clausewitz, *On War*, edited and translated by Michael Howard and Peter Peret (Princeton: Princeton University Press, 1976).

• 2 •

Technology and the Cycles of Land Warfare

The cycles and patterns of war, like practically all of the currents of change in the modern age, have been most influenced by advancements in technology. The expansion of pure science—exploited by inventiveness and expanded by industry—has served to advance the pace of change in the science of war more in the past century than in all other epochs of history. Since the beginning of the machine age in the nineteenth century, this frenetic acceleration of technological advancement has compressed the interval and stretched the amplitude of the cycles of change in warfare. The pace of technical infusion has been so extraordinary that, during the past century and a half, the world has painfully experienced no fewer than two complete cycles of transformation in the art of war. The evidence is compelling that another cycle induced by the arrival of the information age has already begun. Each cyclical rotation has profoundly changed the dynamics of the battlefield, which in turn has equally profoundly changed how military forces fight.

While the forces compelling and sustaining change have been complex, advancements in only a few technologies were responsible for launching each cycle of change. Technology began to dominate patterns of change in warfare with the rise of industrial production and the appearance of precision war-making machinery like rifled weapons. The range and precision of the small bore repeating rifle, the machine gun, and quick-firing artillery initiated this first cycle of change—in effect the first "precision revolution" in warfare. The combined influence of lethality, mass, and range created a battlefield dominated by the killing effects of firepower. The carnage that all belligerents suffered in the First World War taught the lesson that the Americans had already learned in the Civil War: A battlefield dominated by firepower always favors the defensive and inevitably compels the opponents, however reluctantly, to adopt a method of warfare based on attrition.

MOBILITY DOMINATES AND THE CYCLE TURNS

Before the slaughter ended on the Western front in 1918, military professionals on both sides of "no man's land," or "the killing zone," sought to solve the tactical and operational dilemmas imposed by the dominance of precision firepower. The tactical, close-combat problem was to find a way to cross the killing zone relatively intact and capable of continuing the fight. The larger-scale, operational problem was to make a crossing of the killing zone decisive. The classic role of an operational maneuver force is to achieve a quick and overwhelming victory by approaching the enemy indirectly, bypassing his powerful extremities, and attacking his brain. A maneuver of this magnitude and complexity will succeed only if the operational instrument possesses a substantial advantage in agility and speed and the ability to strike deep within enemy territory with enough combat power remaining to fight and win on arrival.

The conceptual solution to the problem of restoring the capability to conduct rapid and decisive maneuver first came to the Germans near the end of the First World War, and it was deceptively simple: Short, highly intensive doses of firepower to prepare the assault; small, mobile units to quickly exploit the shock effect of firepower for infiltrating and bypassing centers of resistance; and operational formations sufficiently mobile, long-ranging, and independent to move through exposed points of weakness to push deep into the enemy's rear. The initial success of the German Army's storm-troop tactics in the 1918 spring offensive convinced the Germans that they had found the doctrinal solution for restoring mobility to the battlefield. The failure of the offensive to achieve decisive results convinced them that, in the future, they would have to develop materiel and technologies to make the most of this new tactical and operational fighting method.

During the First World War, two commercial inventions, the gasoline engine and the vacuum tube, were adapted to warfare and sparked the development of armored vehicles and aircraft. Only after the war, however, did revolutionary improvements in the performance of tanks and aircraft make possible a quantum increase in speed across and over the battlefield sufficient to conduct decisive operational maneuver. The dominance of precision technologies that favored the defensive surrendered to new technologies that enhanced the speed, mobility, and agility of air and ground forces. This remarkable graft of practical science to a tactical concept turned the cycle of war for a second time and shifted advantage on the battlefield from the defensive to the offensive. Large units could now dash great distances into the enemy's rear to strike at his brain while avoiding his powerful extremities. The object of mechanized warfare, or *blitzkrieg*, became the collapse of an enemy's will to resist. Victory was gained through psychological paralysis induced by movement rather than through butchery by massive applications of firepower. Continued refinements in propulsion and communications technologies would guarantee the dominance of the offensive from the Polish campaign in the Second World War to operation Desert Storm in the Gulf War.

But the history of mechanization in the years between the two world wars also carries with it a caution. After experiencing the horrors of the Western front, all Western powers were committed to developing the technologies capable of restoring mobility to the battlefield. They were well aware of which technologies showed the greatest promise. Professional journals of the period were rich with insights and theories on the use of aircraft and motorized vehicles. France, Germany, Russia, and the United States all developed first-rate aircraft and armored vehicles and conducted experiments with mechanization during the interwar years. But only the Germans were able to refine a method of war, *blitzkrieg*, that fully leveraged the technological potential of tanks and tactical aircraft. The Germans succeeded where the Allies failed in large measure because they took the time to scrupulously assess their wartime experiences in order to form a clear and realistic picture of what mobile warfare would be like. They then translated their vision into operational principles and concepts long before they started to build machines and organize units. Concepts came first. As the French and British learned to their dismay during the early battles of the Second World War, if the vision and the concepts are wrong, adding resources simply compounds the error.

PRECISION PRECIPITATES
RETURN TO FIREPOWER DOMINANCE

After victory was achieved in the Second World War, the Western powers found themselves facing a new set of tactical and operational problems forced on them by the prospect of a new conflict with the Soviet Union. The tactical and operational challenge now was not to accelerate friendly movement across the battlefield, but to slow enemy movement in order to halt a Soviet-style *blitzkrieg* across the north German plain. Combat forces needed to develop the materiel and defensive doctrine that would permit them to absorb the initial shock of a massive Soviet armored attack with sufficient remaining combat power to hold in the defensive. The operational problem was to strike deep with long-range firepower in order to slow the rate of arrival of Soviet forces at the front. The invention of the microchip offered a technological solution to the problem. Billions of dollars and the collective genius of a generation of brilliant minds exploited microchip technology to develop a remarkable set of precision and information technologies capable of stopping a mechanized offensive with precise, long-range killing power.

Cold War adaptation of the microchip to military purposes turned the technological cycle of change a third time and precipitated another precision revolution similar, at least in form, to the sinister era begun with the introduction of rifled weapons at the end of the nineteenth century. Western militaries are not far enough into the third cycle to anticipate precisely the impact of this new "information" era on the art of war. But they are far enough along to identify with some certainty which technologies will have the greatest influence. Recent experience in post–Cold War conflicts seems to suggest that there are principally three: stealth, precision, and information.

Stealth and precision are similar in both pedigree and purpose. They were developed by the United States during and immediately after the Vietnam War in an effort to make bombing safer and more precise. The military use of information, on the other hand, was derived principally from technologies developed in the commercial sector. The dramatic evidence of recent aerial campaigns against the Iraqis, the Serbs, and most recently the terrorists in Afghanistan suggests that the combined success of stealth, precision, and information has made today's battlefield enormously more lethal and America's firepower dominance of it absolute. At no time in the history of warfare has the effectiveness of a single dimension of war, in this case firepower, been increased so profoundly in such a short period. Prior to the introduction of precision technologies, the killing effects of "dumb" bombs and artillery were very slight despite the fearsome flames, smoke, and noise that their images invoked. Dumb shells and bombs are virtually useless against troops under cover or on the move. The odds of hitting a soldier in a foxhole with an artillery projectile or an unguided gravity bomb are less than one in a thousand. Add some form of precision to the bomb or projectile, and the odds of destruction go from improbable to absolute. At a minimum, the mathematical difference in accuracy is at least two orders of magnitude, perhaps more in some circumstances. Thus a Vietnam-era artillery strike of several thousand rounds needed to destroy an enemy bunker or fighting position might easily be done in the precision age with two or three projectiles.[1]

It is important to note, however, that the ability to strike with precision demands more than just the ability to launch precision munitions. The target must first be found, positively identified as enemy, and tracked with the same precision as the munition used against it. Second, the decision to strike must be made, the munition and the delivery system selected, and the trip to the target accomplished before the target has had a chance to move away from the footprint of the sensor. As witnessed in Kosovo, and to a lesser extent in Afghanistan, the first task is the most difficult to accomplish. Information technology has not been refined sufficiently to find and track the target with the same precision as the ability to strike. The bombing campaign in Kosovo demonstrated convincingly that modern surveillance and sensing devices can deny an enemy the ability to mass large, static forces. But the Kosovo experience also suggests that even the most advanced sensing and killing technologies have yet to prove effective against smaller, fleeting targets. The Afghanistan experience points out the frustration inherent in a firepower system too clogged with bureaucracy and with too many decision points imbedded in the system. One-meter accuracy has little utility if the missile is directed at the wrong target, or if the target disappears before the missile arrives.

While improvements in information technology will continue to increase the ability to see the battlefield with greater clarity, the technology is not likely to become so good as to make the battlefield completely transparent. Even with continued quantum advances in microchip technology, it is unlikely that enough bandwidth or sensor devices in sufficient abundance will be available to see, sense, and track everything that moves on the battlefield. The Afghanistan experience dramatically reinforced the long-held principle that the killing effect of distant fires is enhanced geometrically by the presence of eyes on the battlefield capable of tracking moving targets firsthand and discriminating between targets real and false and troops friend or foe. A few well-trained and properly equipped special operations soldiers on the ground armed with the authority to call for and direct aerial precision missions from the ground made the difference between success and failure in the firepower campaign in Afghanistan.

In considering the impact of technology on the course of future warfare, it is important to note the technologies and weapons that are not likely to change. The image of half-century-old bombers shouldering the burden of the firepower campaign in Afghanistan dramatically illustrates the truism that platforms—namely, the vehicles that traditionally have been the machine-age gold standard for determining the efficacy of a military force in the past—are not likely to become substantially more potent as machines of war than they are today. Nor should they, necessarily become so. Ships, aircraft, and armored vehicles have reached a technological plateau. Because platforms will continue to rely on fossil fuels for propulsion, the speed, lifting power, range, and agility of land, sea, and air transport will increase only marginally at best. This is not to say that weapons will not become more effective in the years ahead, but only that the effectiveness of platforms will be dependent mostly on the degree to which the three principal catalysts of change—stealth, information, and precision—can be embedded in the platforms themselves.

If platform speed is to remain relatively constant, then the pace and tempo of maneuver—strategic, operational, and tactical—will likely remain relatively constant in the years ahead. Most of the increase in tempo and speed will come from the advantages to be accrued from the reduction in the mass of battlefield systems allowed by the proliferation of precision and information technologies. In Desert Storm, nearly 60 percent of the bulk of land systems was taken up by "dumb" ammunition and the vehicles and equipment necessary to transport and secure it. As precision proliferates in the decades ahead, the weight of munitions that must be carried into a theater of war (or aboard tactical vehicles) will be reduced in rough proportion.

When the ground services become as capable of delivering precision as the air services, the masses of artillery that characterized machine-age firepower systems will disappear. No longer will armies have to mass guns to mass killing power. Guns and rockets will scatter about in groups of two or three for protection. Stocked with a few hundred rounds of precision munitions, each gun will be able to fire with great lethality for long periods without the need for resupply. Properly linked by networks with each other and with supported maneuver units, the guns, though scattered across a vast expanse of territory, will retain the ability to mass the killing effects of their fires without having to mass themselves.

The concept of massed effects will have three limitations. First is the limitation of range. The more fleeting the target, the closer the firing system must be to engage it. Propulsion technologies exist today to deliver ballistic and guided projectiles against point targets literally hundreds of miles distant. But no matter how sophisticated the missile, Newton's laws will continue to reinforce the principle that the more distant the platform, the less able it will be to strike fleeting targets, or those targets in close proximity to friendly troops. The second limitation is cost. Today, precision is very expensive and precision weapons are a limited commodity. The difficulties experienced late in the Afghanistan campaign with striking the Taliban and the al-Qaeda terrorists once they dispersed into the Tora Bora caves serve to highlight the problems inherent in employing million-dollar weapons to engage small, discrete, fleeting targets. Surely in the future when facing assault from American aerial systems, an adaptive enemy will go to ground, entrench, disperse, and attempt to spoof aerial sensors. Such an enemy can only be destroyed by the employment of a large number of cheap, discrete, and responsive precision weapons against him.

Finally, no matter how efficient the network, coordinating the firepower from many dispersed locations will involve friction, confusion, and delay. As long as lives are at stake, commanders will always hesitate before ordering fires close to friendly forces. Experience in recent wars has shown that the more costly and rare a munition, the longer the decision to deliver it. Most of these problems can be largely eliminated by designing cheaper precision weapons and distributing precision down to the lowest tactical levels. As evidenced by experience in Afghanistan, not only will precision in the hands of front-line, close-combat soldiers make tactical engagements cost effective, but the ability of close-combat soldiers to see the target directly will reduce the risks of fratricide and the problem of misidentifying enemy targets.

The availability of robust telecommunications networks in the future will allow fighting units to leave behind in rear areas most of the impediments not needed for the immediate combat tasks of sensing, shooting, and moving about the battlefield. An order of magnitude increase in the ability to see the battlefield will in all probability considerably reduce the density of combat systems necessary to command in all dimensions of war. Numbers will still count, to be sure, but densities on or above the battlefield beyond a certain degree will impede a commander from achieving optimum effects. Reliable information about the enemy and friendly forces will lessen the propensity, common today, for commanders to overcompensate by demanding more firepower than they actually need. A military corollary to the "just in time" principle pioneered by industry will most certainly reduce the weight and bulk of combat forces. The cumulative advantages inherent in precision and information technologies may well allow some quickening of the pace of maneuver.

This disproportionate increase in the lethal effects promised by continued improvements in precision and information-age technologies will increase the effectiveness of firepower systems enormously and will change the nature of land warfare fundamentally. The routine use of unmanned aerial sensors in Afghanistan presages an era, perhaps only a decade or less away, when close-combat maneuver soldiers will have access to sensors on board combat vehicles capable of spotting enemy forces in all directions and within the range of their organic weapons. A battle-force commander will have access to a picture of the battlefield gathered from his own sensors that will offer great clarity. The picture of his more distant surroundings will become more transparent and indistinct because the commander will have to rely on information provided from outside sources. At best, the information will be neither current nor accurate enough to be useful for targeting—although in all probability the commander will be able to use it to track larger formations on the move.

To place these informational capabilities of a future force in a tactical context, imagine for a moment a small unit, perhaps a combined-arms company occupying a circular piece of ground about five miles in diameter. Concentric rings of relative information dominance spread radially away from it and stretch upward, forming a protective info-sphere above the unit. Within the closest ring, the company can see, track, and strike anything that moves and can probably see most stationary targets not completely covered and concealed. Within the second ring, the unit can sense and track small units on the move, but can routinely strike only stationary targets, such as parked vehicles and man-made defensive emplacements. Sensors within the second ring can also track approaching flying objects, including artillery, aircraft, and low-flying tactical missiles. The third ring stretches out to a distance of perhaps a hundred miles and overlaps other units similarly arrayed across the battlefield. This is principally a ring of information networks that keeps the unit aware of all activities around it and allows the unit to act in concert as part of a joint force.

When the unit moves, the protective information sphere moves with it. The ability to sense and track the enemy with precision will permit a unit on the move to avoid surprise and to always gain the advantage of position over the enemy. The ability to see the enemy first from distances outside the range of the enemy's organic weapons will make every close-combat action an ambush. The ability to know precisely the location of all friendly units will permit many widely dispersed units to converge on an enemy formation quickly and efficiently. To a contemporary observer, tactical maneuver of this sort will appear to be haphazard and uncoordinated. But a closer look will show that these many, small, seemingly disparate tactical units will be moving in concert—coordinated through a tactical network and under the control of a single hand.

The ability to gain information dominance and exploit that dominance decisively with tactical precision weapons will eventually influence design and performance of combat systems. Today, tanks and infantry carriers are protected by heavy armor intended to defeat or at least lessen the destructive effects of enemy fire. If the enemy can be seen and tracked from safe distances well away from the lethal range of his weapons, then the need for heavy armor will not be as necessary as it is today. Lighter vehicles are more agile and capable of greater speeds—characteristics that will further extend the survival of fighting vehicles. Similarly, the inherent vulnerability of troop-carrying and attack helicopters will be reduced considerably if these aircraft are able to sense and avoid enemy air defense guns and missiles.

The greatest vulnerability of an information-age battle force will be the information network itself. Any success by the enemy in penetrating the shield of information will have disastrous consequences. The information advantage can be lost most easily by forfeiting the strategic high ground of the atmosphere and space. Most sensors and virtually all telecommunications will be occupying the third dimension. Together, they will form a fragile constellation of manned and unmanned aerial platforms interconnected principally by satellites. The info-sphere will be as vulnerable to technical attack as to physical attack. In a strange twist of irony, it is not inconceivable that a robust and powerful joint battle force could be made impotent by some distant computer hacker hired by the enemy to collapse the info-sphere from a continent away.

Inevitably, stealth and precision weapons will begin to proliferate as they become cheaper and easier to duplicate. Within the next two decades, cheap, stealthy, and precise missiles and bombs will be found in all major arsenals of the world. Likewise, information technologies and the ability to exploit them on the battlefield will most certainly soon become integral to the warfighting doctrines of most of the world's militaries. Unlike that of stealth and precision, the expansion of information warfare technologies among all the major military powers will be substantially independent of defense budgets. The presence of robust and proliferating civilian Internet and cellular communications networks overseas will guarantee that the military application of these technologies will always be close at hand and quickly available to military leaders for rapid exploitation when needed. Developments in information technology by civilian industry are becoming increasingly more suitable for and more easily adaptable to military use. Secure data and voice networks, long the exclusive domain of military telecommunications, have become far more sophisticated and common within financial and commercial markets today. Commercial satellites now offer overhead imagery immediately and make it available by credit card. Continuous improvements in the portability and robustness of cellular technologies and the worldwide proliferation of cellular networks may well have the greatest influence on the evolution of the art of war during the next two decades. By 2020, the capability to communicate with anyone securely, from any location, mobile or stationary, will become practically a universal phenomenon. The dividing line between military and commercial telecommunications will in the near future become virtually transparent.

Thus the technological problem of the future will not be much different in principle from similar challenges in the past: The United States must maintain its advantage in precision and information over an enemy who will have increasingly greater access to those technologies in the future. The challenge is different only in that the demand to win battles in the future at minimum cost in human life will require that the gap between enemy and friendly capabilities be kept very wide indeed. Even a little technological "closure"—perhaps from an enemy who learns to foil or dampen the protective info-sphere—could have disastrous consequences when combined with other non-technological advantages that the enemy will enjoy.

NEW USES FOR OLDER WEAPONS

The image of aging B-52 bombers performing as the platform of choice for the delivery of very sophisticated precision missiles in Afghanistan serves as a useful metaphor to underscore the fact that age is not necessarily an indicator of a weapon's relative usefulness on the battlefield. This principle is particularly relevant if the enemy does not attempt to engage in a contest for qualitative superiority, as has been the case in virtually all wars fought by the United States during this era of limited wars. In fact, since the beginning of the industrial revolution, the armies, navies, and air forces of all the major powers have gone to war armed with a heterogeneous assortment of new and old equipment. The German armored phalanx that crushed Poland and France during the early days of the Second World War was nine-tenths bolt action, horse-drawn, and propelled by the feet of infantrymen. The pace of technological change has been so rapid that fighting forces have never been able to keep up with the constantly accelerating pace of obsolescence. No nation in this century has had the wealth to maintain an entire military at the same comparative level of modernization all the time. But in limited wars, the heterogeneous nature of modern militaries has so far proven to be as much an asset as a liability.

After outliving their utility in high-intensity conflict, weapons (particularly firepower systems) often remain in the arsenals of all services because they are useful for a longer period in the less technologically challenging environments of limited wars. In fact, all too often in this new era of warfare, the services have been obliged to swap the new for the old when they have discovered that older weapons are actually better suited for conflicts of lesser intensity. During the early days of the Korean War, the U.S. Army was particularly adamant that older propeller-driven fighter aircraft from the Second World War were superior to the newer jets that the U.S. Air Force was introducing to perform the close support mission. Fast movers were incapable of spotting a dispersed enemy and bombing with the precision necessary to deliver ordnance in close proximity to friendly ground forces. In Korea, the city-smashing B-29 strategic bomber traded in its pedigree as the aircraft that dropped the first atomic bomb for the more pedestrian mission of inter-dicting Chinese logistics between the Yalu River and the front lines.

The lesson was repeated in Vietnam. The U.S. Air Force and the U.S. Navy were again obliged to bring propeller-driven observation and attack air-craft out of mothballs to meet the same demand. Today, venerable firepower platforms such as the AC-130 gunship (a 1950s-era transport first modified in Vietnam to be a firepower platform) continue to prove their usefulness in Afghanistan. These aircraft and others, such as the A-10 Warthog, seem to reappear time and time again as essential firepower providers just before the decision is made to scrap them in favor of faster, more capable (and much more expensive) systems.

Long after outliving their usefulness for high-seas combat, large-surface vessels such as cruisers and destroyers today still remain the most efficient choice for providing supporting firepower to ground forces ashore. Main-battle tanks, designed originally for fighting other tanks in large-scale war-fare, found useful roles in Korea, Vietnam, Panama, the Falklands, Lebanon, and Chechnya as mobile protected firepower platforms useful for engaging infantry with machine guns and cannon. Because they deliver supporting fires from positions beyond the killing zone, rocket and cannon artillery need to be modernized far less frequently than close-combat systems that must face the more challenging and unforgiving fighting environment inside the killing zone. It is principally for that reason that calibers, basic design, and ballistic performance of cannon have not changed substantially for the past hundred years.

Older, so called "legacy" air, sea, and ground firepower platforms have had longevity in limited wars principally because the enemy has had neither the means nor the will to seriously challenge firepower systems. No enemy to-day or in the foreseeable future will be able to afford first-rate air or sea plat-forms capable of facing American aircraft and surface vessels in direct com-bat. Artillery is more vulnerable to the potential of massive engagement by enemy artillery, but the quality of U.S. counter-artillery and counter-mortar systems lessens this threat considerably. During the past half-century of experience, the U.S. firepower system has had the luxury of being able to stand off from the enemy's direct engagement and enjoy the freedom to con-centrate on the efficiency and effectiveness of its fires. Without serious oppo-sition, the delivery of firepower in limited wars has become something of a routine industrial process.

The greatest gain in weapons effectiveness will not be in platforms, but in the projectiles and the technologies available to find, track, and kill the enemy. The service life of obsolescent delivery platforms such as fighting vehicles, aircraft, and ships can be extended safely only as long as precision and information technologies can be added expeditiously to the platform. While many billions of developmental dollars invested in new platforms in recent years have served to add only a few miles per hour to platforms, the same sums dedicated to information and precision technologies variously attached to fighting platforms have already multiplied their relative effectiveness a hundred times or more, with no end to this multiplicative increase in sight for many years to come.

DOMINATING THE "LAST MILE"

While the primary focus of firepower systems will continue to be to find, identify, track, and kill with great precision, the challenge for maneuver fighting systems will prove to be far more complex and demanding. Therefore, while legacy platforms may work well for firepower systems, maneuver systems—particularly those that must venture close within the lethal reach of opposing enemy maneuver platforms—will have to be modernized continuously to maintain an absolute and unambiguous superiority in all categories of performance. Absolute overmatch in air and land direct-combat systems must be guaranteed in large measure because, in limited wars, approximately 96 percent of all American combat deaths occur within this "last mile" of tactical system-on-system engagement. Close-combat ground forces, principally infantry, account for four-fifths of these deaths.[2] Combat aircrews, principally pilots of fighter aircraft and attack helicopters, comprise most of the remainder. If the United States is to remain true to the commitment to fight successfully at minimum cost in human life, the systems that are most likely to carry Americans into harm's way must never be inferior to those of the enemy.

With the exception of the strategic air campaign over North Vietnam, U.S. airpower has always managed to sweep the skies of enemy aircraft. The U.S. Navy has never had to engage a serious blue-water threat since the end of the Second World War. The uncluttered nature of the air and ocean mediums has made it very difficult for less sophisticated air and sea opponents to gain even temporary advantage. U.S. ground forces have never suffered aerial or sea-borne bombardment in limited wars. Nor has any opponent ever attempted to interdict the strategic logistical lifelines between the United States and distant theaters. It is highly unlikely that U.S. absolute dominance in the air and on the seas will be challenged anytime soon. The stealth, situational awareness, and precision technologies that American air and sea platforms possess today are so expensive and difficult to replicate that no other nation will possess the disposable income or technological and managerial competence to develop competing systems. Should some future competitor find the means to purchase a few high-quality weapons, it seems unlikely that it would be able to demonstrate the competence to employ them effectively enough to contest American air and naval superiority for many decades.

The picture is less certain and comforting for the last mile of combat on land. Unlike air and sea weapons, a ground force must maintain an enormously greater technological edge if technology is to offer any decisive advantage in the close fight. A few meters of range or a few miles per hour in speed accounts for little real advantage because the complex calculus of terrain tends to lessen any technological advantage that one ground force may have over another. Close engagements on the ground tend to be local, compartmented affairs with the advantage most often going to small units led by audacious and creative commanders. A faster tactical vehicle gains little advantage in a crowded defile, or while waiting to cross a bridge. An opponent who manages to maneuver close enough to fire into a flank from point-blank range can overcome superior range and armored protection.

Yet in past limited wars, ground forces, particularly dismounted forces, have rarely possessed the same technological overmatch as that enjoyed by American air and sea fighting forces. In all limited wars since Korea, firefights have all too often been fair fights against an enemy equipped with light weapons just as good as, or in some cases superior to, American weapons. Past experience shows clearly that enemies equipped with simple weapons of comparable quality to American weapons have proven to be the most troublesome and difficult to counter. From Korea through Vietnam, unsophisticated enemies have managed to inflict most combat deaths on Americans with automatic small arms and the lowly mortar—a weapon no more complex than a steel tube capable of lobbing simple iron bombs to a range of less than a mile.

Thus if the United States seeks to fight a future limited war with minimum loss, it must put a premium on the development of systems that will give an overwhelming advantage to soldiers fighting inside the deadly zone where the battle is culminated and the greatest potential exists for serious harm. First in priority must be the development of air and ground fighting vehicles capable of destroying dispersed, entrenched, and hidden enemy formations. The technological challenge for a ground maneuver vehicle will be to build a system light enough to be transported great distances by air, yet robust enough to fight and survive in close contact with an enemy equipped with industrial-age, heavy-armored vehicles. Such maneuver vehicles must not only be able to fight effectively at the tactical level but must also possess sufficient speed and range to reach operational objectives deep in the enemy's rear. Thus, as stated earlier, an aerial maneuver vehicle, most likely a helicopter of some kind, should be employed to achieve the necessary advantage in maneuver, particularly in the remote and inhospitable regions in which U.S. ground forces are most likely to fight limited wars in the future. Experience in recent wars shows conclusively that the advantage in close combat is best maintained while fighting mounted. Occasions will occur, however, when close-combat soldiers will have no choice but to engage the enemy on foot. Since dismounted warfare is so dangerous, it must receive special attention from the technological community to ensure that it can be conducted successfully with the lowest possible risk.

The chapters that follow seek to determine the influence that technology and other factors will have on the course of land warfare in the future. They argue that three challenges—one at each level of war from strategic, to operational, to tactical—will face the architects of change within the next two decades.

The *strategic* level is concerned with the use of military force to achieve national objectives. In the new American style of war, it has come to be interpreted as the highest political and diplomatic level at which decisions are made to collect and deploy military forces to a distant theater. The size of strategic land forces varies, depending on the nature of the topography and the seriousness of the enemy threat. In past limited wars, deployments involved relatively large armies consisting of multiple corps of 50,000 soldiers each. The numbers of soldiers deployed in more recent campaigns have been considerably smaller. The strategic challenge in the years ahead will center on "time versus risk"—that is, the decisions that must be made to balance the size of the strategic force to be projected versus the time necessary for the force to arrive ready to fight. The United States must be able to overcome the problems of distance and time without unnecessarily exposing early arriving forces to an enemy already in place within a theater of war.

The *operational* level of warfare provides a connection between strategic deployments and the tactical engagement of small units. The "art" of maneuvering forces to achieve decisive results on the battlefield nests here. As with the deployment of strategic level forces, the basic elements of operational maneuver have shrunk as the conflict environment has changed since the end of the Second World War. During the Cold War, corps conducted operational maneuver. More recently, the task has devolved to brigades, usually self-contained units of all arms capable of independent maneuver. An independent brigade consists of about 5,000 soldiers. At the operational level, ground forces will face the challenge of determining the proper balance between "firepower and maneuver" resources and technologies to ensure that the will of the enemy's army to resist can be collapsed quickly and decisively.

Battles are fought at the *tactical* level. In the past, the tactical fight has been a face-to-face endeavor; small units of about company size, no more than several hundred soldiers, are locked into combat at close range. The tactical fight is where most casualties occur. The tactical challenge of the future will be to balance the anticipated "ends," or what the combat commander is expected to achieve on the battlefield, with the "means," measured in the lives of soldiers allocated to achieve those ends. Since ground forces suffer casualties disproportionately, ground commanders face the greatest challenge of balancing ends versus means.

All three challenges must be addressed together if reform of the land-power services—the Army and the Marine Corps—is to be swift and lasting. The essential moderating influence on the process of change is *balance*. At the strategic level, the impulse to arrive quickly must be balanced with the need for forces massive and powerful enough to fight successfully on arrival. The impulse to build a firepower-dominant operational force must be balanced and moderated by the realization that maneuver forces will be essential if the transitory advantage of fires is to be made permanent by the presence of ground forces in the enemy's midst. The impulse to culminate tactical battle by closing with and destroying the enemy must be balanced by the realization that fighting too close may play more to the advantage of enemy rather than friendly forces.

NOTES

1. FM 101-60-2, Joint Munitions Effectiveness Manual/Surface to Surface; Effectiveness Data for Howitzer, 105mm M101A1; October, 1970.

2. T. N. Dupuy, *Attrition: Forecasting Battle Casualties and Equipment Losses in Modern War* (Fairfax, VA: Hero Books, 1990), pp. 60–61.

Land Warfare at the Strategic Level
Balancing Time and Risk

$\mathcal{T}$he challenge of time versus risk was aptly if not elegantly conveyed by Confederate General Nathan Bedford Forrest when he stated that the key to success on the battlefield was to always be "fustest with the mostest." In contemporary terms, a U.S. force tailored to arrive early in a theater of war to prevent an enemy from achieving his aggressive intent must be light enough to be projected rapidly, principally by air. The perpetual dilemma of air-delivered forces is that they simply lack the heft necessary to fight effectively against heavy forces. The lighter the force, the faster it arrives, but the greater the risk that it will face a heavier and more massive enemy on arrival. Today, thanks to its central strategic position, access to bases overseas, and large capacity for strategic lift, the United States possesses an unparalleled capacity to meet Forrest's intent by projecting forces into troubled regions both first and with the most. But capacity is not unlimited. The problem of time versus risk was dramatically illustrated during the opening phases of the Gulf War, when a single U.S. airborne division projected rapidly into the theater was all that stood between the heavy armor of the Iraqi Army and the Saudi oilfields.

The challenge of time versus risk is what keeps strategic planners awake at night in peacetime. Strategic projection forces are enormously expensive. The United States simply cannot afford to deploy all the forces necessary to be dominant in every potential contingency and circumstance in every possible corner of the world. Of course the surest means for reducing risk at an affordable cost is to be able to anticipate when, where, and against whom every future conflict will be fought. Unfortunately, throughout the era of limited wars, American strategic planners have established a notoriously poor track record for forecasting precisely where and when the next conflict will occur. Cold War planners knew who the enemy would be and where he would be confronted. But in America's experience in limited wars, the variables of place and time have been so many, and the behavior and intent of limited war enemies so unpredictable, that no one could reasonably have been expected to anticipate, for instance, the North Korean or Iraqi invasions, or the fanatical violation of U.S. territory by Osama bin Laden. Fifty years of experience in fighting limited wars nevertheless do yield enough data to anticipate very generally the characteristics of limited wars in the future. There are enough indicators in the historical record to narrow the options of time, place, circumstances, and probable enemies. Armed with reasonably reliable assumptions such as these, peacetime planners will be able to build and position forces necessary to reduce the risk and increase the speed of strategically deployable forces.

WARS OF ATTRITION AND WARS OF PREEMPTION

The historical record of this new era of limited wars, beginning with Korea and continuing most recently through the war against terrorism precipitated by the bombing of the World Trade Center and the Pentagon, offers frustratingly ambiguous and often contradictory indications of the future course of such conflicts. The soldier's laboratory of actual war experiences reveals an image of a shadowy new age in which failed states become incubators of terrorist nations-in-arms. Other experiences foretell the dark beginnings of a period of cultural warfare precipitated by legions of disaffected and socially disenfranchised urban masses. The geostrategic landscape is cluttered with a confusing panoply of competing states, each with its own hegemonic ambitions, cultural and religious affinities and hatreds, and list of ancient affronts and grievances against neighbors as well as distant Western states—all begging to be set right through force of arms. The potential for extreme violence that characterized the Cold War has given way to a new, kinetic state of aggressive actions by an enormously varied list of actors: Panama, Iraq, Somalia, Haiti, Rwanda, Sierra Leone, East Timor, Afghanistan—the list goes on. While each of these limited conflicts had a specific character, enough examples have been provided by the recent past to permit a few tentative generalizations about why the violence erupts, who controls it, and how such conflicts evolve over time.

The laboratory of practical experience suggests that there are two general types of limited wars: those of *attrition* and those of *preemption*. In most cases, a war of attrition plays to the benefit of the opponent, whose principal advantage rests with the ability to maintain the initiative by controlling the element of time. In a preemptive campaign, the attacker manages to steal the time advantage by striking quickly to collapse the opponent's centers of gravity and secure a decision through the application of overwhelming force. In either case, the chief factor is time. The United States does well when, for whatever reason, it manages to control the variable of time. At least so far in the post–Cold War, limited warfare era, short wars have been successful, while protracted wars have failed.

One immutable characteristic of warfare will most assuredly survive into this new era: States, or at least state-like actors, are now and will continue to be the sources of most organized and sustained violence that threatens America's important interests abroad and at home. Only after his radical form of terrorism managed to take over a failing state did Osama bin Laden have the strategic tools necessary to elevate a regional terrorist movement into a global one. By capturing the organs of state, al-Qaeda gained the priceless trappings of legitimacy. It turned Afghanistan into a terrorist haven capable of providing sanctuary and access to the financial, diplomatic, military, and political organs of power. Through its Taliban surrogates, it gained the vital perceptual high ground that allowed it to attract international money, power, and followers from around the Moslem world. Most important, the takeover of a recognized international entity gave al-Qaeda a moral shield against outside intervention. It took a horrific deed in the form of the World Trade Center and Pentagon attacks to allow the United States to gain sufficient moral justification to violate the sacred barrier of international sovereignty. In the future, the al-Qaeda takeover may even serve as a model for other rogue non-state actors—such as aggressive drug cartels, mafia-like entities, or religion-based fundamentalist groups.

Evidence grows daily to support the conclusion that other sovereign states in the Middle East and Asia continue to harbor terrorists within their borders. The surest way for the United States to deter states supporting terrorism from committing acts similar to those perpetrated by al-Qaeda is to demonstrate the competence, capability, and will to conduct rapid, decisive interventions in those regions of the world where state support of terrorism is most prevalent.

WHERE CONFLICTS WILL OCCUR

Regardless of the means by which a state or state-like entity appears on the global scene, recent history suggests that the most dangerous and persistently violent conflicts between states seem to cluster in distant regions long subject to cultural antagonisms. For the most part, regional violence seems mostly to be the handiwork of a few very bad men who manage to incite populations to action by dredging up long-simmering ethnic, religious, or cultural animosities and directing them against other states. In almost all cases, however, the real motives for regional aggressions are more in keeping with the typical pedestrian motives driven by one state's desire to violate the integrity of a neighbor in the thirst for regional or perhaps global dominance or the hunger for stolen wealth.

Rogue states have a profile. Not one of them is a true democracy. A threatening hegemonic competitor will most likely come from among the poorer, despotic states with long histories of aggressive behavior. Recently, the profile of aggressive states often presumes the presence of a dominant leader, often charismatic and always ruthless, ruling through an elite whose collective survival depends on the largesse of the ruler. The elite maintains control of the under-classes by subtly melding brutal control with a heightened sense of collective outrage at some ethnic, religious, cultural, or territorial menace—the more foreign and abstract the menace, the better. Despotic states will not be vulnerable to the more familiar strategic "centers of gravity," such as territory, the will of the populace, or economic and industrial power.

The behavior of such aggressors as North Vietnam, Iraq, Serbia, North Korea, and Afghanistan suggests that the opinions—or, for that matter, the welfare—of the people have very little influence on the decision making of their leaders. The economy can be destroyed and the territory violated and plundered as long as the resulting hardship never touches the leader or his cronies. As experience in the limited war era has shown, the political "centers of gravity" of a contemporary despotic and potentially aggressive state of this sort increasingly nest inside the source of state power—the leader and the elite who rule the state as if it were a medieval fiefdom. As witnessed in recent Balkan, Asian, and Middle Eastern conflicts, the health and longevity of the ruling elite is dependent solely on its ability to ensure the strength of what Lenin termed the "organs of power": the police and the army. Both institutions give the ruler the means for controlling the population, as well as political and diplomatic legitimacy—the two essential ingredients necessary for continuing in power. Destroy the army of an aggressive, despotic state and the ruling elite is destroyed. The state, which in all probability was the creation of the ruling elite, must fall in turn.

Recent experience with contemporary despotic leaders seems to suggest that, although their behavior may be ruthless and despicable, especially by the standards of Western liberal democracies, their actions are by no means illogical or necessarily unpredictable. Actions are driven by an implicit impulse to remain in power and, if possible, to expand the power of the state by manipulating military means in traditional Clausewitz ways to fulfill regional territorial ambitions. An aggressive leader precipitates a conflict by playing on the cultural and religious antipathies of the population in order to maintain the allegiance, or at least the acquiescence, of the masses. As opportunities present themselves, he will exploit them to violate the territory of vulnerable, less powerful states.

The strategic objectives of the aggressor are now twofold: 1) to employ military power to seize and collapse decisive points inside the enemy's territory as quickly as possible in order to lessen the impact that his aggression will have on international public opinion, and 2) to do whatever is necessary to prevent interference in the conflict by an outside power. Most despotic states, thanks to the availability of information from the global media, possess a finely tuned sense of the limits of tolerance of the Western powers. By clever media manipulation, such states will seek to keep the U.S. reaction below the threshold of active intervention. They may demonstrate just enough military capability—in the form of long range missiles, ships, submarines, mines, and anti-aircraft systems—to create the impression that intervention might be too costly. If the aggressor miscalculates and a response intervention by the outside power becomes likely—as in the case of the Taliban and the United States, for example—the aggressor's task will be to achieve his goal very quickly and go to ground with the intent of making the cost of intervention prohibitively costly. While the prospect of a shooting confrontation with the outside power will be daunting, a determined despotic aggressor regime will not necessarily want to avoid the clash, particularly if it believes it has the means and the will to prevail over time.

Conflicts caused by rogue states or state-like entities seem to cluster in regions where human misery is most pronounced. Nothing about this phenomenon is new. Hunger, crowding, environmental disaster, and economic collapse have always provided a breeding ground for violence among young men with little hope for the future and nothing to lose. The disaffected and dispirited have always found purpose in a charismatic ruler who promises wealth, position, and fulfillment in exchange for loyalty and a resolve among his charges to sacrifice for the cause.

BALANCING INTERESTS AND RESPONSES

In the past, the states best able to manage events beyond their borders have been those best able to avoid the temptation to overreach. Great powers remain great in large measure because they possess the wisdom to temper active involvement in foreign interventions—to remain within the limits of a national strategy that balances ambition with military resources. The first principle of the strategic art states simply that the greatest weight of resources must be devoted to safeguarding the most vulnerable and vital interests of the state. If a vital interest is threatened, the survival of the state is threatened. Generally, the most vital interests of a liberal democracy include, first and foremost, preservation of the territorial integrity of the state. The example of the attacks on New York and Washington should send a message to those with similar ambitions that the surest way to focus the wrath of the American people against them would be to strike this country within its borders again. The second strategic priority is the protection of the national economic welfare by ensuring free and open access to markets for vital materials and finished goods. Other important but less vital interests should be defended by the threat of force only as military resources permit.

Outside the limits of U.S. territory, the strategic problem of defining the geographic limits of U.S. vital interests becomes complex. While the United States may have some interests in every corner of the world, there are certain regions where its strategic interests, both economic and cultural, are concentrated and potentially threatened. These vital strategic "centers of gravity" encompass in the first instance those geographic areas essential to maintaining access to open markets and sources of essential raw materials, principally oil. Fortunately, many of these economically vital centers are secure from serious threat. But a few happen to be located within or astride regions that have witnessed generations of cultural and ethnic strife.

Four regions overshadow all others in being both vital to continued domestic prosperity and continually under the threat of serious state-supported violence. These regions are defined generally by an arc of territories along the periphery of Eurasia: Europe, the Middle East, South Asia, and north East Asia. For the past several centuries, these regions have been the arenas of the world's most serious and intractable conflicts. Points of collision begin with the intersection of Western and Eastern Christianity and continue southward to mark Islam's incursion into southeastern Europe in the Balkans. The cultural divide continues without interruption across the Levant in an unbroken line of unrest and warring states from the crescent of the Middle East to the subcontinent of South Asia. The fault-line concludes with the divide between China and all the traditional cultural competitors along its land and sea borders.

Other countries outside the periphery of Eurasia might, in extreme cases, demand the presence of U.S. forces for peacekeeping or humanitarian operations. But it is unlikely that in the years to come the United States will risk a major conflict that will involve the calculated commitment of forces in a shooting war in regions outside this "periphery of Eurasia," which circumscribes and defines America's global security.

REDUCING RISK THROUGH
GLOBAL PRESENCE AND STRATEGIC SPEED

The ability to get to a distant theater of war quickly will not be enough to address the challenge of balancing time versus risk. To guarantee success, the conflict must end quickly. Because of their superior strategic mobility, air forces today can generally open the campaign often in only a matter of days. But an attack by aerial firepower alone fails to deny the enemy the advantage of time. A determined enemy with a will to win and unchallenged inside his own territory needs only to endure the assault by aerial firepower and wait patiently until it subsides. If left undefeated for too long, an adaptive enemy will find the means to stretch out a campaign and make it too costly. The experience of protracted attrition warfare in Korea and Vietnam demonstrated dramatically that a stalemate for the American side means victory for the enemy. Moreover, prospective competitors have observed the performance of U.S. forces in recent limited wars and know that they do well in short wars and very poorly in wars that last too long.

The complete solution to this challenge, of course, will be to find the means to get there quickly with a balance of combat power sufficient to fight a sustained, continuous, and unrelenting campaign. Therefore the national military objective in future wars will be to execute a strategic *coup de main*— a total "takedown" by first paralyzing the enemy with fire and then collapsing resistance quickly by dropping ground forces suddenly throughout enemy territory. In wars of the future, the passage of time will hinder the intervening force and help the defender. The first objective in future limited wars should be neither to destroy the enemy nor to capture key objectives within his territory, but to deny the enemy the advantage of time. In the opening phase of a campaign, he must be denied the opportunity to react and position his forces. The campaign must then be ended quickly to deny the enemy time to learn, adapt, and improvise an effective method of resistance.

Things can go wrong. Given time, an enemy can turn a strategic takedown into a protracted conflict. While technology in the form of superior information, communications, and precision can be brought into the fight, the enemy will have certain advantages of his own which, if exploited cleverly, could slow deployment of an intervening force and increase the risk of the venture. An enemy familiar with the area of operations will be able to offset American dominance in information to some degree. He will attempt to exploit this advantage by employing deception measures and by using camouflage and strategic feints. He also will be able to leverage his absolute control of the media to spread propaganda and disinformation. In all likelihood, he will do all in his power to impede the arrival of the intervening force, and his efforts will be aided by the fact that ports, airfields, roads, railroads, and other infrastructure in the region will be primitive or perhaps largely nonexistent.

It seems unlikely that U.S. forces will be able to enter a distant theater of war directly from bases in the United States, without first pausing to stage through an intermediate base somewhere safe yet within reasonable reach of the objective area. To be sure, there will be no shortage of safe places from which to launch such an assault. The difficulties inherent in translating such a strategic force into an operational force capable of maneuvering by air will take time and will inevitably reduce the strategic speed of the campaign. An adaptive enemy will most certainly do all in his power to impede access to the theater of war. The pace of arrival will be moderated to a great extent by the paucity of airlift both from the United States to the staging bases and from the staging bases into the operational theater. Surely the ferocity, and to some extent the effectiveness, of U.S. combat forces will be impeded by the restrictions imposed on the use of firepower. In time, as casualties mount, these "rules of engagement" will be made less onerous. But battlefield dominance is best established early in a campaign. Any diminution in early advantage often translates into a longer and more difficult campaign.

The distances that U.S. forces will have to travel to reach a distant battleground along the periphery of Eurasia will likely impede any effort to achieve a quick victory. Yet it is just because Eurasia has so often been a battleground for U.S. forces in this century that America has won the right to retain a string of outposts there. This fortunate inheritance bequeaths to today's generation continued access to key strategic nodes in Europe, the Middle East, and Northeast Asia.

The strategic implications inherent in this gift of permanent presence are enormous. U.S. involvement in conflicts for less than vital interests may occur in regions accessible only from distant bases, as witnessed recently in such remote countries as Rwanda and Somalia. However, thanks to the proximity of bases within reach of all of the most probable points of conflict around America's strategic perimeter, it is extremely unlikely that any conflict will erupt that can be reached only by projecting forces from the continental United States. But regional bases by themselves will neither provide the necessary degree of conventional deterrence to dissuade a despot from violating the territory of a neighboring state nor contain all the fighting power necessary to defeat a competent aggressor should the United States determine that intervention in such a distant conflict is in its vital interest.

Credible deterrence and overwhelming power can be guaranteed in distant regions only by a military that possesses a balance of very lethal, flexible, and projectable strategic forces capable of delivering overwhelming combat power with great speed to each of the three vital centers of gravity along the periphery of Eurasia. Strategic speed in future wars will come from the ability to approach a threatened region of war from many different directions—from the United States and from forward land and sea bases. These forces must be projected in all dimensions: air, sea, land, and space. Any strategic operation that involves the commitment of major U.S. expeditionary forces must be synchronized in such a fashion that all elements of combat power arrive as nearly simultaneously into the area of operations as the availability of strategic transport will allow. The object of strategic projection therefore must be to place overwhelming force directly in the enemy's midst—preferably before he has had the time to seize his initial objectives inside the territory of a violated regional neighbor. Audacity permits preemption and quick victory; caution and deliberation create the specter of attrition and stalemate.

A strategic assault directly at the enemy is essential to achieve a quick and decisive victory. But as experience in Korea, the Falklands, and the Gulf illustrates, a force that seeks to gain the time advantage runs the risk of arriving in the presence of the enemy ill-prepared to fight. A force that intervenes prematurely without the combat power and sustainability to prevail over time may create conditions that lead to excessive losses or failure. An enemy with superior mass may be able to fall on an early arriving force and thoroughly destroy it before the intervening force has had the opportunity to build up superior force. In Korea, only an overextension of the North Korean Army's reach south of the Han River prevented it from pushing the Americans into the sea during the late summer of 1950. In the case of the Gulf War, no one is entirely sure why Saddam halted his aggression at the Kuwaiti-Saudi border. The results would have been catastrophic, however, had the armored columns of the Iraqi Republican Guard continued to advance against the foot-borne, unarmored formations of the 82nd Airborne Division waiting to defend in open, hastily dug desert foxholes.

Time is the essential ingredient in the success or failure of warfare at the strategic level. Time is America's enemy and its enemy's friend. Not until the enemy's centers of gravity are under physical assault can the advantage of time be wrested from the enemy and the essential process of attacking his will begin in earnest. Furthermore, as the Gulf War illustrates, the act of strategic projection, if done with competence, dispatch, and determination, actually initiates the process of psychological intimidation so necessary to collapse the enemy's will to resist. The image of an enormous, seemingly unstoppable monolithic force rising in the distance and closing from all points and every warfighting dimension creates in the mind of an enemy the beginning of a conviction that victory is no longer possible.

Once the act of strategic maneuver begins, the challenge becomes to reinforce the enemy's collective sense of impending destruction by overwhelmingly and consistently defeating his army in the field. The clock starts in earnest once the shooting begins and the casualties start to mount. At first glance, it would appear that a future force with the technology and competence to arrive quickly on the scene of battle would be guaranteed an advantage once serious battle begins. Unfortunately, the U.S. Army's record for fighting the opening engagements of recent limited wars seems to indicate that early success is problematic. Indeed, the examples of Korea and Vietnam suggest that, unless an enemy is unwise enough to forfeit the advantage of time by allowing unimpeded access along with the occasional gift of a few additional months to shake out the bugs, acclimate to the terrain and climate, and train within the theater of war, chances are good that ground forces will find the first battles of the conflict both bloody and indecisive.

THE ENEMY'S ADVANTAGES: MASS, WILL, AND PROXIMITY

Painful experience in wars in this century suggests that the advantage in battle does not automatically go to the side with more sophisticated weapons. An enemy is likely to offset technological inferiority with advantages such as mass, will, proximity, and an intimate knowledge of the battle area. Thanks to a proclivity to emphasize materiel over mass, U.S. forces will most probably fight outnumbered. There is no question that a military force possessing superior technology gains a considerable advantage. But recent experience fighting outnumbered seems to reinforce Lenin's observation that "quantity has a quality all of its own." Superior mass allows an opponent willing to make the sacrifice the luxury of trading lives for time. Victory is difficult to achieve against an enemy who arrays his army in thick, redundant formations. Even if the battle is won, decisive outcomes become more problematic if the enemy can readily replace his losses and fight on.

Clausewitz asserts rightly that war is ultimately a test of will. Future enemies of the United States may have the advantage in will simply because what may be a limited war to the United States may well be perceived by such enemies as a threat to their state, or at least to the survival of the state's ruling elite. Such an asymmetry of purpose can only result in an asymmetry of will. Clausewitz also asserts, again rightly, that the defensive is the stronger form of warfare. The defender can remain hidden and dispersed, while the attacker must be exposed in order to move and mass. Moving about the battlefield induces more friction and complexity into the attacker's fighting scheme compared with the less challenging task of fighting from stationary positions. When firepower dominates the battlefield, the advantage always goes to the defender. When the killing effects of firepower become so great that units are no longer capable of moving across the battlefield, the results are inevitably paralysis, stagnation, and decision only through attrition and slaughter.

Precision-weapon technologies, at present in the possession of only the Western powers, will find their way into the arsenals of lesser powers. When precision proliferates, the battlefield will become a very unfriendly place to the offensive force. Since the United States will probably be obliged, at least initially, to assume the offensive role, success on the battlefield, now relatively cheap in terms of lives thanks to its monopoly in precision weaponry, may have to be purchased at an ever more expensive price.

A global power can tame, but never conquer, the tyranny of distance. While possession of overseas bases and superior strategic mobility might allow Americans to arrive quickly in a theater of war, odds are that the enemy would be closer to the battlefield and able to arrive more quickly. The need to gain public support and build a coalition will inevitably slow the arrival of an intervening force. Thus it may be possible for an aggressive enemy to steal the strategic march, capture the advantage of time, and disperse within his objective before an intervening force can arrive.

The most significant advantage to the other side will come from an asymmetry of ends. To be successful, the United States must force an enemy to capitulate. An enemy, in contrast, can win merely by avoiding defeat. The strategic advantage that goes to the weaker side with nothing to lose is a condition of war as old as the history of warfare itself: Fabius versus Hannibal, Washington versus Howe, Ho Chi Minh versus the United States. To win by not losing, an enemy must, as a first principle, avoid the loss of his army, which represents his most vulnerable center of gravity. As long as his army is secure, a determined enemy will be willing to trade virtually anything for the advantage of time. In 1964, a French journalist asked Ho Chi Minh to explain how he expected his small, backward country to defeat the world's most sophisticated military. He replied, prophetically: "They will kill many of us and we will kill a few of them, but they will tire of it first."

To manipulate the advantage of time to the fullest, a future enemy will likely follow the example of enemies who have been successful against intervening powers in the past. He will first try to slow the arrival of U.S. forces into the theater of war by creating dissension at home in the United States and among its allies. Should that strategy fail, he will likely follow the examples of Saddam Hussein, Slobodan Milosevic, and Osama bin Laden and attempt to limit the U.S. response to a strategic assault by airpower alone. He will realize that a strategic assault with precision weapons will be enormously destructive. Yet as long as he can maintain control of his people and as long as his territory is not violated, he will control the element of time and the strategic initiative will remain his alone. His greatest fear will be that the United States will collect the resolve to put ground forces in his midst. The presence of troops on his territory will signal that the United States seeks a decision by taking the clock, and the initiative, away from him. He cannot simply remain idle if U.S. troops occupy his territory. Forcing him into action will not necessarily guarantee victory. But it will mean that he cannot win simply by avoiding defeat.

Once real shooting begins, an asymmetric enemy will attempt to snatch victory from the jaws of defeat by countering with a defensive strategy based on dispersion, deception, and delay. First, he will employ whatever meager offensive means he has at his disposal, however sparingly, to kill Americans. The longer the Americans take to win, the greater will their losses be on the battlefield. Defensively, the enemy will attempt to protect his army from destruction by seeking sanctuary for his most vulnerable installations—by hiding, deceiving, dispersing his forces, and going to ground. Should all of these efforts fail, he will attempt to regain the advantage of time by appealing to the global community for support and by negotiating for peace when defeat is imminent. If given time, an enemy will learn how to win by not losing. His military leaders will learn to fight in the school of real combat. His soldiers will become inured to the pyrotechnic effects of American firepower, and they will learn how to avoid the worst of the killing effects of precision weapons. The damage done to the social infrastructure by aerial bombardment will be paraded before the global media in an effort to win the battle for public opinion.

In limited wars of the future, the ability of the United States to fight a preemptive campaign rather than a war of attrition will demand the ability to resolve the time versus risk challenge in its favor by properly balancing the application of mass and speed. Waiting too long to intervene in an effort to achieve overwhelming combat power risks arriving after the enemy has had the opportunity to achieve his objectives unopposed. Too quick an arrival, however, risks total defeat at the hands of a more numerous enemy. The strategic focus in any future war must be on mastering *time* rather than terrain or the enemy. Fortunately, the United States has acquired a great deal of experience in manipulating speed and mass in a succession of recent limited wars. To be sure, experience in some of these wars has come at too dear a price. All the more reason, therefore, for the United States to exploit the experiences of recent wars in order to learn from the mistakes of the past and create a realistic image of how future limited wars can be fought and won quickly and decisively.

· 4 ·

Balancing Firepower and Maneuver
Lessons from Vietnam to the Falklands

$\mathcal{T}$he challenge of balancing firepower and maneuver in warfare is as old as warfare itself. Vegetius, in his fourth-century work on the Roman art of war, *De Re Militari*, wrote that one of the essential skills demanded of Roman armies in open warfare was the ability to meld and balance the effects of missile attack and maneuver. The quickness, flexibility, discipline, and agility of the legion allowed the Romans to maneuver the enemy into a disadvantageous position. The final infantry assault would be preceded by a bombardment of arrows, missile engines, and thrown spears. Roman infantry would halt at a distance of about thirty yards from the enemy formation to throw their spears in a single volley and then rush across the deadly zone to close in on the enemy with swords. Missiles would kill very few. But the shock effect and disorganization caused by a steady rain of arrows, missiles, and spears falling into the enemy's formations was usually enough to give the infantry a momentary edge at the critical time when the close combat began.

A Roman centurion reading *Joint Vision 2020*, today's latest vision of how America intends to fight, would recognize the two operative elements of that document, precision strike and dominant maneuver, as nothing more than new words to describe the familiar prime variables of warfare. Firepower is simply a term for the killing and the psychological effects of projectiles and missiles launched from a distance. Since firepower cannot hold ground, its effects are fleeting. Firepower is psychologically intimidating. Its effects cause confusion and interrupt operational tempo and paralyze the enemy in place. Maneuver provides the ability to gain a positional advantage over the enemy. A maneuver force seeks to exploit the momentary paralysis effects of firepower to move against the enemy in an effort to turn him away from his lines of support and back him into unfavorable terrain. An enemy has been outmaneuvered when he finds himself isolated and cut off and no longer able to influence the battle in his favor. He is left with only two alternatives: concede to the opposition or face annihilation. Firepower and maneuver must be orchestrated and applied in balance to ensure success. While both are essential and complementary, they also compete with each other for primacy on the battlefield. At times, when the speed and agility of a force exceeds the ability of firepower to impede it, mobility is dominant. At other times, the range and lethality of firepower becomes so great that the zone that separates maneuver forces becomes too deadly to cross.

KOREA: THE CHINESE ADAPT

The equations that govern relationships between the variables of fire and maneuver differ substantially between limited and unlimited wars. The evolution of a style of war that has become distinctly American began when the U.S. armed forces first discovered and subsequently solved the firepower versus maneuver equations for limited wars. The U.S. Army in particular was obliged to do the math the hard way—in the practical classroom of real combat. The discovery of this new American age of warfare began with two wars of attrition—the first in Korea and the second a decade later in Vietnam. In both conflicts, commanders went into combat handicapped by their experience in fighting and training for large-scale, European-style combat. Habits acquired through generations of practice cannot be changed overnight. But to their credit, once the harsh realities of limited war became apparent, American combat commanders learned quickly to adapt and change.

One of the first lessons they learned was that the limited political ends dictated by the strategic circumstances of the war severely limited the means available to achieve success in battle. The most severe of all limitations, of course, was the imperative to keep casualties to a minimum. The essential doctrinal adjustment made by field commanders to accommodate this new imperative was to increase the firepower available to support maneuver forces and to lessen the exposure of close-combat soldiers to direct attack by the enemy. Early battles in Korea began with the application of doctrinally correct proportions of firepower to maneuver inherited from the Second World War. Very quickly, however, field commanders increased their demand for artillery and air power to support ever more compact and self-contained assault forces. What began as traditional dismounted infantry assaults in 1950 soon became elaborate tank-, infantry-, and firepower-intensive demonstrations intended to gain the objective with minimum cost in lives.

The doctrinal shift between firepower and maneuver in favor of the former was immediate and dramatic. During the Battle of Soryang in the spring of 1951, twenty-one battalions of artillery fired over three hundred thousand rounds in five days in support of a single push by X Corps. Two years later, at Pork Chop Hill, nine battalions fired over thirty-seven thousand rounds in less than twenty-four hours in support of a single regimental assault. Fourteen battalions of supporting artillery fired over two thousand rounds in only eight minutes in support of a single battalion of the 38th Infantry Regiment during the Battle of Bunker Hill in the spring of 1951. General Edward Almond, who commanded the corps that bore the brunt of this attack, recalled instances when entire battalions were saved from annihilation by firepower alone. He spoke of "time on target" concentrations, in which as many as fourteen battalions fired more than 2,500 rounds of different caliber timed to land on a single point within two minutes.

The story was the same for other sources of supporting firepower. The Air Force, in its first conflict as an independent service, quickly overcame its initial reluctance to provide close air support. By the end of 1951, the Air Force had developed the skill and deployed the resources to bomb effectively from directly in front of friendly troops out to the farthest extent of the battle area deep inside the enemy's rear. During the Soryong River battle, the Air Force supported Almond's corps with heavy bombers delivering radar-guided, blind-bombing strikes at night close to U.S. troops. The Air Force flew over 4,500 sorties to beat back Chinese attacks in October 1952.[1]

As the weight of firepower increased, the densities of infantry formations decreased in proportion. By the winter of 1950–51, General Matthew B. Ridgway conducted most of the Eighth Army counter-attacks at regimental level. That spring, Ridgway consistently used nothing larger than company teams to spearhead his advance to the Han River. Fewer soldiers forward supported by a firepower system capable of achieving enormous killing power had the desired effect early in the war. The Chinese were halted, pushed back, and slaughtered in large-scale kill zones south of the Han River. The farther south the Chinese advanced, the more exposed became their lines of supply. By spring 1951, many more Chinese soldiers were dying from malnutrition and exposure than from firepower as the Air Force successfully strangled the overextended and exposed logistical sinews that linked the People's Liberation Army (PLA) to its source of supply in the homeland. U.S. casualties decreased steadily as General Ridgway's firepower-dominant style became increasingly more effective.

As the front stabilized later in the war, the role of infantry increasingly evolved into that of a "finding and fixing force." The infantry held a thin defensive perimeter and patrolled aggressively to ensure that a Chinese attack was detected in time to destroy it with artillery and airpower. Large-scale operations such as the battle for the No-Name Line became carefully orchestrated battles of attrition, the objective of which was to kill thousands using hundreds of thousands of bombs and shells with the least cost in friendly lives. Imperfect as it seems today, the firepower system developed during the Korean War was beginning to be accepted as the proper tactical mechanism for dealing with an intractable foe.

However, as the front stabilized and the campaign settled into a defensive "slugfest," ominous signs appeared on the battlefield suggesting that the firepower-centered doctrine was beginning to be understood and countered by the enemy. The protraction of the war had given the PLA time to assess how the Americans were fighting and to develop methods to mitigate the killing effects of American firepower. U.S. commanders were caught off guard by the swiftness and effectiveness of the Chinese response to a firepower-centered method of war.

The Chinese were quick to adapt because they had been down this road before. Their effort to sustain their army in the face of a technologically superior foe would eventually result in nothing less than a fundamental redefinition and codification of an Eastern approach to defeating the Western way of war. The process began long before Korea in the mountain fastness of Manchuria as Mao Zedong developed tactics for defeating the Japanese prior to the Pacific war. Mao and his marshals developed a body of doctrine adapted from their successful wartime guerrilla campaigns and modified their concepts to fit the demands of a conventional war fought against an enemy superior in technology and materiel. Mao perfected his new way of war against the Chinese Nationalists during the Chinese Civil War fought between 1946 and 1949. His concepts were simple and centered on three tenets, the first and most important of which was "area control." To be successful, Mao's army first needed to survive in the midst of a larger, better-equipped enemy. To ensure survival, Mao divided his army into small units and scattered these across a broad expanse of territory. Controlling and maintaining cohesion among such a disparate and scattered force was and remained his greatest challenge.

Once his force was supportable and stable, Mao proceeded to apply the second tenet, which was to "isolate and compartmentalize" the Nationalist forces. The challenge of this phase was to leverage control of the countryside to such a degree that the enemy gradually retreated into urban areas and along major rail and road lines of communications. The final act of the campaign demanded an ability to find the enemy's weakest points in order to collect and mass overwhelming force against each point sequentially. Maneuver was by infiltration. To avoid the enemy's superior firepower, the Red Chinese would converge on their intended target in small groups from many isolated, dispersed locations all at once. The object was to remain dispersed as long as possible and then to mass suddenly by surprise and only when in the immediate proximity of the enemy's defensive perimeter. Mao's new style of conventional war, while effective, demanded an extraordinary degree of discipline and patience to persevere under extreme hardships. It also demanded the ability to "transition" quickly from an area control force to a force capable of fighting a war of movement.

During the early days of the Chinese intervention in Korea, Mao and his marshals, to their collective misfortune, momentarily forgot the lessons of the Civil War. The PLA badly misjudged the killing effect of an increasingly more effective American artillery and tactical air-power system. Pushed too quickly into maneuver warfare, the Chinese massed in the open, often in daylight, to expand their control over the northern portions of the Korean Peninsula as quickly as possible. The Chinese paid a terrible price for their haste. Their spring 1951 offensive sputtered to a halt as U.S. artillery and aerial firepower killed Chinese soldiers in masses.

The PLA eventually adjusted to the conditions of this new war by returning to the Civil War methods that had served them so well in the recent past. Over the next two years, subsequent Chinese attacks remained limited and controlled. The Chinese high command learned to hold most key logistic facilities north of the Yalu River, well out of reach of U.S. air attacks. South of the river, the Chinese dispersed and hid their forces while they massed only in the period immediately before launching an attack. PLA soldiers moved at night and chiseled their front lines of resistance deep into hard, granite mountains. By the beginning of the "stability phase" of the war, the PLA had effectively altered its operational doctrine sufficiently to change the dynamics of the battlefield in Korea. American casualties soon mounted, while the Chinese stabilized their casualties at a rate acceptable to their political leadership. Far more Americans died in combat during the period of static combat in Korea than during the earlier period of fluid warfare. A cost acceptable to the Chinese became too costly to the Americans. The result was an operational and strategic stalemate. To the Chinese, stalemate equaled victory.

Late in the war, frustration within the American command mounted as it became apparent that the Chinese were becoming increasingly immune to an ever-increasing onslaught of firepower that seemed to have increasingly less effect on the enemy. To some degree, ground commanders in 1953 faced the same tactical problem that French, German, and British commanders faced late in the First World War: how to create a flexible, reliable system effective and destructive enough to restore mobility on the ground. Unfortunately, the actions of the enemy had shifted the firepower-maneuver balance so far to the side of firepower and the defensive that maneuver was no longer possible even with the support offered by shiploads of artillery and bombs. The solution was obvious: If firepower could not be made more effective, then the balance had to be shifted by increasing the ability of ground forces to maneuver. But the mountainous Korean terrain restricted mechanized maneuver to a few primitive roads that could not be traversed without first capturing the surrounding heights. Endless toil and bloodshed were needed to assault and seize steep mountain peaks. Deep maneuver to seize operational objectives by land-bound units was virtually impossible and far too costly.

The only sure way to conquer the mountains and narrow mountain passes in Korea was to go over them. A few soldiers and marines saw in the helicopter a means for maneuvering vertically. The helicopter made its debut for medical evacuation and search-and-rescue missions. These vehicles were mostly small, vulnerable, and slow, and they carried too few passengers to be useful as carriers for large-scale aerial maneuver.

Toward the end of the war, the H-19—a rescue helicopter with the lift capacity to carry most of an infantry squad—became the first aerial vehicle suitable for carrying infantry into battle. Experiments with the H-19 convinced both the Army and the Marines of the potential of aerial envelopment. But there were too few H-19s available to conduct operations above company level and, while choppers might move soldiers to distant mountaintops at a hundred knots, the speed of movement once on the ground was the same as it had been in Roman times: two miles an hour.

Yet the more farsighted soldiers and marines, sparked by the catalyst of their own experience, resolved during the decade that separated Korea from Vietnam to champion the development of an entire family of vertical-lift aircraft. By 1960, the Army was committed to modernizing its aviation fleet to include an all turbine-powered family of medium- and heavy-lift helicopters.

VIETNAM: THE ENEMY ADAPTS

In the first Indochina war, the Vietnamese borrowed extensively from the Chinese experience and found creative ways to lessen the killing effect of French firepower. The Vietnamese also proved highly skilled in adapting to the new challenges posed by their Western opponents. The Vietminh based their tactical and operational approach on Mao's unconventional methods. Their conduct of the battle was remarkably reminiscent of siege operations conducted by the PLA during the Chinese Civil War. In both cases, the secret of success proved to be dispersion and careful preparation of the battlefield. The Vietminh remained scattered in small units whenever possible in order to offer smaller—and thus less detectable and less lucrative—targets, as well as to allow their troops to live off the land. Fewer supply lines and logistic sites offered even fewer opportunities for interdiction fires.

To win, the Chinese and the Vietminh needed to attack. Successful attacks demanded the ability to mass, at least temporarily. The Vietminh needed to exercise great care in massing under the enemy's umbrella of protective firepower. Superior intelligence provided sufficient information to select the right time and place. Their ability to collect and orchestrate the movement of tens of thousands of soldiers at just the right moment allowed attacking forces to collapse their enemy's defenses before French firepower could regain the advantage. This remarkable ability to "maneuver under fire," perfected against the Nationalist Chinese and the French, reached new levels of refinement during the second Indochina war—against the United States. But first the Vietnamese, like their Chinese allies, had to learn a cruel lesson. They discovered early in the second Indochina war that fighting the Americans would be substantially different from fighting the French. The firepower of the U.S. military would be enormously more massive and lethal. Consequently, tactics used against the French successfully at Dien Bien Phu and elsewhere would have to be modified substantially if they were to prevail against a more numerous and technologically advanced opponent.

The U.S. Army went into Indochina burdened with many of the same prevailing attitudes about the relationship between fire and maneuver that it had carried into the early days of the Korean War. During the very early "search and destroy" phase of the war, commanders still favored operations by larger units—usually brigades, sometimes divisions supported by doctrinally correct apportionments of aerial and surface-delivered firepower. As in Korea, they learned gradually to increase the proportion of supporting fires and to lessen the exposure of maneuver elements moving into contested areas.

General William DePuy, commanding the First Infantry Division in 1966–67, was quick to realize that artillery and tactical aircraft were responsible for most enemy casualties. His casualties, on the other hand, came principally from three sources: enemy mortars, concentrations of enemy small-arms fire delivered against infantry units in ambushes, and mines. His common-sense solution was simply to use much smaller infantry units, usually squads or platoons, to locate and fix the enemy, and then to orchestrate a varied medley of supporting firepower systems to do most of the killing.

Once the enemy was located, the infantry's task was to stay out of the killing zone, avoid decisive engagement, and pull back just far enough to allow effective delivery of ordnance but not so far as to allow the enemy breathing space to disengage and escape the firepower trap. The old infantry adage,

"Close with and destroy the enemy," became simply: Get close enough with as few forces as possible to "find, fix, flush, and set up the enemy for destruction by fire."

DePuy was among the first to grasp that modern firepower technology and the imperative to win at lower cost in lives were together sufficient to cause a shift in the relationship between firepower and maneuver. In later years, he was fond of saying: "On a battlefield increasingly dominated by lethality, if you can be seen you can be hit, if you can be hit, you will be killed." Whether traditionalists liked it or not, DePuy believed that the balance had in fact shifted to the point where firepower systems, not infantrymen, had now become the central instrument for achieving decisive effect on the battlefield.[2]

While seeming to offer the promise of less costly victories, DePuy's concept of maneuver supporting fires failed to last as a viable doctrine much beyond Vietnam. There were cultural objections. Commanders rightly feared that training combat soldiers not to close with the enemy might diminish fighting spirit and create hesitation and a loss of decisiveness and élan. The enemy who learned over time how to lessen the killing effects of American firepower offered the most persistent complication to the DePuy doctrine.

After suffering greatly from American firepower during the Tet Offensive in 1968, the North Vietnamese under the command of the chief architect of the North Vietnamese Army (NVA) fighting strategy, General Vo Nguyen Giap, learned quickly to accommodate their strategic plans to the new realities imposed by American firepower. The North Vietnamese relearned the importance of dispersion and patience. They redistributed their forces to keep the most vulnerable units outside the range of American artillery, and they moved logistics installations away from battle areas into sanctuaries relatively safe from aerial detection and strikes.

Thus the Vietcong and the NVA dusted off and applied many of the same methods that had proven useful in previous Asian wars against Western-style armies. They learned to "hug" close to units in contact and to keep larger formations dispersed and positioned just out of artillery range. The enemy soon became very adept at hiding in built-up areas and the jungle. They also learned imaginative ways to deceive reconnaissance and fool even the most sophisticated detection technologies. During the summer of 1969, the NVA, in an effort to kill more Americans at less cost to life on its own side, began to change the focus of its offensive operations from American infantry units in the field to softer targets, such as firebases, logistic bases, and convoys.

As in Korea, over time, the battlefield advantage offered by superior American firepower began to diminish as the enemy adapted the proven lessons of Asian warfare to fit the unique circumstances of war against a Western power. By the end of 1969, the battle for Indochina had devolved into a war of attrition in which the side with the greatest available advantage in firepower found it was no longer able to translate that advantage into success on the battlefield. A dispersed enemy wise to the American reliance on firepower became a far more difficult target. Soon, so much explosive weight was needed to achieve any substantial result that the firepower system itself became an impediment rather than an advantage. As the war dragged on and pressure at home mounted to reduce casualties, commanders had few options other than to rely increasingly on a firepower-attrition strategy that demanded an even greater intensiveness of firepower to accompany offensive action in the field.

Maneuver commanders began to complain that the firepower-attrition doctrine imposed on them had become a millstone around their necks. A single example serves to make the point. The "force-feed fire support system" used by the 25th Infantry Division toward the end of the war relegated the control of every contact, however minor, to the duty officer at division headquarters. He was instructed to automatically dispatch a stream of firepower systems into the fight to include Air Force gunships, tactical airpower, attack helicopters, and even "flame bath" helicopters equipped with napalm. The firepower would come even if the battalion commander felt that such a rich dose was either wasteful or counter to his scheme of maneuver.

Another extreme example of the debilitating influence of firepower late in the war came from a corps artillery commander in the Central Highlands region of Vietnam, who reported that his command fired almost two million rounds in seven months of relatively inactive combat—equating, by his best estimate, a ratio of 1,000 rounds, or roughly $100,000, per kill. Lives were saved to be sure, but infantrymen on the ground rightly lamented the resulting loss of flexibility and control.[3]

In Vietnam as in Korea earlier, maneuver commanders regretted their inability to restore the balance between firepower and maneuver. The problem was with a tactical method that offered them too much firepower and too little maneuver. Vertical-lift technology in the form of the ubiquitous UH-1H "Huey" helicopter gave them a huge advantage over their Korean predecessors in getting to the battle area. But once on the ground, the same old problem of local mobility prevented the infantry from maneuvering to halt and surround and fix the enemy in place. Both sides were moving at the pace of the Romans. Maneuver commanders learned again the old tenet of operational maneuver: "If the attacker can move no faster than the defender, then the defender can always refuse to fight unless the circumstances of battle are in his favor."

Yet despite their frustration with the firepower system, maneuver commanders returning from Vietnam supported DePuy's hypothesis. The new limited war imperative to win at minimum cost in life demanded that the traditional balance between firepower and maneuver be altered significantly just as DePuy suggested. A remarkable study done by a group of returning infantry commanders at the Army War College in 1969 concluded that firepower was now the dominant factor on the American battlefield. They wrote that maneuver is performed primarily to pinpoint the location of the enemy and to increase the effectiveness of the massive application of fire on the enemy. Ideally, the enemy should be killed at the maximum effective range of organic weapons. The need to advance infantry to "zero" range will proportionately increase friendly casualties and decrease the ability of foot infantry to maneuver or use fire support. They concluded that, in this new age of limited wars, the traditional proportion between firepower and maneuver on the battlefield must at least be rebalanced. The dynamics of fighting such wars in the future might even have been altered to the extent that the established principle of "firepower supporting maneuver" was now reversed. But the unsolved problem remained: How can a force in the field maintain the initiative and maneuver if it is increasingly burdened by a cumbersome firepower system that limits the speed, agility, and flexibility of the force? As they would soon discover, the United States was not the only Western power to face such a problem.

THE RUSSIANS LEARN IN AFGHANISTAN

Half a decade later, and half a continent away, in Afghanistan, the Soviets learned the same harsh, firsthand lessons of overconfident industrial-world military organizations confronting Third World militaries that have the will, tenacity, and skill to remain effective in the field despite complete firepower inferiority. Year after year, the Soviets arrayed themselves for conventional combat and pushed methodically up the Panjir Valley only to be expelled a few months later by a seemingly endless and psychologically debilitating series of methodical and well-placed ambuscades and minor skirmishes. Mounted mostly in tanks and infantry carriers, the Soviets had the maneuver advantage in the valleys. But they remained buttoned up and road bound and never were particularly effective at locating the enemy with any precision. Once pressed, the Mujahidin simply dispersed into ever-smaller aggregations and moved into the mountains, where Soviet main force units were reluctant to follow.

Borrowing a page from the American textbook in Vietnam, the Soviets attempted to make up for their maneuver disadvantage on the ground by exploiting the firepower, speed, and intimidating potential of armed helicopters. They employed helicopters principally as convoy escorts and to provide fire support. At times, Hind helicopters proved enormously lethal and effective, particularly early in the war, when the Mujahidin were psychologically unprepared. But the Mujahidin themselves eventually borrowed a page from the Vietnamese textbook. They first learned to employ heavy anti-aircraft machine guns, and later Stinger shoulder-fired missiles, to shoot the gunships down in increasing numbers. Military frustration and defeat in Afghanistan presaged the collapse of the Soviet Union.

THE ISRAELIS LEARN IN LEBANON

The Israeli Defense Force forged its freedom and maintained its regional military dominance by prosecuting an unbroken series of victories in four wars of preemption from the War of Independence in 1948 to the War of Atonement in 1973. After nearly three decades of failure in preemptive campaigns, an alliance of Arab state and non-state actors pushed Israeli mechanized forces out of Beirut and precipitated a series of attrition campaigns that continue to plague the Israelis to this day. Back streets, tall buildings, and other forms of urban clutter provided the Arabs just enough respite from the firepower-intensive methods of the Israelis to wear away Israeli morale both in the field and at home. Unable to bring the full force of their superior maneuverability and shock effect to bear, the Israelis paused just short of their operational objectives. Excessive casualties and public images of bloody excesses on both sides eventually resulted in an Israeli withdrawal from Beirut. Their success in Beirut soon provided Israel's enemies in the region with a new and promising method to offset Israeli superiority in open mechanized combat. Now a spectrum of low-tech threats—ranging from weapons of mass destruction delivered by crude ballistic missiles, to random acts of terrorism, to children throwing rocks at soldiers—confronts an increasingly frustrated Israeli military and public.

BRITISH EXPERIENCE IN THE FALKLANDS

Fought during the late spring of 1982, the Falklands War was Britain's first experience with serious war since the Suez Crisis. The circumstances surrounding the campaign and the manner in which it was fought serve as a remarkably prescient prelude to other limited wars destined to occur during the next two decades. In a period of a few months, and within the confines of two small islands isolated in the South Atlantic, the British fought a war of strategic preemption. Much like the Americans, they found themselves involved with the challenge of balancing the three primary variables inherent in modern limited wars. Trained to fight in Europe, the British made many of the same tactical mistakes in the opening battles of the campaign that the Americans had made elsewhere. Chief among these was a propensity among maneuver commanders to underestimate the difficulties inherent in close combat and to rush into firefights without pausing to secure adequate firepower support or precise, target quality intelligence.

Faced with the problems of time and distance, and without the means to arrive quickly, the British sought to isolate the islands with sea power in an effort to keep the Argentines from reinforcing their relatively small island garrisons. Once on the ground, the British Army fought two series of land engagements—one to eliminate the Argentine Marine's positions protecting the settlement at Goose Green, and the other to culminate the campaign by eliminating Argentina's final resistance at Port Stanley (at the easternmost point of the islands). The contrast between the two battles in many respects parallels the experience of the U.S. Army in Korea and Vietnam in coming to grips with the realities of fighting the new and unfamiliar form of limited wars, in which firepower predominates on the battlefield.

Goose Green was an infantry battle fought in haste.[4] The assault force of the 2nd Parachute Regiment (Paras) hoped that darkness and surprise would offset the considerable disadvantage of attacking a reinforced battalion of Argentines dug into hillsides in well-prepared bunkers and trenches. The terrain was cold, stark, and completely devoid of cover. Enemy resistance slowed the advance of the Paras until daylight found them in the open, exposed with nothing but three light artillery and two mortars for support. The assault group of four rifle companies began to break into small clusters of riflemen who, without the benefit of covering fire, were obliged to inch their way up to within 50 meters of the enemy positions. From there, the men would rush each position, firing continuously and throwing hand grenades. The commander, Lieutenant Colonel "H" Jones was shot dead by the Argentine defenders as he crawled to within three feet of an enemy position.

The Paras eventually prevailed in the fight for Goose Green—principally because of their superior morale, leadership, and training. But it was a fight that did not have to be so close. Intelligence failed to accurately identify the numbers and the quality of the Argentine resistance. More than enough firepower was available to support the assault in the form of light tanks, naval fire support from frigates offshore, and artillery. But very little of it came into play during the firefight.

The British adapted very quickly after their close encounter at Goose Green. They would not fight again without an overwhelming advantage in firepower. The culminating battle on the main Argentine center of resistance at Port Stanley was conducted as a series of unrelenting attacks by infantry and light armor supported by copious amounts of firepower delivered by artillery and from ships stationed off-shore. It was only fitting that the final act that broke the back of Argentine resistance should come from the veterans of Goose Green. This time, the mission for the Paras was to seize Wireless Ridge, located astride the most direct route into Port Stanley. If they learned no other lesson from Goose Green, the Paras certainly learned the absolute need for overwhelming firepower. They gathered about them all manner of fire support for the final assault, including two batteries of artillery (this time supplied with plenty of ammunition), a frigate for naval gunfire support, and a troop of Scorpion and Scimitar fighting vehicles. This was anything but a silent night attack. From the moment the first company crossed the start line, Wireless Ridge erupted in a volcano of exploding shells. Six thousand rounds of all types eventually landed on the ridge. Compared to Goose Green, Wireless Ridge was a "cakewalk."

The most important lesson for the British, however, was that first-class infantry, well motivated and well led, could make up for most deficiencies in mobility and firepower. Although Argentine artillery at times inhibited British movement, the effects were fleeting at best. The effect of British fires on the poor-quality Argentine troops, on the other hand, was paralyzing. The psychological impact of firepower broke the will of the Argentines on Wireless Ridge. The British also learned that supporting firepower steels *good* soldiers. To infantrymen about to risk their collective lives, the sight and sound of exploding shells signals that they are not alone—that, indeed, they are part of a larger, massively competent organization whose overall power is clearly superior to the opposition. For soldiers on the receiving end, particularly poor ones, firepower creates a sense of stress and alarm made all the more fearsome by its impersonal and anonymous nature. A soldier cowering alone in the bottom of his foxhole finds himself alone and isolated from his buddies. This feeling of isolation leads inevitably to vague imaginings and apprehensions—not only of dying, but of helpless inaction and the intense fear of being left to die alone.

One might ask why comparable if not greater doses of firepower failed to have a similar effect against the North Vietnamese. Part of the answer is that, on many occasions, particularly early in the war, the psychological effect of sudden and precise firepower strikes did induce some enemy to flee. But in a war without fronts, a fleeing soldier, however demoralized, most often could retreat, recover, and fight another day. The Argentines, however, had no option but surrender after their flight. The soldiers of the North Vietnamese Army were also better than the Argentines, and experience in combat tells us time and again that poor units are infinitely better candidates for firepower shock than tight, cohesive units. Time and experience also play a significant part in the ability of fires to intimidate psychologically; over time, soldiers become inured to firepower's shock effect. They soon learn that the sound and pyrotechnics of a firepower strike are far greater than the actual killing effects of artillery and bombs. Consequently, as a conflict progresses, more and more firepower is needed to intimidate as well as to kill. The British were fortunate that only a single dose of fire was needed to end the campaign. Had the fighting lasted much longer, the need to increase the amount of firepower to achieve the same effects against the Argentines might well have bankrupted the meager firepower available to the British.

The Falklands campaign brought to an end the period of the Cold War in which all of the major participants except for Germany experienced the realities of limited war. The United States, Israel, France, and the Soviet Union learned painfully the frustrations inherent in fighting wars of attrition in which the enemy managed to maintain the initiative by controlling the advantage of time. The British, thanks to their favorable geographic position and an enemy without the competence or the will to fight a protracted campaign, managed to achieve their strategic objectives by conducting a short, relatively bloodless campaign of preemption. In all cases, the powers engaged considered these conflicts to be distractions from the real purpose of Cold War states: a bipolar showdown between the United States and the Soviet Union and their respective allies.

Not until two nearly simultaneous events—the unraveling of the Soviet Union and the involvement of the United States in three successful preemptive campaigns—would the United States begin to realize the importance of the lessons of past experience with limited wars for future land warfare strategy.

NOTES

1. Billy C. Mossman, *Ebb and Flow: November 1950–July 1951* (Washington, D.C.: U.S. Army Center of Military History, 1990), pp. 238–39, 350–54, 442; S.L.A. Marshall, *Pork Chop Hill: The American Fighting Man in Action, Korea* (New York: Morrow, 1956), p. 196.

2. Paul H. Herbert, *Deciding What Has to Be Done: General William E. DePuy and the 1976 Edition of FM 100-5, Operations*, Leavenworth Papers, No. 16, (Ft. Leavenworth: Combat Studies Institute, 1988), pp. 19–23.

3. Robert H. Scales, Jr., *Firepower in Limited War* (Novato, CA: Presidio Press, 1994), pp. 143–44.

4. For a more complete depiction of the battles of Goose Green and Port Stanley, see Robert H. Scales, Jr., *Firepower in Limited War* (Novato, CA: Presidio Press, 1994), pp. 199–233.

• 5 •

Getting It Closer to Right
From Panama to Afghanistan

$\mathcal{T}$he American invasion of Panama in December 1989—operation Just Cause—is the only limited war that the United States has won conclusively since the end of the Second World War. In the laboratory of contemporary campaigns, it still stands as the truest model of the art of preemptive warfare. To be sure, the victory was gained in large measure because the Americans had many significant advantages. It was an operation with a clearly identifiable and assailable strategic center of gravity in the person of Panama's leader, Manuel Noriega, and his henchmen. It was a preemptive campaign launched from strategic distances, but those distances were not all that far from bases in the United States. American forces possessed secure sanctuaries in the midst of the enemy and had nearly a century's worth of experience in the region. Moreover, the United States had a hugely disproportionate military advantage.

Because Just Cause was not much of a military contest, the campaign did not seem at the time to be worth much attention—particularly when the larger-scale conflict in the Gulf, Desert Storm, captured the attention of the American military only eighteen months later. But the ease with which the Panama campaign was won masked its importance as a prospective window on the way armies might fight in the future. The Army's failed effort to put troops on the ground in Kosovo resurrected interest in Just Cause. Perhaps the operational method used so successfully in Panama might serve as a useful analog for determining how to do "a Kosovo" better in the future.

From an art of war perspective, the experience in Just Cause taught the lesson that success in a preemptive campaign is dependent on the ability of the intervening side to apply overwhelming force nearly simultaneously with the object of collapsing the will of the enemy very quickly. The American experience taught the lesson that simultaneous operations can be achieved

61

only by orchestrating all of the instruments of war so that they play the score in harmony. Land, sea, air, and space forces converged on Panama from many locations—some from within Panama, others from the continental United States—in a single, continuous, strategic maneuver.

On the ground, the campaign took the form of a very complex joint operational takedown. Ground, sea, and air forces arrived at night, striking and capturing targets scattered across the entire expanse of Panamanian territory. Special operations forces led by the 75th Ranger Regiment parachuted into Rio Hato, Torrijos, and Tocumen airfields to preempt effective reaction and to open the door for the follow-on 82nd Airborne Division. The Marines seized the key Bridge of the Americas to isolate the west bank of the canal. Navy SEALS attacked over the beach to capture Patilla airfield and to disable the patrol boats of the Panamanian Navy. Airborne, mechanized, and light infantry task forces from within Panama moved out quickly on the ground to seize the Panamanian Defense Forces headquarters, the Commandancia, and other key facilities inside Panama City and its suburbs. Strategic maneuver was balanced with firepower, also delivered from strategic distances. Two F-117 stealth fighters flying from Nellis Air Force base in Nevada each dropped a laser-guided, two-thousand–pound bomb near the infantry barracks at Rio Hato to distract the enemy forces there just before the Rangers parachuted from 500 feet onto the Rio Hato airfield. The most effective firepower system proved to be Air Force AC-130 gunships, which circled continuously over friendly troops, destroying enemy vehicles and delaying the arrival of enemy reinforcements.

In other respects, operation Just Cause had about it the look and feel of subsequent limited conflicts. Maneuver was non-linear and focused on the control of the entire operational area rather than on the sequential capture of key terrain and high ground characteristic of more traditional forms of maneuver. The Army, in particular, was introduced to the challenges of post-conflict operations when it was obliged to care for the needs of thousands of displaced Panamanians who needed food, shelter, and protection for months after the shooting phase of the operation was over. The United States also had to explain its actions to the public—literally as it was fighting the operation—because over fifty members of the media were on the ground in Panama to observe and report on the operation in real time. Street fighting in Panama City again raised the disconcerting prospect of close combat inside Third World urban areas, foretelling all the horrors and risks that the U.S. Army would meet again soon in Somalia and Haiti.

In time, the U.S. Army would begin to appreciate the significance of the Panama experience as the first and perhaps most compelling signpost of the future course of land warfare. At the very moment when the Army turned to concentrate seriously on the lessons of Panama, however, another war in the Middle East deflected its attention toward a more strategically significant but operationally less relevant analog of future war.

THE GULF WAR: DESERT SHIELD TO DESERT STORM

The Gulf War was as much a symbol of vindication for the U.S. Army as it was a victory for the nation. The Army's reputation, tarnished in Vietnam, was restored in the blowing sands of Iraq and Kuwait. The obvious quality of American soldiers, doctrine, and materiel on display in the Gulf gave the Vietnam generation of Army leaders the opportunity to answer a legion of critics who, even on the eve of the air war, still doubted the Army's ability to fight.

The certainty of the victory had only just begun to permeate the collective conscience of America's military leaders when all of the services began to analyze the Gulf War experience to find relevant signposts for the future course of warfare. Definitive conclusions were slow to emerge at first because the signals were often contradictory. To those inclined to hold on to the past, the war appeared to play out much as if it had been fought on the plains of Central Europe. The efficacy of the Army's Cold War AirLand Battle doctrine and the suitability of the equipment to support it were seen as sufficient to carry the Army into the future with little change. To others, the war sent different signals. While the specifics were as yet indistinct, those who studied the war with a more open mind were beginning to see the difficulties facing the future U.S. Army expressed in terms of the three military challenges set out earlier.

Most dramatic and troubling was the challenge of balancing time and risk. At the very beginning of the emergency, the Joint Chiefs of Staff agreed, with some trepidation, to dispatch a brigade of the 82nd Airborne Division to the border area between Kuwait and Saudi Arabia to establish America's strategic "line in the sand." The line served the useful purpose of demonstrating American resolve. But it was a very thin and tenuous line. Early deploying units dodged a bullet thanks to Saddam's incredible strategic ineptitude. Had the Iraqi Republican Guard continued south into Saudi Arabia, the poorly protected, foot-mobile airborne infantry would have had a difficult time stopping them. The inability of light infantry to stop tanks turned a risky scheme into a very dangerous gamble with soldiers' lives—a gamble commanders do not like to take. The time-risk challenge for the early stages of the campaign centered on the natural tension that derives from two conflicting imperatives: one, to arrive early in order to preempt the enemy's aggressive action, and two, to arrive with sufficient killing power, mobility, protection, and sustainability to fight effectively once on the ground. Thanks to superior airlift, light forces could arrive in any theater of war within hours. But the airlift was inadequate to transport the heavy vehicles and substantial ammunition, fuel, and spare parts necessary to allow the 82nd to fight effectively on arrival. In a word, light forces were strategically but not tactically mobile, and heavy forces had the opposite problem. The paradox could be solved in one of several ways. Light forces could be made more mobile, lethal, and survivable, or heavy forces could be made lighter and thus more deployable. In any case, neither could occur to any substantial degree unless both forces had access to faster sealift or more substantial airlift.

The time-risk challenge also presented a longer-term problem that was just as troubling. After about a month, the first armored units arrived in theater and lessened the immediate danger to the 82nd. Yet almost half a year was needed to build up sufficient combat power in Saudi Arabia before offensive operations could begin. As already noted, the operational ineptitude of Saddam and his field commanders intervened to nullify the consequences of the delay. But those who watched the deployments proceed concluded that six months of preparation and more than a month of aerial bombardment before decisive operations began would most certainly give a more competent and aggressive enemy time to find ways to make a buildup and subsequent offensive very costly in lives. What if Saddam's SCUD missile attacks—directed at ports, airfields, and installations—had been more numerous and accurate? What if Saddam had taken the time given to him to reposition his forces in depth to better absorb air strikes and to readjust the location of his reserves to better position them to counter-attack?

The Cold War U.S. Army was simply too bulky and unwieldy for operations such as this, in which strategic speed is the essential imperative for success. Half a year was needed to place a third of a million troops on the ground and to build the huge complexes in the desert to support them. Fewer than 10 percent of these soldiers were fighters. There were more medics and communicators in Saudi Arabia than combat soldiers. An armored division in the Gulf weighed almost a hundred thousand tons. Ammunition and the trucks and guns to haul and shoot it took up over two-thirds of the weight of the division. The Army took almost 27,000 shipping containers into the theater and delivered over 350,000 tons of ammunition to fighting forces; of this total, fewer than 80,000 tons were actually expended in the campaign. Fuel was another problem. Mileage on the 70-ton Abrams tank was about one gallon per mile, and an attack helicopter burned 2.5 gallons per minute. What if the war had *not* been fought in a region where the bulk of the world's fuel is extracted and refined?

The weight and bulk of the U.S. Army in the Gulf also seriously affected the balance between primal elements within the firepower-maneuver challenge. The Army had a serious problem with "the logistical tail wagging the operational dog." Television images of tanks sweeping across the deserts of Iraq misrepresent the actual dynamics of an armored force maneuvering across open terrain. Even in the open, maneuver is highly directional and limited by the rear area supporting it. Think of an arm hinged at the shoulder, elbow, and wrist, with each finger representing the 5,000 soldiers and 1,500 vehicles of an armored brigade, the essential element of operational maneuver. The fingers can be opened and closed quickly, yet the hand can only be traversed left or right within a limited arc. The rest of the extremity is relatively fixed, and days are often needed to unhinge a wrist or shift an elbow in a new direction. The more the fingers are thickened by the density of the formation, and the more ungainly the logistical tail becomes, the more difficult it becomes to maneuver freely. In the Gulf War, the open desert terrain lessened the impact of the problem of tactical, or retail, logistics to some degree. But to those who thought about war in the more restricted terrain of Europe or Asia, the experience of supporting the Great Wheel movement in Iraq gave pause.

The increased range of engagements in the Gulf War also affected the firepower-maneuver balance. The ability to see and strike at great distances, particularly at night, made it possible for advancing maneuver forces to stand off from the enemy and deliver overwhelmingly destructive fire. In the Second World War, an average of 18 rounds was needed to destroy a tank at a range of 800 yards. During the 1973 Arab-Israeli War, the average was two rounds at 1,200 yards, and in Desert Storm, one round at 2,400 yards. Tank commanders were aware of their range advantage over the enemy and took special precaution to ensure that initial engagements were opened by surprise and at distances just beyond the maximum range of the Iraqi T-72 tank. The combined effects of more distant air- and surface-delivered artillery and tactical-air and attack helicopter fires, when orchestrated together properly, produced a carpet of precision killing power that extended from about two to three miles in front of advancing troops out to the limits of the corps boundary—in the case of the VII Corps, a distance of about 180 miles.

The battlefield in the Gulf continued to thin as the firepower quotient rose. The range and lethality of modern tanks and the ability of maneuver forces to see vast distances in the desert allowed armored formations to open up to an unprecedented degree, thereby exposing forward maneuver elements as little as possible. The propensity to spread out and disperse when faced with the increasing lethality of firearms is nothing new in warfare. In the Civil War, both sides at Gettysburg adhered to doctrinally correct Napoleonic frontages of about 26,000 men per mile of front, including skirmishers and local reserves. By the First World War, the improved precision of rifled arms had forced armies to disperse to about 4,000 men per mile. In the European theater of operations in the Second World War, the figure was 1,000, and in the Gulf War, about 240. What might have constituted a corps front at Gettysburg became a battalion front in the Second World War and was occupied by a force as small as a platoon in Desert Storm. Instinctively, when faced with the realities of real war against a clever enemy, the U.S. Army exploited information-age and precision-age technology fully in order to return to DePuy's maxim of minimum exposure to achieve maximum killing effect.

During the Gulf War, it became apparent that the shape of battle formations had become less geometric and more organic in appearance. In the Gulf, individual armored formations had opened up to the point where constant visual contact between fighting elements was no longer considered necessary to maintain cohesion in the close battle. Linear formations were still considered necessary, mainly to lessen the chances of fratricide when fighting at night and during periods of limited visibility. After the war, it was apparent that, if the technology could be developed to permit positive identification of friendly units, the need for linear warfare would be a characteristic of wars just past.

The changing dynamics of the battlefield had already begun to change the roles and purposes of each of the layers of operational command. A space once occupied by a division of 16,000 soldiers and 5,000 vehicles could now be commanded by a brigade of about a third that size. Thus a *brigade* of 5,000 in the Gulf had begun to take on the characteristics of a Cold War *division*. Increasingly, brigades were becoming more autonomous entities with their own organic fire support and logistical structures, giving them the ability to operate separately for longer periods. Divisions were also beginning to act more like *corps* (typically 50,000 or more), taking on many of the non-combat functions previously performed by a corps. Finally, it appeared that, in the Gulf War, there was little or no justification for any fighting echelon above corps. Clearly, the problem of layering slowed the arrival of fighting forces into the theater. Why was it necessary to build a structural analog of the army in Europe or the United States if the intended purpose of fighting forces in the region was merely to fight a brief campaign and return home? A finance or personnel soldier in Saudi Arabia required just as much food, shelter, and comforts of home as a combat soldier. Surely the strategic speed and agility of the U.S. Army could be increased if many of these support functions were left behind. Perhaps, some argued, entire layers of command had been made redundant by the information age. Take out a single layer, and the speed of the army could be accelerated without compromising effectiveness.

The hidden hand of popular acceptance and political control continued to moderate allowable means to achieve the strategic ends of the campaign. The cost of a conflict in lives lost must remain in proportion to the perceived value of the endeavor. The war demonstrated the need for a protracted preliminary aerial bombardment to wear down and demoralize the enemy sufficiently to make the land campaign as casualty-free as possible. Commanders went to extraordinary lengths to ensure that soldiers were protected from chemical and biological attack. But the ends-means dilemma had some deleterious effects on the execution of the war as well.

Immediately after the ground war began, fratricide became a problem—caused in part by the inability of attacking forces to track and follow units on the move at night in the open desert. Pressure to avoid killing friendly troops created friction and tactical timidity. Air and artillery strikes were kept miles away from advancing formations and close support missions of any sort were extremely rare. Advances were often halted mid-stride as commanders readjusted formations and counted soldiers before continuing. Even though Saddam's SCUD attacks against Saudi cities caused little physical harm, the psychological impact of these very public strikes was substantial. Consequently, almost 40 percent of allied air sorties were dedicated to finding and destroying SCUD launchers. For Saddam, the fear of civilian casualties and the political impact of Iraqi SCUD attacks gave a very handsome return on a very limited investment. The ends-means dilemma may well have limited the decisiveness of the campaign. Nearly real-time television footage of surrendering Iraqi soldiers and the horrible images of the so-called highway of death brought home the plight of enemy forces, and fear of excessive Iraqi deaths created pressure to end the conflict perhaps prematurely.

Despite the overwhelming incompetence displayed by Iraqi military leaders at the tactical level, some Iraqi units displayed considerable capacity to adapt on the battlefield. As the U.S. air campaign began to focus on the destruction of the Iraqi ground forces in the Kuwait theater of operations (in early February), the Iraqis almost immediately began to construct berms around their tanks and to scatter them widely across the desert. These simple acts ensured that an aircraft dropping precision-guided bombs at best would be able to destroy a single vehicle with each pass. The Iraqis also fooled their enemies by burning tires next to operational vehicles. Moreover, by employing anti-aircraft weapons effectively, they kept a substantial portion of coalition aircraft at an altitude where they were unable to do substantial damage.

The best-trained Iraqi units endured several weeks of allied air bombardment with will unbroken and combat capability intact. The most impressive indication of Iraqi ability to adapt came in the operational movement of a substantial portion of the Republican Guard during the first hours of Desert Storm. Elements of two divisions shifted from a southeastern defensive orientation to defensive positions facing to the southwest along the Wadi al-Batin. In those positions, the U.S. VII Corps would destroy the Tawakalna Republican Guard Division and the 50th and 37th Armored Brigades. Nevertheless, sacrifice by these units provided time for the remainder of the Republican Guard to escape. Significantly, the Republican Guard carried out this movement in terrain and weather conditions ideally suited to destruction by firepower and despite the overwhelming superiority of coalition air power.

SOMALIA

The operation in Somalia, conducted in the fall of 1993, is the most striking example yet of what can happen in limited wars when an intervening power fails to understand the complexities of balancing ends and means. The presence of soldiers on the ground in an unstable region immediately makes the ends-means dilemma capable of spiraling quickly out of balance, particularly if the purpose of the soldiers' presence changes over time. Soon after the Army and Marine units arrived on the scene, the strategic ends of the operation shifted from humanitarian relief to the elimination of a ruling elite. The early involvement of special operations forces, tailored for fighting wars in the shadows, momentarily masked from the American people how quickly the intervention in Somalia was drifting from the task of feeding the starving to open warfare against armed gangs on a Third World urban battlefield. The presence of the media in force in Somalia became an instrument of amplification as images of soldiers handing out food to starving villagers were suddenly replaced by images of dead American soldiers being dragged through the streets of Mogadishu. The loss of eighteen Ranger soldiers in close, back-alley fighting dramatically underscored a corollary to General DePuy's maxim: A tactical engagement fought for too high a price for too little return might very well by itself determine the strategic outcome of a national endeavor.

The long-term strategic implications of the "fight and flight" phase of the operation still affect perceptions of America's fighting resolve today. Those who fail to understand the interrelationships between ends and means falsely conclude from the Somalia example that the United States has become so averse to casualties that the level of tolerance is now zero. They forget that, prior to the Gulf War, the media reported that the U.S. Department of Defense estimated as many as 20,000 or more casualties should Saddam employ chemical weapons. In the Gulf War, where the expected end-state demanded nothing less than the security of the world's access to oil, the American people were willing to tolerate casualties. The popular reaction to casualties from the SCUD attacks against Riyadh also suggests that, while the American people may tolerate casualties in future wars, they will never tolerate wasting the lives of its young men and women.

The reaction that foreign armies had to the American withdrawal from Somalia is also instructive. Just as video images of exploding "smart bombs" have inflated opinion of American prowess with firepower, images of the withdrawal from Somalia have caused foreigners to overestimate American sensitivity to casualties. During the height of the air campaign in Kosovo, the Serbian man in the street could be heard to say that America would stop the bombing and the war could be won if only the Serbian armed forces could kill eighteen Americans. It may well be that the ability of the United States to build a credible conventional capability to deter future limited wars will depend on how well it manages to correct both misperceptions.

Unfortunately, the remarkably heroic performance of the U.S. special operations forces was largely lost in the dust of the hasty retreat from Somalia. For more than twelve desperate and bloody hours, a small, company-size band of Delta Force and Ranger soldiers fought off thousands of Somali "technicals" in a fight remarkably reminiscent of the famous defense of Rourk's Drift by the British Army during the Zulu War. Supported by Blackhawk and UH-6 Little Bird gunships, the Americans fought from behind buildings and walls both to rescue downed helicopter crewmen and to keep the Somali irregulars from swarming over their small perimeter and destroying them completely. The experience taught the sobering lesson that, in this new era of limited wars, even the most technically advanced army in the world must be prepared to fight the old-fashioned way at point-blank range against an enemy perfectly willing to die in large numbers.

But the bloody action in Mogadishu may also tell something about the kind of maneuver forces that the U.S. Army may need if it is to get the most from the small number of such forces that it will be able to put on the battlefield in the future. The most obvious lesson is the same one learned by all armies faced with the prospect of fighting close: Elite soldiers who are carefully selected, trained, and well led always perform to a higher standard. The Mogadishu fight just underscored dramatically how much of a difference high-quality infantry can make to the outcome of a very serious firefight. Had lesser quality soldiers faced such a vicious attack by overwhelming numbers, casualties surely would have been much greater and the prospects of success much more problematic.

The experience of special operations soldiers demonstrated that just a bit of modest technology applied to the task of fighting close can make an enormous difference in keeping soldiers alive and improving their effectiveness. Simple devices such as good radios, night observation and identification devices, first-rate body armor, and state-of-the-art customized small arms all gave combat soldiers in Mogadishu a substantial edge when it mattered most. Superbly effective and very close support by mini-guns and rockets fired from specially equipped gunships reminded the Army of a lesson first learned in Vietnam. The armed helicopter still remains the instrument best suited to delivering fire in very close proximity to friendly troops in contact. Likewise, the extra attention given by aircraft designers to make the Blackhawk helicopter capable of absorbing "punishment" was a worthy investment. The Somalis downed two Blackhawks, but only after the aircraft suffered hundreds of hits from small arms and rocket fire. Others managed bravely to fly directly into a hail of bullets, hover long enough to deliver troops and supplies, and then fly away to safety despite being riddled with gunfire. Vietnam-era helicopters would have disintegrated when subjected to such intensive ground fire. Finally, the sobering experience of Somalia taught that even the bravest dismounted soldier fights at a disadvantage when unable to exploit fully the mobility advantage offered by the helicopter. The force was able to escape only after the arrival of an armored convoy of Pakistani and Malayan tanks and infantry carriers. The lesson is clear: If time and circumstances permit, all the combat power available should be applied overwhelmingly when the lives of soldiers are at stake.

KOSOVO

U.S. experience in Kosovo suggests that, while improvements in precision munitions may continue to tilt the firepower-maneuver equation in favor of the former, the nature of the enemy and the immutable character of war continue to argue for the preservation of balance between the two classic components of war. Placed in suitable historical context, the Serbian response to the NATO onslaught is nothing more than another data point along a continuum of progressive, predictable adaptation by technologically dispossessed militaries that are willing to challenge Western militaries armed with superior precision firepower. Like their Asian counterparts, the Serbs sought victory by avoiding defeat. In a similar fashion, the Serbs conceded the vertical dimension of the battlespace to NATO. They were content with an approach that only hoped to shoot down a few allied aircraft, using ground-mounted guns and missiles. This hope was underscored with the expectation that a few dead or captured allied airmen would contribute to the gradual degradation of NATO's resolve. Even if a shootdown was not possible, the Serbs sought to keep their anti-aircraft assets intact in order to force NATO aircraft to bomb from as high an altitude as possible.

The surest way for the Serbs to avoid defeat was to keep their army in the field viable—both to act as a defiant symbol of national resolve and to be the legitimate Serbian guarantor of sovereignty over the occupied territory. To maintain an effective "army in being," the Serbs likewise borrowed from successful past precedents. Units quickly went to ground and dispersed across a broad expanse of territory. They quickly computed the pace at which the allies could find, target, and strike uncovered targets and then devised the means to relocate mobile targets inside the allied sensor-to-shooter envelope. Camouflage, decoys, and spoofing techniques, proven so effective by Asian armies, were repeated with varying degrees of success by the Serbs. As the allies became more proficient at spotting troops, the Serbs sought even greater dispersal and went deeper to ground.

Toward the end of the conflict, significant success from the air came with the appearance of an infant ground presence in Kosovo in the form of the Kosovo Liberation Army. The KLA was not terribly effective in open combat against the better armed Serbs. But the presence of large-scale KLA units in their midst on occasion forced the Serbs to come out of protective cover and mass. The results were predictable and remarkably consistent with past experience in combat against the Chinese and NVA. Troops moving, massed, and in the open present the most lucrative targets for destruction by fire from the air. However amateur and ineffective the KLA, its presence forced the Serbian Army to reluctantly trade the security of its hiding places for battle in the open. Only after Serbian armor and artillery were exposed in daylight did the air campaign become moderately effective in taking out tactical targets.

Yet the Serbian Army was never severely damaged by the aerial onslaught; it was simply too large and well protected to be completely destroyed from the air. Since total destruction was not feasible, the contest in Kosovo soon devolved into a test of time and will characteristic of attrition warfare. The side that could endure the longest without collapsing its national resolve would achieve victory. Once it became evident to Milosevic that NATO's political resolve would not be broken before a threatened ground assault could materialize, he chose, as always, the most expedient path. Seeking to ensure his own political survival, the Serbian leader ceded Kosovo to the allies.

AFGHANISTAN 2001–02

There is no question that the success achieved by the Afghan warriors of the Taliban and al-Qaeda gave them confidence that, should the United States be foolish enough to follow the bombing of the World Trade Center in New York and the Pentagon in Washington with an ground invasion in Afghanistan, it would suffer the same humiliation and defeat as the Soviets had a decade before. Anecdotal evidence in fact suggests that the al-Qaeda leadership in particular had in mind an apocalyptic war of attrition against the Americans as a hoped-for strategic goal of the bombing. The U. S. military managed to avoid the fate of the Soviets by capitalizing on superior technology and by adhering to a method of fighting that proved to be effective across the entire spectrum of conflict.

The campaign in Afghanistan would become a virtual proof of principle and the surest confirmation yet of the universality of the newly emerging American way of war. No place on the planet is more distant and inaccessible. Nowhere is the terrain more inhospitable or the enemy more inured to hardship and war. Nor could any defense planner devise a prospective warfighting scenario as far removed from the pattern of past conflicts that had shaped the way Americans have fought limited wars for the past fifty years. If the new style of war accommodated the extremely atypical circumstances of enemy, terrain, weather, and mission, then the confidence would be there to conclude that the U.S. military has at last developed a style of war that might fit, within reason, practically all of the strategic circumstances likely to be encountered in future limited wars.

The strategic velocity of operation Enduring Freedom was metered more by the ability of political and diplomatic forces to set strategic conditions than by the lifting capacity and readiness of the projected force. For military and political planners alike, the campaign was a cold start. No one ever imagined that American forces would have to fight in such a distant and inhospitable place. Thus the speed with which coalitions were formed and basing rights negotiated was a remarkable testimony to the ability of the military and political leadership to work together for a common strategic end. To be sure, the United States never achieved full basing and overflight rights in the region. Attack aircraft had to fly enormous distances from faraway bases in Diego Garcia in the Indian Ocean and from carriers offshore. Some fighter aircraft would have to execute as many as six aerial refuelings during a single mission that might last up to six hours. But difficulties gaining access to the area of operations should not overshadow the fact that Central Command succeeded in conducting a strategic basing and deployment exercise in absolutely the most taxing strategic, geographic, environmental, and military circumstances.

From the very beginning of the planning process, it was apparent that the Afghanistan campaign plan developed by Central Command in Tampa, Florida, adhered faithfully to the concept of trading firepower for manpower. Firepower necessary to defeat Taliban and al-Qaeda forces would come from the air. Killing power would be delivered in about equal proportion from tactical fighters launched from carriers stationed off the coast of Pakistan and from Air Force strategic bombers, called again as they have been so many times in the past to launch conventional weapons against tactical targets on the ground. From the beginning, it was apparent to commanders planning the operation that this was not to be another Somalia. Universal revulsion at the horrific deeds of September 11 served to raise the bar of tolerance for the price to be paid in blood and treasure in Afghanistan. Yet despite the greater latitude offered tacitly by the American people and the government to accept losses in order to bring the terrorists to justice, the U.S. Command chose to do all in its power to limit the cost of the campaign in lives of friend and foe alike.

Experience with the difficulty of achieving decisive results using aerial attack against tactical forces in Kosovo convinced the U.S. Command that any aerial assault would have to be complemented with a substantial ground effort. Putting substantial U.S. ground forces into such hostile terrain against an unbroken enemy would have played into the Taliban's strategic plan. Fortunately, resistance to the Taliban still remained on the ground in Afghanistan in the form of the 3,000 or so militia of the Northern Alliance. These soldiers, properly bolstered by U.S. precision firepower, logistics, and intelligence, were to constitute an effective if unusual surrogate maneuver force.

The shooting phase began on October 7—with all the frictions typical of previous American campaigns. Initially, success was hampered by the usual tendencies to overcontrol and overcentralize the delivery of expensive and rare precision munitions. The delivery problem was made more difficult by the enormous distances that Navy fighters and Air Force bombers had to fly in order to reach the target areas. Unfamiliarity with the region and a dearth of intelligence infrastructure in the region greatly hampered intelligence gathering during the early days of the campaign. An elusive enemy, very bad weather, and terrain rough and inhospitable enough to defeat some of history's most competent invading armies made a smooth transition into the combat area extraordinarily difficult and time-consuming.

What made this campaign different from previous campaigns was the short time needed by units in the field to improvise a doctrinally incorrect yet innovative and effective firepower system capable of overcoming seemingly overwhelming environmental and political friction. The essence of the campaign was captured on film, with the image of Special Forces sergeants, equipped with the latest laser and satellite technologies, moving about the battlefield mounted on shaggy Afghan steppe ponies. In a very short time, these soldiers became the glue that cemented the U.S. forces to the militia of the Northern Alliance. Initially, the teams found it difficult to gain the trust of a group of Afghan fighters who were inclined to be skeptical of the degree of U.S. commitment as well as the ability of U.S. forces to influence the course of a campaign from aircraft orbiting in the stratosphere. Trust became much easier to establish once the Afghans witnessed how devastating precision bombardment could be when controlled by soldiers with a direct view of the target.

Only a few days were needed for this very small group of Special Forces teams to improvise a system for controlling aerial fires and directing them against Taliban positions south of Mazur-e-Sharif. The teams used hand-held, global position system (GPS) locating devices, matched with compasses to derive the exact locations of the Taliban positions. They transmitted the target coordinates by voice to the bomber crews orbiting overhead. The crews manually punched locating data into their arsenal of GPS-guided bombs before launching them toward the targets. To guide fighter aircraft with precision, the teams used hand-held laser designators to "paint" the targets sufficiently for the fighters to pick up the "spots" and transfer them to the aircraft's internal laser designation systems. Many of the more discrete Taliban and al-Qaeda targets were taken out by AC-130 gunships. These updated versions of the venerable Vietnam-era "Specter" aircraft possess the ability to sense and track the smallest enemy target using a variety of infrared and low-light devices. Killing is done with frightening efficiency by 40mm Gatling guns and 105mm cannon.

By the end of October, the combination of twenty-first-century precision firepower complemented by an indigenous maneuver force consisting of Northern Alliance militia mounted aboard commercial trucks and antique Soviet armor succeeded in forcing the Taliban to cede all critical terrain in the north and to retire into the city—their last stronghold being in the city of Kandahar. Operational maneuver by U.S. forces began shortly thereafter, with the insertion of a reinforced Marine battalion, Task Force K-Bar, by Air Force C-17 and C-130 transports into a forward operating base on the outskirts of Kandahar. The successful establishment of the aerial bridge from Pakistan and Uzbekistan to Camp Rhino, and subsequent helicopter-borne raids by Marine, Army, and special operations forces from the base outward into the far reaches of Afghan territory testifies to the ability of U.S. ground forces to conduct aerial maneuver in even the most distant and inhospitable settings.

The greatest concern of forces on the ground in Afghanistan was intelligence. Special operations direct-action units were hunting individuals, not armored formations. Traditional Cold War overhead sensors designed to locate fixed sites and slow-moving masses of armor simply lacked the capability to provide timely and precise target-quality intelligence to operators seeking to locate a scattered and dispersed enemy. The problem was compounded by the fact that many of the enemy sought to hide among the innocents inside cities and villages. The intelligence problem was solved to an extraordinary degree by the employment of an assortment of unmanned aerial vehicles. Long-endurance unmanned air vehicles (UAVs), such as the Air Force's Global Hawk and Predator, established an unblinking eye over the battlefield that provided an image of sufficient granularity to find, identify, and track individual terrorists. The ability of these UAVs to loiter for long periods gave U.S. forces in Afghanistan a constant eye over the battlefield that allowed analysts to watch for patterns of activity in order to anticipate enemy movements and avoid surprises. Immediacy was achieved by linking UAVs directly to operatives in the field—and in some cases directly into the command consoles of attacking aircraft.

More than any conflict of the "American era," operation Enduring Freedom will become both a metaphor for the character of conflicts to come and a template for how such wars will be fought. In Afghanistan, all of the elements of future preemptive wars were represented: rapid projection of firepower and maneuver capabilities by air; the use of carefully selected, trained, and bonded small units; the establishment of an unblinking aerial eye over the battlespace; and tactical maneuver by air from forward-operating bases deep inside the enemy's territory.

THE ENEMY WATCHES, LEARNS, AND ADAPTS

With the exception of the truncated expedition to Somalia, the U.S. military has put together a string of extraordinarily successful campaigns since the end of the Cold War. Success has come easily—in large measure due to the ineptitude of the enemy and the ability of the United States to bring overwhelming force to bear against him. But the unfortunate example of American experiences in less successful campaigns suggests that future victories against more competent and capable enemies are by no means guaranteed. Non-Western militaries understand that the United States does have vulnerabilities: an aversion to casualties and excessive collateral damage, a sensitivity to domestic and world opinion, and an apparent lack of commitment to prepare for and fight wars that are measured in years rather than months. These militaries also perceive that Americans, in particular, still remain committed to a style of war focused primarily on the single offensive dimension of precision strike. Moreover, they are already thinking about how to target Western vulnerabilities while capitalizing on their own five intrinsic advantages: time, will, the inherent power of the defensive, proximity to the battlefield, and greater familiarity with the theater of war. Taking a page from Mao's and Giap's strategy, potential opponents have learned the value of time and patience. From their perspective, swift success is not essential to achieving ultimate victory.

Future U.S. adversaries have also discovered the apparent advantages that can be gained when they interfere with an intruding power's intention to end the conflict quickly and at minimum cost. Consequently, the logic of their strategy will lead to efforts that impede rather than prevent the intrusion of a Western opponent. In recent wars, non-Western armies have learned to limit the damage and duration of air campaigns by dispersing their forces and by distributing telecommunications, logistics, and transportation infrastructures as widely as possible. Moreover, they understand that sophisticated air defense networks, whose effectiveness depends on airfields, surface-to-air missile sites, and complicated and vulnerable command and control nodes have become more of a liability than an asset.

Once conflict on the ground begins, potential opponents understand they must capitalize on their superior mass to offset the lethal firepower and precision technology of Western armies. They will capitalize on the positional advantages of being on the defensive in or near their own territory. As they gain confidence, they will search for opportunities to mass sufficient force to achieve local successes. As in the air campaign over Afghanistan, the enemy will seek to frustrate U.S. ground forces by employing just enough modern weaponry to extend the campaign indefinitely. A few precision cruise missiles against major logistic bases will add to the casualty bill that the U.S. government must explain to civilians back home.

As non-Western militaries develop concepts for defeating the American firepower-centered method of war, the character and composition of their forces will slowly change. The Cold War impulse to mimic Western force structures is rapidly disappearing. Foreign militaries that were once Cold War clones are taking on identities unique to their own cultures and societies. The mountains of metal, consisting of expensive yet often second-rate air, sea, and ground machines of war that today serve as potentially lucrative targets in a conflict against the United States are rapidly disappearing. Non-Western armies, in particular, are getting lighter. The need to survive and remain effective against the threat of overwhelming American killing power is forcing them to develop means to disperse, hide, or if possible eliminate vulnerable logistics, transportation, and telecommunications facilities.

Clausewitz provides a harsh and accurate warning about the fundamental nature of war. War is not the action of a living force upon a lifeless mass (total non-resistance would be no war at all), but always the collision of two living forces. The ultimate aim of waging war must apply to both sides. Once again, there is interaction. As long as I have not overthrown my opponent, I am bound to fear he may overthrow me. Thus I am not in control: He dictates to me as much as I dictate to him. It is this fundamental Clausewitz point that American military organizations, confident about their performance in recent conflicts, might well forget. Potential opponents have thought long and hard about how to attack American weaknesses. The United States must not allow its more recent successes in campaigns from Desert Storm to Enduring Freedom to cloud the reality that future adaptive enemies, armed with the means and the will to win, are seeking new ways to defeat America's new style of war.

· 6 ·

Tactics and the Human Dimension
Balancing Ends and Means
in the Close Fight

$\mathcal{L}$ ieutenant Colonel Harry Kinnard was operations officer of the 101st Airborne Division during the Battle of the Bulge in the Second World War. Two decades later, in 1965, General Kinnard commanded the 1st Cavalry Division during the U.S. Army's first major encounter with the North Vietnamese Army at Fire Base X-Ray and Albany in the I Drang Valley. Reflecting on the I Drang many years later, General Kinnard commented, "I lost more men in one day during the Bulge than I lost in the entire battle for the I Drang. We won both battles. Yet while the Bulge is celebrated as a great victory, the I Drang is still considered a defeat."[1] Kinnard was a brilliant soldier—a pioneer in the newly developed science of aerial maneuver on a firepower-intensive battlefield. Yet he was one among many veterans of America's total-war era who failed to appreciate that, in limited wars, the price paid for victory must be tempered by the relative value that the American people place on achieving the victory. With each succeeding war since Vietnam, the bar of tolerance has been consistently lowered.

For the past half-century, most combat deaths in limited wars have been suffered by close-combat soldiers. Clearly, the burden of balancing the ends (measured by the success of a battle) with the means available (measured principally in soldiers' lives) will fall most heavily on close-combat units and leaders. The enemy already knows that casualties constitute America's single most vulnerable and assailable "center of gravity." Killing America's soldiers, therefore, has become for America's enemies not a means to an end, but an end in itself.

To meet the challenge of winning at minimum cost of life, the U.S. Army must accomplish two essential tasks. First, it must break from the traditions of its Cold War past and place an unprecedented priority on the

79

selection, training, and bonding of close-combat units. Second, it must develop and codify a doctrine that changes the way close-combat soldiers fight from a force that closes with and destroys the enemy to one that "finds and fixes"—that is, one that seeks to identify and hold the enemy in place so that supporting firepower can do the killing while close-combat forces remain at a distance.

The "last mile" of the struggle has long been mystical ground shrouded in the lore of the warrior. Centuries of accumulated dogma teach that closing with and destroying the enemy in a face-to-face engagement must be the manner in which all engagements are culminated. Military theorists and philosophers from the French Colonel Ardant du Picq in the nineteenth century to Ferdinand Foch and George S. Patton in the twentieth have measured the depth of the soul of an Army by the willingness of its infantrymen to literally face the enemy in order to kill him. Close combat is intimate and very cold and demands the absolute in personal courage and devotion to duty.

But myths and mystique may no longer be useful as a means for determining how to fight the close battle in future limited wars. In fact, a dispassionate and analytical look at how the art of the tactical battle has evolved during recent limited wars suggests that, once the shooting begins in earnest, mystique very quickly gives way to methods that are both more pragmatic and less costly in life. In fact, during the past half-century of practical war experience, American field commanders have consistently altered their tactical methods in combat to accommodate the imperative to fight at a lower cost in human life.

The task of developing new methods for fighting close with minimum loss of life is made all the more difficult by three factors. First, no one truly understands how much more lethal the battlefield will become as the enemy begins to acquire Western weapons technologies and eventually, with experience, learns how to fight more effectively. Second, the U.S. armed forces, and ground forces in particular, must learn new methods of fighting against an enemy who will become more experienced and competent with each successive engagement. Third, if timidity and loss of aggression and the spirit of the offensive become the price of attempting to win "cheaply," the actual result may be the opposite of what was intended. An enemy may be encouraged to fight more fiercely if he perceives any diminution of fighting spirit among his American opponents. An enemy who senses that casualties are a critical point of weakness will try all the harder to kill as many Americans as possible. The U.S. Army and the U.S. Marine Corps in particular must walk a very fine path as they begin to balance the realities of ends and means to meet the realities of fighting at the tactical level. They must be able to continue to inculcate courage, aggressiveness, and risk-taking in the minds of their soldiers while at the same time developing a new doctrine that accepts the additional imperative of preserving life.

Certainly there will be occasions on most future battlefields when an intractable enemy must be rooted out of cities or sanctuaries in inhospitable terrain. On such occasions, close-combat troops will have to move into the killing zone to confront the enemy on his terms and kill him in very bloody and very hazardous circumstances. Recent American experience in Afghanistan and Israeli experience in the West Bank suggest that, even in a firepower-intensive environment where precision killing is the preferred method for achieving the strategic objectives of a campaign, firepower alone is not enough. The presence on the ground of a few superbly trained and bonded close-combat soldiers determined and courageous enough to face death as they close on the enemy will still make the difference between success and failure.

MANEUVER SOLDIERS

As a ground-combat force approaches the deadly zone and moves within range of the enemy's rifles, mortars, and machine guns, the dynamics of war become more art than science. Intangibles such as training, confidence, leadership, and cohesion provide a more secure mantle of protection than the possession of superior equipment. The magnificent stand by Colonel Joshua Chamberlain's Twentieth Maine at Little Round Top during the battle of Gettysburg and the incredible performance of the American Rangers who scaled the Normandy heights at Point du Hoc are only two of many instances in the history of warfare when maneuver units, usually infantry and cavalry (or armor today), performed far more effectively in close combat than numbers or circumstances could have predicted.

There is as much folklore as science in the accounts of maneuver units that do exceptionally well in close combat. Empirical and anecdotal evidence gathered from combat studies of the Second World War, Korea, and Vietnam has shown conclusively that elite maneuver units, carefully selected and trained, not only perform better in combat but do so with many fewer casualties from all sources of combat incapacitation (for example, from disease and combat fatigue). Such units fight so effectively because they are composed of soldiers of exceptional quality—better trained and better led as well as coalesced through long-term association that builds familiarity and mutual trust. The difference between carefully trained and led units and those of lesser quality is dramatic.

One of the reasons why General DePuy, as a division commander in Vietnam, became so vehement about the need to save soldiers' lives was his experience as a regimental commander in the 90th Division in Normandy. In his oral history, done years after his retirement, DePuy recalled that the 90th was the greatest killing machine in Normandy. The only problem was that the division did the dying, and the Germans did the killing. The division suffered over 100 percent casualties among enlisted maneuver soldiers and 150 percent officer casualties in these same units during the first six weeks of combat. The story was the same for most of the infantry and armored divisions landing in Normandy and pushing ashore during the opening days of the crusade in Europe. The poor performance of the 90th and other similar units at Normandy, unlike that of divisions sent to fight early in the war, was not due to a lack of resources or time to prepare. The 90th had over two uninterrupted years to train for war in Europe, and by 1943 the shortages of equipment and ammunition to train were substantially a thing of the past.

The great nineteenth-century military intellectual and creator of the modern military staff system, Helmuth von Moltke, once observed: "An Army that learns to fight by fighting, fails." The example of the 90th Division in Normandy was an extreme example of the U.S. Army's historical propensity to violate Moltke's axiom. Although German units in Normandy were understrength and exhausted from four years of continuous fighting on other fronts, they had all been educated in the tough school of real war and were quite skillful in the practical art of close combat. American units, on the other hand, were new to the realities of modern infantry combat and were unprepared for the harshness and the ruthless nature of fighting the Germans in the close confines of Norman hedgerows. After a few months, the learning curve of U.S. units steepened sharply, to be sure, but the price paid in blood for the experience was enormous.

As in all wars fought in the twentieth century, U.S. maneuver units in the Second World War were neither manned nor led by the most qualified people. The infantry had last call on the best qualified soldiers and leaders, while the Air Corps got first choice of the most intelligent and most fit of each year's cohort.[2] Thus the branch that required the most robust and physically able recruits to do the tough work of maneuvering in close proximity to the enemy actually received soldiers who were below the average height and weight for army recruits. The huge number of casualties suffered by the infantry early in the European campaign exacerbated the quality problem—as it has in all of America's wars before and since. Casualty rates of 100 percent per month were not uncommon. An infantry division in combat required as many as 3,500 replacements a month to keep rifle companies up to strength. A chronic shortage of infantry, caused by a gross underestimation of the requirement for close-combat units, prevented the leadership from taking units out of the line to rest, refit, rebuild, and adequately integrate soldiers and leaders. This anachronistic system for replacing maneuver soldiers was both tragically wasteful of human life and deleterious to combat effectiveness. Infantry units in particular often became collections of strangers. New soldiers, pushed individually into depleted platoons and companies, poorly acclimated to combat, and not part of the social bond of the unit, often had only a few days to live. The morale of veterans was often severely affected by the realization that the only relief from the endless horrors of front-line combat was a wound or death. Yet the Army's policy of individual replacements and unrelieved time in combat continued until the war's end.

It seems strangely illogical that the U.S. Army has held on so long to such an inefficient and archaic system for procuring, training, and replacing maneuver soldiers. Apart from the humanitarian argument, the cold strategic realities of balancing ends and means would argue that America gains or loses strategic maneuver room in a conflict in direct proportion to the severity of the cost of the conflict in human life. If casualties are the greatest vulnerability, then maneuver soldiers, specifically infantrymen, constitute the most assailable point within America's "center of gravity." In wars in the past century, most of those from all services who died have been infantrymen—not just soldiers or Marines, but infantrymen. In Korea and Vietnam, infantry soldiers alone accounted for over 80 percent of all combat deaths in both wars, even though infantrymen comprised only about 11 percent of Army and Marine forces and less than 4 percent of all servicemen in theater. Anyone other than a pilot or an infantryman in fact stood a far greater chance of dying from accidents or disease than from contact with the enemy. It is also important to note how these soldiers were killed. The greatest killers of Americans in wars in this century were automatic small arms and the lowly mortar.

In future conflicts, the American people will watch and measure the relative cost of each war and never will tolerate the waste of lives. Once war begins, the clock starts ticking. Every dead American shown on CNN will contribute to the process of accounting. Enemies know from watching America's strategic reversal in Somalia that the most vulnerable center of gravity for the United States will most certainly be its willingness to tolerate casualties.[3]

As is evident from numerous combat examples in past wars, bonding (the long-term association of men within a small unit) is useful in all units, but it is absolutely essential to those that are to remain effective in combat. Yet the personnel system still treats close-combat soldiers as replacement parts—just as it did a half century ago. New soldiers come as individuals and strangers to their first units. Once there, in today's turbulent environment, infantrymen are fortunate to spend as much as a few months together before being reassigned to other duties. Often they are transferred away to other units after only a few years in a single duty station. Likewise, officers are lucky if they are allowed to stay in command of small units for more than a year.

Maneuver soldiers are also still selected and trained with little regard for the demanding nature of close combat. The public continues to harbor the image of Willie and Joe as archetype infantrymen. In reality, the tasks of a modern maneuver soldier are not only the most dangerous on the battlefield but also the most complex, demanding, and difficult. Moreover, saving the lives of close-combat soldiers has never been a terribly high budgetary priority. Infantry weapons are not very different today from what they were in an earlier era. It should come as no surprise, then, that all too often in the past, the close fight became an even contest that usually resulted in a tactical "draw" once infantry soldiers moved inside the lethal range of the enemy's small arms and mortars. Moreover, the realities of balancing ends and means, in which losses cost the enemy less in strategic capital than they did the United States, meant that every draw was a defeat.

Despite the searing experiences of recent wars, programs to increase the survival of maneuver soldiers in combat have been few, and the money devoted to these programs minuscule compared to others having substantially less return on the investment in human life. It is ironic and instructive that, while the United States has spent billions to develop the technology to sense and track strategic targets thousands of miles away and to destroy them with million-dollar cruise missiles and bombs, an infantry platoon leader still cannot take out a mortar firing from behind the next hill without exposing his soldiers to direct fire from the enemy.

On future battlefields, the difficulties inherent in maneuver units will become even more severe. The examples of Panama and Somalia demonstrate the truth that infantry units will be required to fight on short notice and often in distant, unfamiliar, harsh, and unforgiving places. As the battlefield expands, it will become more isolated, and soldiers will find themselves increasingly alone. As enemies become more familiar with the new American style of war, they will become increasingly more competent in minor tactics and more difficult to fight.

A glance at the recent conflicts in Bosnia, Kosovo, and elsewhere suggests that, often in this new global environment, tactical actions by soldiers at the lowest level can have strategic consequences. In Kosovo, a squad leader is the one responsible for determining whether or not to fire on men in civilian clothes who may be threatening his position. A mistake in judgment will bring immediate, global attention and may undermine the entire strategic outcome of the U.S. presence there. In Afghanistan, when an infantry sergeant identifies a village as the source of incoming fire, a mistake of only a few meters in locating the source of fire may result in civilian rather than enemy dead.

On every future battlefield, infantrymen will be required to perform many complex tasks formerly reserved for other branches of the service. They will be expected to become forward observers, medics, communicators, mechanics, sappers, and intelligence gatherers. Maneuver soldiers will be required to manipulate information and precision-age weapons of ever-increasing complexity. The Army will not be able to fully exploit the potential of this new age of warfare unless maneuver soldiers are fully capable of using the technology at their command.

All soldiers are not the same. The Army is no longer so large as to be able to afford to differentiate the unique and demanding needs of close-combat soldiers from those of all the other soldiers who support them. If the next war is to be won at minimum cost of life, then past experience suggests that those selected to go into harm's way must be protected by resorting to the most extraordinary measures. They must be exceptionally proficient in battle. The examples of Sedan, Point du Hoc, Bastogne, and Mogadishu demonstrate conclusively that elite soldiers man-for-man fight better and suffer fewer casualties. Close-combat units therefore must be made as selective as budgets and policies will allow. In terms of total budget priorities, the challenge is not all that great, as maneuver soldiers make up only a very small proportion of the total force. Today, infantry soldiers comprise less than 4 percent of all military manpower—fewer than 50,000 total, of whom approximately two-thirds are Army and a third Marine personnel.

If the number of maneuver soldiers is so small and the consequences of loss are so great, it is important to take the time to develop every combat soldier individually—much like professional sports teams select and develop prime athletes. The process of developing the best possible maneuver soldier begins by selecting only those best suited to the task of close combat. Decades of rich data on the selection of Special Forces and Delta soldiers collected by the special operations community suggest that the selection criteria for maneuver soldiers should be quite different from those of the general population of new recruits. Obviously, physical strength, agility, and stamina are qualities that come first. One of the ironies of warfare in the information age is that today's soldier carries far more on his back than his grandfather did in machine-age wars. U.S. Rangers and paratroopers dropping into Grenada and Panama as well as the British in the Falklands carried more than 115 pounds of gear in their rucksacks. As we have seen recently in professional sports, physical stamina and strength are no longer the preserve of younger men. Careful selection matched with modern physiotherapy will extend the active career of close-combat soldiers perhaps well into middle age. In future wars, the wisdom of age need no longer be separate from the strength of youth.

In his classic work on soldiers in battle, *The Anatomy of Courage,* Lord Moran was the first to explain the dynamics that influence a soldier's performance in close combat. He writes of two competing influences that constantly tug at the psyche of a soldier as he advances against the enemy. The native instinct for survival pulls him back, while the induced, moral-social imperative pushes him forward. Every soldier goes into battle with a capital investment of moral compulsion, or courage, collected from his commitment to his leaders and his friends. His capital is depleted by intangibles such as fatigue, hunger, thirst, uncertainty, fear of the unknown, and distrust of leaders and peers. His account empties very quickly once combat begins.[4]

The historical record shows that battle-fatigue casualties often can be greater and more debilitating to a maneuver unit than casualties from wounds. The recent experience of American units in close combat suggests that Moran's crucible of courage can be measured and manipulated to some degree—and that battle fatigue can be reduced substantially as a consequence. Soldiers can be acclimated, or psychologically hardened, to raise their threshold to battle fatigue. The special operations community has learned that psychological testing and role-playing in high-stress combat simulations can give a fair appreciation of the depth of a soldier's crucible of courage. In addition to constant and realistic field training, every maneuver soldier should be carefully and continuously profiled and routinely exposed to comprehensive psychological evaluations to ensure that he continues to maintain the emotional balance to perform effectively in the most stressful of all human endeavors.

Lord Moran also reinforced what all veterans of real combat know to be true: The more cohesive and well led a unit is, the better it fights. There are no secrets here. It is an article of faith within the leadership of all major armies that the single initiative most likely to increase the ability of close- combat units to fight and survive on the battlefield would be the adoption of a "band of brothers" approach to the selection and training of close-combat units. If soldiers are to be expected to sustain themselves and fight on this new battlefield, they must be recruited and trained together and then stay together—not for months or even years, but maybe for a decade or more. A unit-based training and rotation system would bring together small units, perhaps platoons of some thirty to forty soldiers, and keep them together through the end of the first enlistment—a period of at least four years. The combination of talents, courage, strength, agility, intelligence, required of close-combat soldiers in future wars demands better soldiers who are better trained. The extra time would permit unit as well as individual training. It would also allow enough time for the unit to adequately coalesce. Early acclimatization of soldiers to U.S. Army culture should take on the character of an apprenticeship rather than the traditional image of basic training familiar to soldiers today.

A year or two might be needed to put together platoons of new soldiers and to teach them all the exacting skills they need to perform well the moment they join regular units. Junior leaders might be permitted to join their platoons in training, so that young soldiers might begin the essential process of bonding with their first-line leadership and gaining confidence in their abilities. Leaders should expect to be a part of the apprenticeship process and stay with the same platoons for many years. Platoons will become smaller as the battlefield becomes more dispersed and direct command becomes more difficult. The traditional ratio of leader to led within the noncommissioned ranks will decrease from approximately one to ten today to perhaps one to two or three in the future.

Maneuver units also must have a "bench." Even units successful in combat will lose soldiers steadily to wounds, sickness, accidents, and necessary transfers. Experience in combat shows that replacements brought forward from within a unit stand a much better chance of survival than those who arrive as strangers. Units entering combat with extra fighters would be able to remain effective much longer. Units deploying into combat in the future should expand their ranks enough to permit double-crewing of combat vehicles. Extra crews would serve not only as casualty replacements but also as substitutes during combat to relieve exhausted crews and allow the unit to fight continuously.

The same double-crewing principle should apply to commanders and their staffs. Past experience has shown that units in combat hit an emotional wall after about seventy-two hours of continuous combat. Thus the pace of operations is usually driven as much by exhaustion as by the tempo of operations. Any pause in the pace of combat gives the enemy a respite that can make continuation of the attack costly. Information dominance will make it easier and faster to rotate command teams. Near-perfect situational awareness will allow shadow staffs to follow the action in real time from a distance. The time-consuming briefings and lengthy reconnaissance that have characterized the provision of "reliefs" in past operations will no longer be necessary. It would make sense to build redundant command groups capable of taking up the operation seamlessly once one team becomes too fatigued to command effectively.

The nature of future limited wars will often require that early deploying forces be thrust into close combat in some unfamiliar part of the world, often with little or no notice. Unfortunately, in wars of the modern era, the U.S. Army has established an uneven record of performance fighting the opening battles of major wars. The examples of the disastrous opening battles of Bull Run in the Civil War and of the Kasserine Pass in the North African campaign in the Second World War tell of the price to be paid for entering a conflict unprepared.

The destruction of Task Force Smith during the first few days of American involvement in Korea and the uneven performance of U.S. Army units in the opening campaigns of the Vietnam War serve as somber reminders that inadequate preparation could be just as catastrophic in limited wars.

The best insurance against suffering any more "Task Force Smiths" is to deploy a fully trained force made up of all appropriate services capable of fighting effectively on arrival. A hastily put together team simply will not work when success in battle will most certainly be decided by the timeliness of the arrival of the intervening force. All too often, units have forfeited cohesion and competence as they have been subjected to last-minute reshuffling and reorganization to make up for shortages of trained people. The problem is simply that not every unit can be prepared and carried at a peak of readiness all the time. The cost in spare parts, training resources, and soldier wear and tear is simply too high. Many decades of U.S. experience with rapidly deploying units in all the services during the Cold War have proven that sustained, affordable readiness can best be achieved by adopting some form of rotational deployment scheme for the entire U.S. Army both at home and overseas.

Today, all services use some form of a "red-amber-green" rotation cycle that allows one-third of the unit to be immediately ready to deploy, another third to stand down from a deployment just completed, and a third to train for the next cycle of deployment. Moreover, the concept of rotational readiness is not exclusive to the military. Fire and police departments follow this same procedure. They, too, have learned that, while some organizations collectively may be able to "peak" for short periods, sustained performance can only be maintained by the continuous rotation of groups engaged in high stress, dangerous activities.

The problem today is that only a few of the U.S. Army's combat divisions and brigades are engaged in a rotation cycle scheme. All too often, as a crisis unfolds, the temptation to strip less ready units to fill those preparing to deploy creates a wave of instant unreadiness that inevitably grows as it moves through the force. The solution to the problem is simple: The U.S. Army of the future must be organized so that *every* rotational unit, whether maneuver or support, is made part of a global deployment scheme.

MANEUVER LEADERS

Good soldiers perform best under good leaders. The future combat environment, so challenging for soldiers, will be even more stressful for those who command them. It is hard to imagine today how strange and fearsome this battlefield will appear to a young infantry or armor leader. He may well find himself and his unit transported literally overnight to a very distant and inhospitable spot on the globe. Time from notification to deployment may be so short that the leader will have to do planning, rehearsals, and troop briefings while flying to the objective area. Once on the ground, he will find himself fighting an enemy who has been waiting for him, dug in, camouflaged, and arrayed for combat. The battlefield will be not only hostile and unfamiliar but empty as well. The leader may be located many miles from his higher headquarters, and his soldiers will be out of sight and scattered in small increments over a vast area. When close combat begins, he will be expected to orchestrate a panoply of weapons and sensors. He will have to maneuver his sub-units to converge on the target at precisely the right time and place. While the leader may have a sizable information advantage over the enemy, the rush of real-time information will force him to make life-or-death decisions within a decision cycle measured in minutes if not seconds. His standards of performance will be high. The media will be everywhere on the battlefield, and he may well face the emotional trauma of seeing a video of his unit—and perhaps pictures of his dead soldiers—on the global network immediately after the battle. This new "climate" of warfare will demand that a young maneuver leader learn and practice a different style of leadership—a style reserved for officers of much greater maturity and experience in past wars.

During the Civil War, many generals, Union generals in particular—Hooker, Pope, McDowell—performed well at the division and corps level but failed miserably when elevated to army command. Ironically, after failing as army commanders, many of them later redeemed themselves by returning to command at lower levels and there performing well until the war's end. One reason for this phenomenon was due to the geometry and dynamics of Civil War battlefields. A corps stretched across a front of about a mile. A corps commander was close enough to the action and had time enough during the battle to see the enemy's actions, make decisions, and order soldiers about by direct contact in real time.

During the nineteenth century, corps command was the highest level of command to still require the skills of an operator for success. A corps commander was still able to see a problem develop and to dispatch soldiers or artillery to solve it on the spot. But at the army level of command the dynamics of war were for the first time different. The army commander was much more distant from the battle and consequently had no ability to act immediately or to control soldiers he could not see. The distance of the army commander from the action slowed responses to orders and created friction such that the commander was obliged to make decisions before the enemy's actions were observed.

Civil War army commanders were now suddenly required to exhibit a different set of skills. For the first time, they had to think in time and to command the formation by inculcating their intent in the minds of subordinates with whom they could not communicate directly. Very few of the generals were able to make the transition from direct to indirect leadership, particularly in the heat of combat. Most were very talented men who simply were never given the time or opportunity to learn to lead indirectly. Some, like Generals Meade and Burnside, found themselves forced to make the transition in the midst of battle. General Lee succeeded in part because, as military advisor to Jefferson Davis, he had been able to watch the war firsthand and to form his leadership style before he took command. General Grant was particularly fortunate to have the luck of learning his craft in the Western theater, where the press and the politicians were more distant, and their absence allowed him more time to learn from his mistakes. From the battle of Shiloh to that of Vicksburg, Grant was largely left alone to learn the art of indirect leadership through trial and error and periodic failure without getting fired for his mistakes.

The implications of this phase of military history for the future development of close-combat leaders are at once simple, stark, and self-evident. As the battlefield of the future expands and battle becomes more chaotic and complex, the line that divides the indirect leader from the direct leader will continue to shift lower down the levels of command. The circumstances of future wars will demand that much younger and less experienced officers be able to practice indirect command. The space that held two Civil War armies of 200,000 men in 1863 would have been controlled by a reinforced mechanized battalion of about 1,000 soldiers in Desert Storm, and it may well be only a company or platoon position occupied by fewer than 100 soldiers in a decade or two. This means that younger commanders will have to command soldiers they cannot see and make decisions without the senior leader's hand directly on their shoulders. Distances between all the elements that provide support, such as fires and logistics, will demand that young commanders develop the skill to anticipate and think in time. Tomorrow's tacticians will have to think at the operational level of war. They will have to make the transition from "doers" to thinkers, from commanders who react to what they see to leaders who anticipate what they will see.

To do all this to the exacting standards imposed by future wars, the new leaders must learn the art of commanding by intent very early in their stewardship. The concept of "intent" forms the very essence of decentralized command. A senior commander must be assured that, in his absence, subordinates will make decisions he would make were he on the spot. Inculcating the commander's intent involves more than giving and receiving orders. To act in concert and to adhere to the will of the senior commander, subordinates must understand the commander's bias, his personality, and how he thinks. They must be able to understand intuitively how an operation will be executed. There must exist between seniors and subordinates such a bond of trust and mutual understanding that detailed conversations are not necessary. Actions need to become instinctive and follow a general line of direction rather than a narrow path. In the heat of combat, the situation will change so fast that assumptions that might have prompted an order hours before will no longer be valid. A commander will know he has been successful when subordinates believe they are free to selectively disobey.

The U.S. Army must begin very early to find and prepare the young leaders who exhibit the ability to command by intent and move them along the track to higher command very quickly. Time is short; the brigade battle force commander of 2020 was commissioned two years ago. The process can be very selective without harming the readiness of close-combat units because the Army needs relatively few with the special talents—the "right stuff"—of close-combat command; in a U.S. Army the size of today's, perhaps no more than two hundred will be needed to lead at battalion level and above.

The immediate challenge will be to identify those characteristics of a leader that will provide the highest probability that those chosen will be up to the task. The measured judgment of superiors is useful, but no longer enough. Initial selection must not be left solely to chance, or to the subjective opinions of senior officers—or even, for that matter, to the individual desires of the aspiring close-combat officer. The system of command selection must reinforce subjective observations with the addition of more objective factors. The first essential ingredient is intelligence and the ability to apply the gifts of intellect to achieving success in war. Actual experience in past wars suggests that the most likely candidates to succeed at the art of indirect command will be those officers who are intelligent, self-confident, and comfortable with uncertainty and ambiguity. Given enough time and patience, those less gifted can be trained to perform in a predictive fashion when exposed to familiar circumstances. But only those who are highly intelligent and well educated can be relied upon to demonstrate consistently the creativity and the capacity of independent thought that are essential to act under pressure in the presence of uncertainty and ambiguity.

While the relationship between intelligence and performance is a tenuous one to prove empirically, no one would deny that smart officers tend to make good combat leaders and that dull ones stand a disproportionate chance of getting their soldiers killed. Yet at a time when intellectual credentialing has become essential for professional certification within the teaching, legal, and medical professions, the U.S. Army remains one of the few major military organizations in the world that does not require accountability in the form of certifying examinations. Officer education has been a subject of endless debate and deserves a volume of its own to do justice to the subject. To be sure, U.S. Army officers today do devote a significant portion of their time in service to schooling. But the schools lack both rigor and accountability. School attendance should not be the principal means for measuring the quality of an officer's intellect. The brightest can best be identified and nurtured by being given a first-class education, honed continuously through a lifetime of learning and assessed periodically by rigorous, objective examinations that measure an officer's knowledge of the art and science of war and his or her ability to think clearly under the stress of combat.

Intelligence alone cannot be the sole factor used to select the best and the brightest. Military history is replete with examples of intellectually gifted officers who simply lacked other attributes necessary to be successful in combat command—such as courage, integrity, charisma, or (rarest of all) the ability to sense terrain and to anticipate intuitively the pace and tempo of battle. The Special Forces method of screening candidates using physically and emotionally rigorous selection programs could be adapted as a general means for identifying those who possess these special attributes. Such a system would go a long way toward eliminating subjectivity and bias from the selection process. Rejection rates would most certainly be high, and it is probable that those who did "survive" the process would not meet today's accepted profile of a model combat arms officer.

Breaking the cultural mold in order to select officers with just the right qualifications and credentials will require a significant change in U.S. Army "culture." But experience with the quality of close-combat officers in previous wars tells us that past practices have allowed too many unsuitable officers to assume command in combat. Often the inadequacies of these commanders have become evident only when they had failed in actual battle. The U.S. Army can no longer afford the luxury of shedding soldiers' blood to find the right man for the job.

Command in combat is not only demanding and at times dangerous; it can be lonely as well.[5] Commanders are expected to maintain distance from their subordinates. Yet a glance at the lives of great commanders suggests that most of them did establish a relationship with a peer—with someone whose opinions and counsel they knew to be genuine and not self-serving. The global internet would allow field commanders to establish a long-term and continuous working relationship with a senior mentor, perhaps a retired senior officer whom the commander could consult before making key operational decisions. A mentor located far from the terror and discomfort of the battlefield, with access to all the analytical tools, records, and lessons learned—and perhaps linked via the Internet with a group possessing expertise in various aspects of the operational environment—might be able to add calm wisdom and secure counsel at the time when a commander in combat needs it most.

The argument for keeping small units together for long periods applies even more strongly to command teams and operational staffs. In the past, certain successful command relationships were so close that military historians have indicated the bonding by hyphens. The Grant-Sherman and Hindenberg-Ludendorf phenomena, for example, illustrate the synergy gained when understanding and communication between commander and principal deputy are right. Science simply cannot anticipate such effective personal combinations. But when they do emerge and prove themselves in battle, they should be recognized at the earliest possible command level and respected and utilized as the particular team rises in rank and authority.

CLOSE COMBAT FROM A DISTANCE

No portion of the Gettysburg battlefield evokes more drama and pathos than the "Angle"—the northern extension of Cemetery Ridge where General Robert E. Lee's last effort to win the Civil War left over seven thousand Confederate dead and maimed strewn between the fences of Emmitsburg Pike and the low stone wall that traces the main line of the Union defenses. Looking west over the 980 yards of cornfield that the Confederate infantry had to cross to reach the Angle, professional soldiers with firsthand experience in war invariably ponder the same question after only a few quiet moments of reflection: If Lee knew about the superior range and killing power of modern rifled weapons, why did he order an attack that he most surely must have known would fail?

The answer is of course shrouded in the ambiguities of history written long ago. But it must be suspected that, despite his genius, and even at this late stage in the war, Lee still remained handicapped by the experiences of his past. He was educated in the art Napoleonic warfare, when the battle could be decisively won only at the point of a bayonet. He learned the practical dynamics of war firsthand in the war with Mexico—possibly the last major war in which Napoleonic-era tactics still worked. Then, suddenly, at the age of fifty-seven, he found himself fighting a war in the crease between an epoch he understood well and one that was only faintly

familiar. The lesson is instructive: Even among men of genius, merely recognizing that conditions have changed does not guarantee that changes
will be made. For another fifty years after the Civil War, the best and the
brightest among the army leaders and intellectuals of European society
would still fail to act on what science was telling them about the increased
killing power of the machine gun, quick-firing artillery, and smokeless
powder. Generals would continue to order soldiers to march to their deaths
with bayonets fixed until the end of the First World War.

Perhaps it is because the closer soldiers get to each other, the more personal and less scientific war becomes. Just as in the Civil War, analysis too often yields to emotionalism and myth. A realistic picture of the dynamics inside the killing zone caused by the effects of modern arms still eludes us as
much today as it did Robert E. Lee, Ferdinand Foch, and Douglas Haig during the opening decades of machine-age warfare. But while generals and theorists may yet have a problem understanding the intricacies of an infantry
firefight, the common soldier has long understood it very well. A young veteran writing home after witnessing the horrors of Antietam expressed the impulses of close-combat soldiers succinctly:

> When bullets are whacking against tree trunks and solid shot are cracking
> skulls like eggshells, the consuming passion in the breast of the average
> man is to get out of the way. Between the physical fear of going forward
> and the moral fear of turning back, there is a predicament of exceptional
> awkwardness from which a hidden hole in the ground would be a won-
> derfully welcome outlet.[6]

Flawed though it may be in some scientific details, S. L. A. Marshall's
work, *Men Against Fire*, presents the most compelling firsthand empirical evidence on the performance of men engaged in close combat. Marshall's observations generally align with the anecdotal evidence of later-generation soldiers and more recent contemporary combat histories. In the Second World
War, only a very small percentage of soldiers actually fired their weapons at
the enemy during firefights. Most of the fire was delivered from weapons
manned by crews, such as automatic rifles and machine guns. In later conflicts, the story was much the same. Infantrymen in Vietnam fired few aimed
shots at an enemy they could actually see. As General DePuy discovered with
the First Infantry Division in Vietnam, most close-combat engagements in
limited wars were precipitated in an effort to find the enemy. The second
most common precipitant were ambushes—total intelligence failures resulting in firefights at the greatest disadvantage. A distant third precipitant were
deliberate attacks made against a known enemy strongpoint—usually done as
a last resort, when the attacking unit ran out of other alternatives. Only in ex-

ceptional circumstances did soldiers stand erect and walk across the killing zone in doctrinally correct firing lines, firing aimed shots as they advanced. In the overwhelming number of cases, soldiers were content to hold back and let supporting weapons do the killing. In the Gulf War, combat crews exploited the superior range and sensing power of their weapons to stand off outside the enemy's effective arcs of fire and to kill the enemy at a safe distance. In an aerial corollary to the Desert Storm example, air strikes in Kosovo could be delivered with great precision from safe altitudes and distances thanks to the standoff and precision capabilities of modern guided munitions. "Sweeping the killing zone" has been a task reserved for those occasions when most of the enemy have either fled or been killed or wounded, and no willingness remains among them to continue the fight.

Both the warnings and the promise of past experience are very important signposts for the future. As we move into the third technological cycle of war, the changing dynamics of close combat will make massive small-arms engagements at close range as obsolete as massive bayonet charges were at the beginning of the first cyclical turn in the changing character of war. Just as the precision of rifled arms expanded the killing zone to the point where bayonet attacks were impossible, the killing power and range of modern precision weapons will allow American close-combat units to achieve decisive effects without having to move inside the lethal zone of an enemy's small arms and mortars.

Most of the technology necessary to fight the close battle at greater distances and lower cost of life is available today. Multiple layers of small, unmanned aerial vehicles linked directly to units in contact hovering directly over the close battle will offer the immediacy and fine granularity of information essential for target-quality intelligence. An image of the ground in front of a small unit will allow the unit to approach cautiously and define the outline and content of the enemy unit. At this point, the object will be to fix the enemy in place to prevent escape. Perhaps robotic vehicles could be sent forward to verify the details of what the aerial vehicles have seen. Scouts would move forward to direct observation only if remote reconnaissance fails to provide all the necessary details.

Once the enemy has been found and fixed, the close engagements will begin by directing precision weapons against the enemy formation from distant platforms. While under the umbrella of the tactical Internet, every close-combat soldier will have the means and the authority to call for remote fires. If the system works as it should, the source of supporting fires will be transparent to the soldier who requests them. One fire support coordinator will monitor the calls for close fires and ensure that the munition has been matched properly to the nature of the target. By 2010, the development of precision-weapons technology will have advanced to the stage where many different precision options will be available to support the close fight. By then, the preponderance of cannon and rocket artillery projectiles will be guided to the target either inertially or by terminal guidance using laser designators.

When the enemy's major close defensive weapons have been destroyed, it will be safe enough to move cautiously into the killing zone about one to three kilometers from the enemy's closest elements and to repeat the precision attack—this time using a combination of small arms and precision weapons. Main guns from fighting vehicles, or perhaps from precision shoulder-fired weapons similar to today's Javelin tank-killing missile, will be employed to finish the fight. Once the enemy no longer returns fire and sensors tell the commander that all of the enemy's major systems have been destroyed, it will be safe to sweep through the killing zone.

It is important to remember when imagining the close fight of the future that an enemy will array his formation differently from what we are used to seeing today. He will attempt to avoid destruction by fire by occupying as large a space as possible, and his major systems will be spread over a large area and dug in, camouflaged, and hidden. The critical point in the battle therefore will be the reconnaissance phase—when the attacker attempts to pinpoint the enemy's systems with enough accuracy to destroy them and to sort out from the clutter of the battlefield which targets are real, important, and threatening enough to strike. While sensors will be able to do most of the dangerous reconnaissance work, verification and refinement will still have to be done by direct observation using live scouts on the ground.

War is the most unpredictable of all forms of human endeavor. There will be times in even the most carefully planned, rehearsed, and executed offensive operations when everything will go wrong. An adaptive enemy does not offer combat unless he thinks he can win and survive. The enemy will therefore exploit every possible advantage to lessen American technological advantages in the close battle—by spoofing sensors, deflecting the track of guided weapons, and luring U.S. forces into the killing zone, where the fight will be on more even terms. Specific pieces of ground, such as cities, forests, and mountains on home terrain will clearly favor a weaker enemy.

The wisdom to make the choice as to how the Army will fight in the future will abide, as it always has, with senior leaders. The memory of the slaughter at Gettysburg and in the trenches of the First World War should act as a caution to those leaders who still cling to machine-age memories of how close battles were fought. General Lee was, arguably, the greatest military genius that the United States has ever produced. Yet even Lee became a victim of his past and failed to recognize and accommodate the futility of closing with the bayonet. Surely the possibility of making such a mistake is with us still in this new age of warfare.

As mentioned in the previous chapter, the most significant break-throughs in military capabilities in recent years have been not in maneuver systems, but in technologies that have begun to tilt the firepower-maneuver balance back toward firepower and attrition warfare. Signs foretelling the return to dominance of the defensive began to appear as early as the closing days of Vietnam. A few laser-guided bombs destroyed targets that had previously required hundreds of unguided "dumb" bombs. The air campaigns over Kosovo and Afghanistan again dramatically reinforced how precision and information technologies have made the battlefield enormously more translucent, lethal, and expansive.

The shift in the balance in favor of the defensive has not had much effect on how the United States has fought its most recent wars because Americans alone have possessed the technology and skill to use these weapons effectively. Hence the challenge of the firepower-maneuver dilemma for future generations: How will the American military win quickly and cheaply against an enemy who has gained possession of post–industrial-age weaponry? If precision will proliferate on all sides of a future battlefield, what technologies can be leveraged to increase the speed of maneuver so that the deadly zone—already hundreds of miles wide and enormously more lethal—can be crossed without suffering terrible casualties? The following chapter will offer a concept to hypothesize how the American military will succeed in such a hostile environment.

NOTES

1. Personal interview with LTG (ret) Harry W. O. Kinnard, November, 1984.

2. Robert R. Palmer, Bell I. Wiley, and William R. Kest, *The Procurement and Training of Ground Combat Troops* (Washington, D.C.: Department of the Army, 1948), pp. 2–4.

3. I owe special thanks to Colonel David Lamm, Army War College Class of 2000, for providing many of the thoughts contained in this section dealing with the need for tightly bonded and carefully selected close-combat units.

4. Lord Moran, *The Anatomy of Courage* (London: Constable, 1945), p. x.

5. I owe a special thanks and recognition to Lieutenant General (Ret.) Don Holder for many of these ideas concerning the special requirements for developing operational-level commanders.

6. Jay Luvaas and Harold Nelson, *The Army War College Guide to Antietam* (Carlisle, PA: South Mountain Press, 1987), p. 246.

· 7 ·

The New American Style of War

In the late winter of 1991, General William DePuy began to succumb to the final stages of Creutzfeldt-Jakob (Mad Cow disease), an affliction he had contracted two decades earlier during a mission to Laos. Unable to move and barely able to speak above a whisper, he would sit for hours, often in the company of friends, patiently watching and reflecting upon the implications of the Gulf War playing out before them on CNN. General Paul Gorman, the architect of the Army's post-Vietnam training revolution and a frequent companion to his mentor during those final days, recalls that:

> General DePuy talked often about the "style" of an army, pointing out that those armies acknowledged by historians to have been exceptionally efficient had a distinctive *modus operandi*—the methodical operational and tactical thrusting of Roman infantry, the mounted sweeps of the Parthians or the Moghuls, the combined-arms operations of the Byzantines under Belisarius, the amphibious raids of the Vikings. He [believed] that there is emerging such a style in the armed forces of the United States—a way of waging war that combines the arms of our land, sea, and air services, draws adroitly on advanced technology, concentrates force from unprecedented distances with overwhelming suddenness and violence, and blinds and bewilders the foe.[1]

DePuy's unique gifts of intellect, common sense, and long, firsthand exposure to the harsh realities of war allowed him to be among the first to see emerging from fifty years of experience with limited wars a body of evidence pointing to the conclusion that, like all great powers in the past, the United States had at last evolved a method of fighting wars distinctly its own. This new style of war was crafted in the laboratory of real war by practically minded commanders like DePuy, who, reacting to the immediate demands of combat, found practical solutions to pressing battlefield problems. From the dramatic evolution in the functions of maneuver and firepower arms in Korea to the equally dramatic alteration in the relationship between ground forces and strategic airpower in Afghanistan, U.S. combat leaders have demonstrated a particular genius for innovation on the battlefield.

The clearly discernible patterns that have emerged from the laboratory of war offer several signposts pointing toward the direction of future conflicts. The most clearly marked signpost tells U.S. ground commanders of the need to accelerate the velocity with which forces arrive in the battle area without endangering forces that are first to arrive. The second demands that Army and Marine commanders must fully leverage their overwhelming firepower advantage to achieve an equally dramatic and decisive advantage in maneuver on the ground. They must continue to take full advantage of the overwhelming killing power of precision weapons without allowing the firepower system to become so physically cumbersome or procedurally ossified as to be a millstone. The third signpost, similar to the first, urgently highlights the need to find a means to reestablish a significant differential in speed and agility of maneuver over the enemy's ground force. The fourth, recalling experience in past limited wars, strongly suggests that American field commanders must be able to improve their ability to watch and track the enemy well enough to anticipate his movements and his intent. The ability to know more than the enemy will become all the more important in the future, when the power of knowledge will be relied upon increasingly to compensate for the enemy's superior mass and numbers. The fifth reminds ground commanders that they must be able to maintain aggressiveness and offensive spirit while practicing methods of close combat that emphasize the tactical defensive and rely on supporting fires to do the close-in killing.

TIME VERSUS RISK: STRATEGIC MANEUVER

Quick and certain victory against an adaptive enemy with a strong will to win cannot be cobbled together at the eleventh hour by calling on a pickup team. Seeds of success must be sown decades in advance by building a base of trust among prospective allies *in every region* of vital interest to the United States. Long-term association, particularly between armies, begins the process of building trust and professional respect that can be exploited fully if and when both sides begin to perceive the presence of a mutual threat. A trusting ally will allow Americans to train its army in American methods and to acquire proficiency with U.S.-provided weapons and equipment. Trust likewise hardens allies against an enemy seeking to create distrust and acrimony on the eve of conflict. As witnessed in Afghanistan, trust also gives U.S. forces early access to the region to enable close-in, firsthand, clandestine observation of the enemy.

Experience in the Gulf War, in Kosovo, and particularly in Afghanistan reinforces the age-old axiom that there is no substitute for friendly eyes directly on the target—particularly during the early days of a campaign. But such access can be gained only through patient, soldier-led diplomacy and years of soldier-to-soldier contact. The hard-won gifts of access, trust, and familiarity gained before the crisis begins will provide suitable opportunity for clandestine special operations forces to infiltrate into a theater to establish a robust system of strategic surveillance. The mission of strategic reconnaissance forces is not to duplicate what overhead observation can provide from satellites and high-flying unmanned aircraft. By 2020, these technical instruments will be able to provide timely images of very fine granularity. Clandestine forces will verify what can be seen from the air and, most importantly, derive the enemy's intentions from firsthand observation. Once the shooting phase of the campaign begins, observers on the ground will be able to increase the lethal effects of precision fires by verifying the nature of the target and ensuring that the enemy's attempts to hide his forces and fool with decoys are not successful. Direct observation will help prevent tragic targeting mistakes due either to faulty intelligence or to the enemy's intentional efforts to deceive and embarrass.

Commanders on the spot will prefer to win the conflict quickly and decisively by conducting a strategic *coup de main* generally following the precedents established in Panama and Afghanistan. Such a preemption (or preclusion) strategy will seek to rapidly project firepower and maneuver forces directly into the path of the invading aggressor forces in order catch them in the open before the enemy has had the opportunity to capture his operational objectives and go to ground. Preemption offers the surest means of winning quickly at minimum cost of life. For example, the outcomes might have been very different had the United States possessed the means to place just two armored brigades, a force of approximately 10,000, between Saddam Hussein's Republican Guard and Kuwait City in early August 1990—or perhaps the same number of brigades between the Serbian Army and Pristina in March 1999.

Unfortunately, two factors virtually ensure that a preemption strategy will be the exception in future wars. The first is the problem of asymmetric distances. The odds are great that the enemy will have to travel only a very short operational distance to set his forces in place long before U.S. and allied forces will be able to transport a fully capable force of similar size in order to preempt him. The second factor relates to asymmetries of will. The enemy regime will not need to prepare its population for war with the United States. It will care little for public opinion and will rely on the army and police to keep its citizens under control. The challenge for the United States most likely will be far more complex and probably more time-consuming—requiring building support at home and alliances abroad. Even after such an outrageous and unambiguous violation as the assaults on the World Trade Center and the Pentagon, the Bush administration needed at least a month to conduct the diplomacy necessary to gain both access to and consensus among the region's powers to allow an attack on Afghanistan.

Superior American technology cannot accelerate the pace of political and diplomatic consensus-building. Thus an enemy will enjoy a period of reprieve useful for positioning forces to receive the U.S. and allied aerial attack. He will move his larger armored forces off the roads and into initial operational objectives before the first waves of U.S. air and ground forces are poised to intervene. At this point, the enemy will own the initiative. He will be in sole possession of the time advantage. The first task for the United States in this instance will be to wrest the initiative from him by regaining control of the clock.

Although the enemy may control time, the Americans, armed with superior situational awareness, will dominate the battle for information. Human and technical sources will be positioned over and within the enemy's territory long before intervention begins. These sources will offer commanders a fairly clear picture of the battlefield. Slowly, images of the enemy's movements and the location of his major forces will come into focus. By the year 2020, a theater commander will have the means to sense and track all movements by air, land, and sea vehicles. As invasion comes closer, a series of pictures will emerge that collectively form a collage of the enemy's patterns of ground movement. Commanders will watch in real time as the enemy moves off road and disperses across the countryside. Eventually, his forces will break into increments too small and too numerous to mark individually from the air. But, as experience in Afghanistan and Kosovo demonstrated, the presence of friendly coalition eyes on the ground, assisted by special operations soldiers, will allow commanders preparing for arrival from distant places to follow the movements and define the outline of the enemy's major formations. Most important, U.S. commanders will be able to find those areas of enemy territory where there are no forces. Finding and monitoring these "blank spaces" will allow the intervening force to arrive in the enemy's midst without having to fight for the privilege on arrival.

Once an unblinking eye is fixed in place over the enemy's territory, the task of strategic maneuver can begin. As long as the process of transformation goes as planned, over the next two decades, the U.S. military should possess a joint force with the strategic velocity essential to arrive at any point along the periphery of Eurasia within a matter of days. By then, the machine-age structures that comprise most deployable forces today will have been transformed into discrete projectable entities capable of rapid movement overseas, followed by the ability to fight a sustained battle once on the ground. It is probable that these entities will be combined arms brigades of about 5,000 soldiers each. Experience in the preemptive campaigns in Panama and most recently in Afghanistan suggests that a force any smaller is not sustainable for long periods, while a force much larger becomes too cumbersome and difficult to tailor for rapid projection. Brigades will form the land force building blocks for standing joint task forces composed of land, sea, air, and space forces—all of about equal size and capable of relatively similar strategic velocities.

To be sure, by 2020, not all U.S. Army brigades will possess the same degree of strategic velocity. The most modern "tip of the spear" formations responsible for the early-entry operational maneuver will be capable of the greatest strategic speed. Self-contained and armed with light armored vehicles, attack helicopters, precision fire support, and minimal logistic infrastructure, these brigades will weigh in at about a quarter of the heft and bulk of the armored brigades dispatched to the Gulf in 1990. A substantial portion of the U.S. Army's remaining maneuver formations, responsible for follow-on and reinforcement of the early-entry forces, will be equipped with modernized versions of today's U.S. Abrams tanks and Bradley Fighting Vehicles. Streamlined logistics and the savings in weight allowed by next generation precision weapons will allow these formations to be projected at about half their current weight and bulk. The heavier follow-on brigades will have to accelerate their strategic velocities in order to avoid creating a projection gap between early arriving operational maneuver brigades and follow-on forces. Heavier units should arrive in theater long before the fighting strength of the early arriving brigades begins to diminish. Otherwise, an enemy near defeat might be given a dangerous breathing spell to collect his forces, restore his will, and regain the operational initiative.

A heterogeneous variety of light, medium, and heavy forces is actually an advantage to an army charged with global responsibilities. Light and medium forces arriving by air will possess the necessary operational speed to strike quickly to collapse the enemy's operational centers of gravity. Slower and perhaps less capable heavy forces will provide the self-protection and sustained combat power necessary to secure the advantage gained by the early arriving forces. As witnessed in Chechnya and Afghanistan, an enemy driven from his operational positions by the overwhelming killing power of precision-fire and maneuver forces may seek to prolong the conflict by withdrawing and condensing his force inside cities, or within complex terrain such as mountains and forests. In these circumstances, information-age advantages of superior mobility, precision, and situational awareness are diminished considerably, and old-fashioned, machine-age attributes such as mass, armor protection, and heavy, concentrated firepower become proportionately more useful. The United States must avoid the temptation to put its all in the preemption basket and risk fighting a more conventional and protracted campaign of attrition with a force too light and fragile for the task.

No matter how quickly the intervening force arrives, the first to fight in a regional conflict will most likely be coalition partners or forward-stationed U.S. air and land forces in the region. The Army After Next strategic wargames taught the lesson time and time again that no degree of strategic velocity could begin to compensate for the advantage offered by forces already present in the region. By 2020, all ground units, regardless of their degree of modernization, must be packaged and prepared for the most rapid projection at the fastest speed commensurate with their relative weight, bulk, and degree of readiness. In 2020, the U.S. Army will be so small, and the threat of a major competitor so serious, that every brigade, regardless of where it is stationed, should have the capability to be packaged and prepared for rapid transport to any threatened theater. For instance, a stability force in Korea should be tailored and equipped to be able to move very quickly to the Persian Gulf, or to South Asia, should the strategic situation be sufficiently serious to demand it.

The strategic deployment phase of the campaign must be quick, continuous, and overwhelming. Perhaps armed forces from friendly regional states or from resistance forces within the violated nation, assisted by forward-stationed U.S. air and land forces, will have the wherewithal to prevent the enemy from achieving total control of the objective area before the preemptive force arrives in theater. With the enemy stalled momentarily, a balanced force of air and land forces, projected initially by strategic airlift, will begin to collect in safe regions along the periphery of the theater of operations. A closer look at the regions peripheral to Eurasia, where serious conflicts are most likely to occur, gives considerable confidence that, even in 2020, sanctuaries suitable for use as strategic staging bases will be available for use by U.S. forces and their allies. Bases and long-term allies are present in or near those portions of Europe, the Middle East, and Asia most likely to be points of conflict in the future. The strategic challenge will be to get close enough to the area of operations for the entirety of the enemy's territory to be within range of tactical airlift yet far enough away to lessen the threat of enemy terrorist action or attack by ballistic and cruise missiles. (The most recent strategic games and studies suggest that the distance between a staging base and the operational area appears to be about a thousand kilometers.)

In any future war, air, land, sea, and space forces will begin to assemble immediately from the United States, from within the theater, from floating bases off shore, and from other distant theaters. Within days, air and land forces will collect in sanctuaries and make final preparations to enter the combat area. The object of strategic maneuver is to descend on the enemy in a single act of overwhelming power with a balanced force of air and land power. The intensity of the attack will be so great that the enemy will be paralyzed in place and unable to regain the initiative. The act of getting there in fact will begin the process of psychological intimidation. The enemy will see an image of overwhelming competence and unstoppable force arriving from every point on the globe. Increasingly isolated by the swiftness and completeness of the U.S. strategic maneuver, the enemy leadership will begin to sense that the question is no longer one of defeat versus victory, but of how soon defeat will come and how great the loss will be.

FIREPOWER VERSUS MANEUVER: OPERATIONAL-LEVEL WARFARE

The objective of warfare at the operational level is to collapse the enemy's military center of gravity—the portion of his military force that, if destroyed, will result in the collapse of his will to resist. Thus the center of gravity is usually defined in psychological rather than physical terms. The enemy will make his center as unassailable as possible by protecting it and keeping it secure and distant. Throughout the history of land warfare, a deep strike or operational maneuver force has been the instrument most suitable for striking the center of gravity. The classical role of an operational maneuver force is to achieve a quick and overwhelming victory by approaching the enemy indirectly, bypassing his powerful extremities and attacking his brain. A maneuver of this magnitude and complexity will succeed only if the operational instrument possesses a substantial advantage in the ability to strike deep within enemy territory with enough combat power to fight and win on arrival.

In future, to achieve decisive results, an operational maneuver force must be substantially more mobile and physically and mentally more agile than the enemy's best formation. Without an overwhelming edge in speed and agility on the part of the intervening force, an enemy force will be able to parry an operational deep thrust or, failing that, dash quickly away into a protected sanctuary. In machine-age warfare, well-handled mechanized formations were generally capable of striking deep and surrounding foot-mobile formations. The challenge of achieving the same decisive results in the precision age is more complex and problematic, however. No longer does one ground force have a substantial maneuver advantage over the other. One reason why the operational maneuver phase of the Gulf War proved indecisive was that the speed of a U.S. armored division led by Abrams tanks and Bradley Fighting Vehicles was only marginally faster than Iraqi formations led by Soviet T-72 tanks.

Another potential impediment to decisive operational maneuver will be a shift in the balance between maneuver and firepower in favor of the latter. Precision munitions and a battlefield made more transparent by information-age technologies will expand the distances that an operational force will have to travel to reach the enemy's military centers of gravity. Moreover, the increased lethality of the battlefield will make transit across the killing zone enormously more dangerous. The advantage to the defender gained by dominance of firepower on the battlefield will be offset to some degree by advances in the speed and agility of future ground systems. Nonetheless, the collective speed of a ground unit is governed more by the vagaries of terrain than by the individual speeds of various vehicles within a formation. Mountains, forests, and cities will slow the pace of movement. Bottlenecks such as passes and narrow roads will canalize formations and cause even the most agile and swift combat vehicles to wait their turn to pass through. The velocity of the swiftest combat vehicle halted by a blown bridge is zero.

In the future, the only sure way to restore the firepower-maneuver balance in favor of maneuver and accelerate the pace of movement across the killing zone will be to break contact with the friction of the ground and shift the maneuver battle into the third dimension. Operational maneuver by air will allow a ground force to leap over the vast and lethal killing zone to occupy the enemy's military centers of gravity directly. The longstanding drawback to aerial maneuver in the past has been the loss of mobility experienced by heli-borne soldiers once separated from their source of aerial delivery. Until recently, the problem with maneuver by air has been that aerial vehicles did not have the lifting capacity to carry armored vehicles and heavy materiel into the battle area.

The successful delivery by air and sustainment of a Marine mechanized force and an Army heli-borne brigade in Afghanistan offers the surest evidence yet that technology does offer the opportunity for air-delivered, close-combat soldiers to arrive quickly into an operational area yet maintain the maneuver and firepower advantage over an enemy armored force.

Challenges still remain. The laws of practical physics continue to limit the lift capacity of modern tactical transport aircraft to about twenty tons. Any aircraft carrying much above that weight requires fixed airfields with long, hardened runways and access to ground support equipment. Heavier cargo aircraft, such as the U.S. Air Force's C-17, can land on some unimproved airfields, but they are expensive, vulnerable, and scarce. The example of the Marine base, Camp Rhino, built around the former Soviet fighter base near Kandahar, Afghanistan, testifies to the utility of the C-17 as an operational maneuver platform if a suitable hardened airfield can be captured and if the enemy's air defenses are minimal.

In most cases, an aero-mechanized force of the sort that was delivered into Afghanistan would likely have to enter enemy territory by force. Among all the choices on hand, the C-130, a veteran of all American limited wars beginning with Vietnam, best fits the requirement for a vehicle capable of conducting operational maneuver into unimproved airfields under fire. During the siege of Khe Sanh, the venerable Hercules proved its ability to deliver cargo and troops under extremely hazardous circumstances. In the Gulf, too, these rugged "birds" extended the reach of rapidly maneuvering ground forces by delivering supplies well forward into landing areas that were little more than flat spaces in the sand. Improved versions of the C-130 are capable of delivering the obligatory twenty tons to operational distances and into the most austere and primitive airfields. While perhaps not the most perfect solution, this aircraft offers the best immediate solution to the problem of restoring the operational maneuver advantage to ground forces on a future battlefield.

Close-combat soldiers must in the future fight mounted whenever possible. Tactical battles fought on foot are simply too costly in life. Images of smoking hulks in the Six-Day War and burning tanks and armored carriers transmitted from the battlefield in Chechnya create the false impression that modern armored warfare is as hazardous or perhaps more dangerous than fighting dismounted and in the open. The facts argue the contrary. Over four-fifths of all American casualties suffered in recent wars were infantrymen, whereas less than 1 percent were mounted soldiers. In fact, the mobility, protection, and firepower inherent in modern armored vehicles all save lives in combat.

Mounted combat has been the exception in recent limited wars because, with the exception of the Gulf War, all American limited wars beginning with Korea have occurred in terrain and strategic circumstances that favored the deployment of dismounted rather than mounted units. The U.S. Army developed combat vehicles to fight on the plains of Western Europe. During the Cold War, the weight and bulk of armored fighting vehicles increased steadily as additional armored protection was added to offset the improved killing power of modern anti-tank weapons. A Second World War main battle tank weighed about thirty tons. The latest version of the Abrams main battle tank weighs over seventy tons. Practical experience with armored warfare in Korea,

Vietnam, Somalia, Grenada, Panama, Afghanistan, and elsewhere continues to highlight the difficulties inherent in maneuvering cumbersome machines designed for European terrain on battlefields in areas of the world where roads, bridges, and mountain passes can accommodate nothing larger than trucks and buses. Likewise, tanks weighing seventy tons are too large and fuel-thirsty to move and sustain in large numbers over great distances by air.

Fortunately, science today offers the promise that the weight and lift problems inherent in aerial maneuver can be solved by combining several emerging technologies to produce a fighting vehicle light enough for transport by C-130s, yet sufficiently lethal and mobile to retain much of the self-protection of heavier armored vehicles. To be sure, a seventy-ton armored vehicle will be better protected against anti-tank projectiles than a twenty-ton tank. But the degree of protection in modern armored warfare is measured by more than just the thickness of armor. Superior situational awareness and greater lethality permitted by precise, long-range, on-board weapons will allow a lighter combat vehicle to win surprise engagements instantly and consistently well outside the lethal radius of the enemy's weapons.

OPERATIONAL OFFENSIVE, TACTICAL DEFENSIVE

On the battlefield of the future, even smarter and more lethal fighting vehicles will not be enough to overcome the disadvantages imposed by a firepower-dominant battlefield. As the balance between fire and maneuver continues to shift in favor of firepower, the task of maneuvering across a more expansive and more lethal battlespace will become enormously more challenging. The imperative to win quickly at minimum cost will demand a change in the way the battle is fought at the operational level of war.

The surest way for an offensive force to succeed on a firepower-dominant battlefield is to employ an operational offensive–tactical defensive method of fighting. A return visit to Gettysburg will help to put the concept in perspective. As mentioned earlier, Gettysburg was fought at the beginning of the first precision revolution. The appearance of the muzzle-loading rifle and rifled artillery extended the killing zone an order of magnitude, while the speed of maneuver across the killing zone remained at the pace of a marching soldier. On the second day of battle, General Lee, "with his blood up," gave the order for his old warhorse, General James Longstreet, to make a frontal attack against the left flank of the Union Army firmly positioned along Cemetery Ridge. Longstreet did not want to obey. Experience at Malvern Hill, the Bloody Lane, the Cornfield at Antietam, and Marye's Heights at Fredericksburg had proven to his satisfaction that the increased range and accuracy of modern rifled arms had made the deliberate attack against unbroken formations of troops virtually suicidal.

Longstreet thought that his discussions on the subject with Lee during the previous winter had convinced Lee that new circumstances of war demanded new methods of fighting. The South, with its much smaller pool of available manpower, was recognizing that more "glorious victories" like Chancellorsville, fought just two months before Gettysburg, would bleed the South white. Perhaps the way to win cheaply, Longstreet argued, would be to use the superior mobility of Southern infantry to maneuver between the Union Army and its railhead at Westminster, Maryland, just twelve miles south of Gettysburg. Both generals knew that the Union Army, cut off from its source of supply and with the enemy positioned between it and Washington, would have no choice but to abandon Cemetery Ridge and turn to face the enemy now sitting astride its line of communications. In such a battle, the South would be able to exploit the advantage of the defensive by forcing the Union to attack in the open against Southern troops secure behind entrenchments. The long range and precision of their muzzle-loading rifles would guarantee victory, but victory at a much lower cost in human life. But despite his genius for war, Lee failed to understand the influence that machine-age technology held over the outcome of tactical engagements. Nothing could avert his attention from the Union positions on Cemetery Ridge. He ordered Longstreet into a frontal attack against Cemetery Ridge and the heights at Little Round Top. Lee's defeat there cost him a third of the attacking force.

Longstreet's operational offensive–tactical defensive concept is both simple and timeless and remains as relevant to the circumstances of today's second "precision revolution" as it was for the first. An attacking force maneuvers to place itself between the defender and his line of communications. The defender can then either remain static and wither, or leave the security of his defenses to attack the force to his rear now set firmly in place and ready to receive him. If the defender chooses to attack his way out of this predicament, he must face the prospect of crossing the killing zone against an opponent who now has both the firepower and the positional advantage.

A modern version of the offensive phase of Longstreet's offensive-defensive maneuver is a rapid, unexpected, and overwhelming insertion of ground forces deep inside the enemy's territory. The maneuver is a contemporary analog to Lee's missed opportunity of putting Longstreet's corps between Meade's army and his source of supply at Westminster. An aerial precision strike phase of the operation paralyzes the enemy long enough to allow a ground force delivered by air to occupy multiple points throughout the enemy's area of operations. Ground forces then saturate the enemy's most vital areas with small, discrete, autonomous, and highly lethal mobile combat elements.

Operational transport aircraft, including C-130s and C-17s, carry armored forces into the operational area from a distance, and medium- and heavy-lift helicopters converge from sanctuaries closer in. The objectives of the aerial assault consist of dozens of relatively safe enclaves scattered throughout the depth of the enemy's territory. Each enclave has been chosen carefully to be devoid of enemy forces yet within easy reach of a key enemy center of gravity. Adhering to the spirit of Longstreet's operational intent, the ground force commander is to occupy uncontested terrain close enough to control and thus dominate these vital centers through direct observation and the use of short-range precision weapons. Such a violent, unanticipated, and overwhelming act will take the form of a strategic takedown or *coup de main* rather than a conventional form of linear maneuver. Non-linear maneuver at the operational level of war demands that the intervening force be able to build up combat power on the ground faster than the enemy can converge on and destroy the enclaves when they are thinly manned and vulnerable.

Success depends on the intervening force's ability to establish an aerial bridge that delivers forces into the theater very quickly and smoothly. Within hours, armored vehicles disgorged from transport aircraft rapidly push outward from the airhead to occupy an ever-increasing portion of the enemy's territory. Depending on the nature of the terrain and the relative strength of the enemy, a brigade airhead can eventually occupy a "security zone" about ten kilometers in diameter. Artillery, attack aviation, sensors, and an austere, mobile assortment of logistics will seek protected areas to occupy within this relatively safe perimeter. Once the security zone is free of residual pockets of resistance, each brigade can begin to establish a control zone: a relatively unoccupied ring of territory that expands the ability of the brigade to influence the battle out to a distance of about another forty kilometers beyond the perimeter of the security zone. As its name implies, the "control zone" is the concentric area outside the security zone that the brigade controls but does not occupy. The brigade concentrates its organic sensors and firepower to isolate and destroy enemy forces contained in the control zone. The distance at which the brigade can find and engage targets somewhat limits the extent of the control zone.

The control zone is not, however, devoid of the brigade's presence. In the air, attack helicopters roam continuously over the area, constantly seeking isolated groups of the enemy in order to destroy them with laser-guided precision missiles. The eyes of the attack helicopter pilots are reinforced by the presence of a swarm of unmanned aerial vehicles orbiting over the most dangerous areas and providing a reliable and constant "unblinking eye" over the control zone. On the ground, the brigade scouts make constant forays into the control zone with the mission to verify the sighting of aerial systems and to positively identify enemy formations, with particular emphasis on tracking and engaging small, mobile targets such as individual vehicles and defensive fighting positions. Standing back and remaining hidden, the scouts methodically take out each enemy position by calling in remote precision fires from artillery inside the security zone or, if the target is on the move, from unmanned aerial platforms hovering directly overhead.

The influence of the brigade continues outward to a third concentric area—a zone of observation which, under the right circumstances, might extend the ability of the brigade to maintain visibility over its surroundings out to a radial distance of a hundred kilometers or more. However, this zone's very size and distance from direct observation and influence makes it very porous. At such distances, enemy forces are not easily seen; nor are they readily engaged, because most of the means available to observe and strike them are no longer directly under the influence of the brigade. The enemy can only be sighted and tracked using strategic and national systems such as satellites or Air Force and Navy aerial platforms. Killing within the observation zone will be done principally by systems that come from a distance, such as fighter and bomber aircraft, cruise missiles launched from surface ships and submarines, and armed drones loitering above the battle area at high altitudes.

The price paid for relying on external sources for information and killing power inside the observation zone is one of granularity and response time. By 2020, the ability of aerial sensors to find and track targets will be much improved. But the systems available then will not be able to track every target—particularly not targets belonging to an enemy who hides, digs in, and deceives. Likewise, the maneuver brigade will not have total control over which targets are struck within its zone of observation. Long-range precision munitions capable of reaching into the observation zone are expensive, and the zone will contain many more targets than weapons to attack them. The brigade's best hope for influencing the battle at this great distance will be to tap into the strategic means of observation, such as special operations teams or coalition forces present in the observation zone and ready to spot and designate targets for engagement by orbiting unmanned aerial platforms. Virtual experience in recent strategic wargaming, as well as combat experience in Afghanistan, suggests that a brigade can reasonably expect to see within the zone of observation with enough clarity and responsiveness to detect movement by enemy formations of about platoon size.

With a multitude of human and machine eyes available to him, the brigade commander will have the confidence to maneuver freely about his area of operations—secure in the knowledge that the enemy will not be able to mass against him any unit above platoon level without risking total destruction from attack helicopters, armed UAVs, tactical aviation, and cruise missiles. The operational implication of this capability is simply that the brigade will be free to close to decisive ranges against enemy formations without risking being ambushed, outmaneuvered, or outnumbered. Thus, a clever enemy might with luck be able to achieve isolated tactical victories if also able to take advantage of occasional lapses in attention or tactical mistakes. But the odds of an American ground force suffering catastrophic defeat when armed with this degree of battlefield dominance are extremely remote.

A pattern of maneuver that follows the spirit of Longstreet's offensive-defensive concept will be one that maneuvers against the enemy with audacity to gain the advantage of position but closes to decisive tactical distances with great caution. The knowledge that the precision advantage will keep the enemy dispersed into small units permits the brigade's maneuver units to divide into similar small formations without risking being overwhelmed and defeated in detail. Groups of two or three armored vehicles will use on-board sensors to locate seams, or empty spaces between the enemy's defenses. Maneuvering very rapidly to take advantage of the paralysis imposed on the enemy by his inability to move without being seen, these small, autonomous formations will select commanding positions outside the range of the enemy's weapons but among and between the discrete autonomous segments of the enemy's larger formations. The object of this style of maneuver is to separate, dissemble, and keep apart all of the essential components that collectively comprise a cohesive fighting body of enemy ground forces. A once cohesive body would now be divided into isolated pockets, each a sub-critical mass severed from its parent body and unable to communicate or to maintain itself for very long without resupply and unable to be reinforced. Once the intervening force gains the advantage of position over the enemy, the factor of time also shifts to its favor. The enemy cannot linger very long in a fractured state. His choices are either to fight or to wither. But fighting will be a problem. Once set within the enemy's critical area, the intervening force, now possessing the advantage of the defensive, will be in a position to call the tactical shots.

Modern precision technology strengthens the inherent power of the defensive phase of an offensive-defensive stratagem. The range and lethality of superior firepower weaponry expands the killing zone, making it far more expensive for a less sophisticated enemy to move across unprotected and in the open. The defender is stationary and has the advantage of watching and engaging with firepower from positions well out of the enemy's much shorter lethal reach while remaining relatively secure in fixed, covered positions. The enemy is trapped and can escape only by massing to attack. If he masses, he becomes a perfect target for destruction by precision strike; check and checkmate.

ENDS VERSUS MEANS: WINNING THE TACTICAL FIGHT

Just as it was necessary to exploit the third dimension in order to restore a balance between fire and maneuver at the operational level, when the occasion demands it, ground forces must be prepared to elevate maneuver into the air to achieve the same advantage at the tactical level. In precision-age warfare, success in the close fight will depend on the ability of the tactical commander to maintain the same proportionate differential in speed against the enemy that he maintains in lethality. If the enemy is limited to maneuvering on foot, then an intervening force mounted in light armored vehicles is sufficient to maintain this advantage. But if the enemy is able to fight mounted, then the advantage of tactical speed belongs to neither side. Under no circumstances should U.S. tactical maneuver forces be subjected to the condition—last experienced during the Gulf War—when American foot soldiers faced a mounted enemy.

Only tactical heli-borne forces can maintain a decisive advantage over a mounted enemy. They will be able to strike very deep into enemy territory, well inside the observation zone, to seal off the routes of retreat and, if the enemy's formations are demoralized and sufficiently vulnerable, destroy them in close combat. The example of the 101st Airborne Division's attack deep into Iraq demonstrated the effectiveness of aerial encirclement. Such a maneuver can be repeated in the future as long as maneuver forces, once on the ground, can culminate the tactical fight quickly and remain under the protective umbrella of aerial fires delivered by supporting attack helicopters, tactical fighter aircraft, and armed UAVs. Armed helicopters will use their sophisticated surveillance devices to extend the maneuver commander's direct view of the battlefield out to the limits of the observation zone—a distance of a hundred kilometers or more. On-board precision munitions will allow attack helicopters to attack targets of opportunity well beyond the limits of tactical vehicles restricted to maneuvering inside the security zone. Attack helicopters will exploit their superior range and mobility to prevent large enemy formations from surprising and massing against maneuver forces. Should attack helicopters discover an approaching formation too large for their on-board weapons to destroy, the advantage offered by their commanding position and direct connection with maneuver forces will make them ideal platforms to call for and coordinate fires delivered by more distant platforms capable of delivering more massive doses of precision fires.

The presence of tactical helicopters will be essential inside the brigade area. But during the early phases of an intervention operation, the use of tactical maneuver by air will be limited by the high fuel consumption of these machines. The limited capacity of Air Force transport to deliver aviation fuel inside the security zone will ensure that neither attack nor troop-carrying helicopters will be able to stay in the air long enough, or in sufficient numbers, to meet all tactical demands. The needs of the commander for aerial support can only be met by supplementing manned aerial platforms with more fuel-efficient, unmanned aircraft capable of performing some of the same observation and strike tasks performed by manned aircraft today.

As the size, lethality, and lift capacity of helicopters improves in the decades ahead, ground maneuver will increasingly begin to conform to and exploit the advantages of aerial maneuver. Foot and mounted units will move into territory already swept and cleared by aerial platforms roaming about and loitering overhead. Aerial maneuver platforms shifting and darting about quickly at the outer fringes of an enemy formation will define and mark it and hold the enemy down until mounted forces arrive to tighten the noose and close avenues of escape.

The helicopter is the only vehicle available within the next two decades capable of giving light forces a decisive tactical advantage in maneuver over heavy, mounted forces. Helicopters can maintain an enormous advantage in velocity and agility yet still retain the ability to fly low and slowly enough to see and track the enemy—often with the same discrimination and immediacy as soldiers on the ground. Information and precision technologies will only amplify these advantages in the future. In particular, the increasing ability of armed helicopters to track and kill will change their role in the future to be as much a maneuver as a firepower platform. While armed helicopters will not be able to occupy ground in the traditional sense, they will be able to command ground by paralyzing and forcing enemy units to disperse, hide, and dig in.

Future aerial maneuver systems should be designed with the maneuver function in mind. The day will come when the role of dismounted close combat will be taken over by small, quiet, stealthy, very low-flying and enormously lethal "birds" capable of maneuvering quickly about the battlefield and taking advantage of the vagaries of terrain to close on the enemy and perform the traditional "find, fix, flush, and finish" functions formerly performed by more vulnerable dismounted infantry.

On occasion, maneuver by dismounted infantry lifted into the fight by helicopters may be necessary—particularly when operating in close terrain, such as jungles and mountains. But under no circumstances must the tactical close fight by foot soldiers be an even match. A close-in, dismounted fight within the lethal range of the enemy's small arms and mortars will only allow the enemy to snatch tactical victory from defeat. Once the intervening forces are successful at gaining positional advantage and paralyzing the enemy with operational and tactical fires, the fight must be finished in close combat with the smallest possible loss of life. General DePuy's maxim that maneuver supports fire on a firepower-intensive battlefield will continue to influence the manner in which the close battle is fought. The purpose of close maneuver is to place the enemy force in such a position that its small arms are ineffective while its force is exposed to the full killing power of superior precision firepower.

PRECISION FIREPOWER FOR TACTICAL FORCES

Heavy precision firepower offered by distant ground and aerial platforms will be essential to deny the enemy the maneuver advantage. By 2020, firepower platforms in the form of guns and rockets will be able to deliver precision firepower from distances measured in hundreds of miles or more. But distant sources of firepower will never eliminate the need of maneuver units inside the battle area for tactical, carry-along precision firepower. Such firepower will still be necessary on the future battlefield because technology will not be able to eliminate shortcomings inherent in fires delivered from great distances.

The time it takes for a missile to travel from launcher to target, or "time of flight," must be less than the time it takes for a target to move out of sight of, or within range of, friendly ground units. Since the laws of physics cannot be repealed, the longer the range, the longer the time of flight and the less effective the missile will be against fleeting targets. In warfare, geography counts. The more detached a firepower source is from the front lines, the less able it is to sense the ebb and flow of the ground battle. Moreover, missiles that travel great distances are both expensive and rare. Cruise missiles cost more than artillery shells and must be employed selectively and with deliberation. The more expensive the missile, the longer it takes to decide to use it.

As tactical units spread out within the control zone, supporting firepower units must follow and conform to the pattern and pace of the maneuver force. To provide coverage for as large an area as possible, firepower units will divide into the smallest possible entities capable of providing effective fire support—perhaps groups as small as pairs of guns and rocket launchers, accompanied by mobile ground and aerial sensors. Many of these firepower systems will be unmanned. Self-contained rocket pods will be delivered by air and scattered about within the security zone. The pods will self-locate and identify themselves to fire-support officers within the brigade tactical operations center in order to be fired remotely on command from the supported brigade.

Today, the artillery provides its own eyes. In future wars, however, the need for responsive fires will demand that the maneuver units increasingly assume the task of identifying targets to engage. Maneuver units will be spread over too vast an area, with too many discrete targets scattered within their midst, to rely on artillery forward observers to see and respond to all of their needs. The role of artillery will evolve into that of umpires who moderate and judge which targets are most likely to interfere with the scheme of maneuver. They will orchestrate the pace of delivery and make decisions on the allocation and distribution of precision firepower when there are too many targets for the number of delivery systems and munitions available.

Sensing and killing technologies will most certainly make the "find and fix" function easier for maneuver units in coming decades. The challenge ahead is that an adaptive enemy and the changing geometry of the battlefield will collude to make the task of killing with firepower increasingly more difficult. As the enemy disperses and goes to ground in order to survive, the battlefield will become so large and porous that the conventional schemes for ground maneuver may well play to the advantage of the enemy.

On an expanded battlefield, an adaptive enemy, armed first and foremost with patience and guile, might well be able to offset a disadvantage in firepower with a countervailing tactic centered on the occupation and control of large, thinly occupied areas of territory. To win the tactical fight, the intervening forces must maintain pressure on the enemy to prevent him from regaining his balance. A commander must exhibit a superbly tuned ability to manipulate time and distance. Time is critical, because he must be able to keep pressure on an enemy who is trying everything in his power to stretch out the campaign and cause as many casualties as possible. Distance is critical, because the attacker must maintain enough separation between his forces and the enemy's for his troops not to be drawn within the lethal arc of the enemy's firepower and risk destruction by fire. Yet the attacker must keep the enemy close enough to observe him directly—to control and conform to his movements, and to ensure that he keeps the enemy well within the more expanded arc of his own firepower.

A tactical commander will in the future confront the same ends versus means conundrum that General DePuy faced in Vietnam. DePuy realized that no matter how hard he tried to protect his scouting elements, the task of finding the enemy still necessitated face-to-face contact. DePuy was frustrated by the high cost of these initial contacts and by the ability of the enemy to escape before supporting firepower could be brought to bear. All too often, the enemy managed to slip away before friendly ground forces could be assembled to cover all avenues of escape—particularly in the rugged Vietnamese terrain.

In the future, a commander will be able to considerably reduce the cost of finding the enemy—thanks to information-age technologies that will allow him to substitute mechanical eyes for the eyes of his scouts. UAVs will precede the advance of tactical formations. They will peer over the next hill and into dense undergrowth to seek out dispersed, hidden enemies. The presence of sophisticated surrogates to do the most dangerous part of the finding function will free the scouts to stand well back and methodically call on distant precision fires to destroy significant points of resistance.

The tactical phase of a non-linear battle will play out very differently from the familiar massive dense battles of machine-age warfare. Seen from above, the tactical battlefield will appear to be virtually empty. There will be no front lines—only areas occupied by thinly spread groups of maneuver elements scattered amoeba-like across a wide expanse of territory. Small, sharp, and discrete battles will be fought continuously, with no apparent center of focus or culminating point. Enemy and friendly forces may well be intermixed, with friendly units taking advantage of their superior situational awareness to move in between the enemy to separate, confuse, and paralyze his tactical units in place.

Machine-age concentrations and barrages familiar to veterans of Korea, Vietnam, and the Gulf War will occur only rarely. In the future, fires will strike suddenly, with no warning, and steadily. A tactical fight of the future against a dispersed enemy might appear in the mind's eye like a distant prairie ablaze with a thousand fires. All of the individual fires would be surrounded simultaneously by groups of firefighters building fire lanes and pouring on flame retardant selectively—to keep the smaller fires from combining to form larger conflagrations. Most enemy points of resistance would be left to burn themselves out, particularly those in difficult areas such as close terrain, forests, and cities. Those points that are both assailable and vital to the enemy's defensive would be fought aggressively, but from a distance. Firefighters would move in close enough to be effective, but not so close as to be trapped by the flames.

Close combat of this sort will be decisive, to be sure—but decisive from a distance. Close-combat units will maintain just enough contact to surround, contain, and feel out the shape and size of each enemy formation. As precision strikes begin to wear away the will of the enemy, close-combat forces will converge methodically, with deliberation. By this stage of the fight, time becomes the ally of the intervening forces. Beyond this stage, the intervening forces can lose only if impatience causes them to be careless and allows a desperate enemy to inflict more casualties than the intervening force can afford. Eventually, surrounded, unable to mass, out of touch with adjacent units and higher authority, each discrete enemy force will slowly collapse.

FIGHTING IN CITIES AND COMPLEX TERRAIN

The enemy will know that the days of his regime are numbered when follow-on echelons of U.S. and allied heavy-armored and mechanized forces begin to arrive by land and sea to add permanence and mass to the advantage already gained by early arriving forces. When weight of metal is added to an overwhelming dominance in mobility and information, the enemy will lose his ability to control time. He will no longer be able to fight in open warfare, or to seek sanctuary in the countryside. As he slowly loses control of his ability to maneuver, he will be left with only three strategic alternatives to control his destiny. All three are predicated upon the intent to shift the variables of the ends versus means equation back into his favor. First, he may seek to negotiate a cease-fire, which he will use either to end the conflict on the best possible terms, or to buy enough time to regain his balance, reconstitute his army, and reestablish control over a portion of his territory. Second, he may seek to dissolve his forces completely into small guerrilla bands capable of fighting a lower-level conflict. A shift to the guerilla alternative demands that the leadership rely on the power inherent in the popular will of the people to support continuance of the conflict—an increasingly unlikely prospect in rogue states ruled by tyrannical elites. Third, he may seek to snatch victory from the jaws of defeat by withdrawing remnants of his army into complex terrain, such as cities.

Urban warfare offers the enemy the best prospects for shifting the balance of ends and means into his favor. Experience in recent wars tells us that city fighting can be a great equalizer for armies fighting at a technological or numerical disadvantage. The battle to seize Berlin in the Second World War cost the Soviets a hundred thousand dead. The siege of Hue during the Tet Offensive in Vietnam was lifted only after the Marines and their South Vietnamese allies suffered 500 dead. More recently, in the first Chechnya War, a semi-trained and poorly equipped force successfully waged a war of attrition in the city of Grozny that eventually wore out the larger, technologically superior Russian Army.

It seems likely that opportunities for urban warfare will increase in the decades ahead, as the sprawl of urban centers continues to grow. Some estimates indicate that, by the year 2020, between 60 percent and 70 percent of the world's population will reside in urban areas. If current global demographic trends continue, we will see the growth of huge urban masses, with many cities exceeding 20 million inhabitants. The enormous problems of infrastructure and the demand for social services that threaten to overwhelm governing authorities in urban centers today will continue to worsen. Moreover, the proximity of the disenfranchised to the ruling elite will provide a spark for further unrest and sporadic violence.

The future urban center, like today's, will contain a mixed population, ranging from the rich elite to the very poorest. The day-to-day existence of most of the urban poor will be balanced tenuously on the edge of collapse. With social conditions ripe for exploitation, even a small unfavorable tilt of circumstances may be enough to instigate starvation, disease, social foment, cultural unrest, or other forms of urban violence. Some urban areas sit astride cultural points of intersection along the periphery of the Eurasian landmass— the region most likely to host serious conflict in the future. A few of these cities also command territory of vital interest to the United States.

Although a retreat into cities might seem to hold a decisive advantage for a lesser military power, there are also some serious political and operational downsides to such a strategy. First, by withdrawing and concentrating inside the cities, the defender forfeits the advantage of time and thus the operational initiative. No large urban mass is self-sufficient. By ceding the surrounding countryside to intervening forces seeking to restrain it, the defending regime cannot maintain its force in the confines of the city for very long before the city begins to lose its capacity to sustain both the army and the population. Cities are generally a state's cultural, social, economic, and political centers of existence, and the popular will of the people to support a furtherance of a conflict will certainly be eroded as they witness the systematic destruction of the prize possessions of their society. With both ruler and ruled captive together inside the city, the prospects of civil insurrection will certainly increase as the prospects of victory diminish.

If the intervening force is patient, the time advantage will prove to be the key to winning against an opponent hiding inside the city. Instead of conducting a direct assault and massive strike, the attacking force can establish a loose cordon around the city while it continues to maintain absolute control of the countryside. All avenues into the city, including air, sea, and land arteries, will be occluded as much as possible. But a completely airtight seal will be both impossible and unnecessary. The intervening (now the "investing," or surrounding) power will seek to control sources of food, power, water, and sanitation. Using the advantage of superior information science, all internal media sources as well as commercial, financial, and government agencies will be as tightly suppressed as possible. Only information coming from the outside will be available to the city's population.

Throughout the cordon operation, the investing power will exploit its advantage in precision and information by selectively seizing and striking decisive points inside the city while being careful not to allow forces to become trapped or too decisively engaged in urban close combat. High-altitude UAVs orbiting over the city will maintain constant close surveillance with a minimum of manpower. Ground-mounted cameras will observe areas susceptible to infiltration. Unless the enemy attempts to escape from his urban terrain, the investing force will not engage in close combat. Instead, using greater stand-off technologies, it will continue to wear down and diminish the enemy's ability to sustain himself by striking selected point targets, such as key leadership and weapons of mass destruction.

The investing force will not attempt to achieve complete destruction of the enemy force, or to inflict substantial destruction of the city and its infrastructure. Instead, it will focus destructive effects on those targets that have the greatest impact on the government, the army, and the population. The purpose of these strikes will be twofold: to demonstrate the futility of further resistance and to create conditions that will lead to collapsing the enemy's will to continue the struggle. By clever use of psychological intimidation through captive media, the investing power will create an environment in which the enemy army is no longer tolerated by the local population. The underlying purpose will be to demonstrate to the population that its existence is most threatened by the continued presence of that army.

As the investing force achieves control of the surrounding countryside, it may collect resources to support the establishment of sanctuaries and safe havens around the city. Humanitarian organizations, both governmental and non-governmental, will be encouraged to construct protective camps. The city's population will be encouraged to leave, and surrounding forces will allow free passage through the cordon to the relative security of the camps.

For those who stay, the isolation of the city will over time create a refugee problem for the surrounded enemy. With the steady depletion of resources, the remaining population will eventually see the government as impotent and unable to meet their needs. It is unlikely that the ruling elite sequestered inside the city will suffer much, and the population closely surrounding them will surely be reminded daily of where the real sources of power and privilege abound.

Although this "indirect" approach to urban combat may not fit all future circumstances, it does offer an alternative to a wasteful street-by-street battle of attrition that only the enemy can win. Even if a city collapses under a close-combat assault, past experience tells us that the enemy may well be the one to benefit most from a victory too dearly won. Regardless of the tactics employed, a future land force must treat urban warfare with caution and not fall into a casualty trap set by a clever and desperate enemy.

NOTE

1. Paul F. Gorman, *The Secret of Future Victories*, (Fort Leavenworth, KS: Combat Studies Institute, 1992), p. IV–1.

· 8 ·

"Kosovo, 2020"
A Wargame

*T*he art of anticipating the course of warfare is a soldier's most difficult and problematic endeavor. Soldiers have two tools to assist them in the task. The first is practical observation and study of both recent and historically more distant cases. At best, however, history offers metaphors rather than analogies. It is such an imperfect predictor, that the military analyst must look closely to discern consistent patterns and trends from the evidence—to seek relevant incidents that successively repeat over time and in different circumstances of climate, terrain, and enemy action. Only when the path behind is straight, clear, and unambiguous can the analyst conclude that it can be extended forward into the fog of the future. The historical record of the experience of the United States in recent limited wars, as described in chapters four and five, suggests that the path of the past points with remarkable clarity to a future that calls for a unique and distinctly different fighting force.

Wargames are a second important instrument in the soldier's analytical toolbox. They are expensive exercises, but they yield valuable lessons. Originating as a military chess game in the late seventeenth century, wargames—and, later, gaming simulations—have evolved to become the most useful means for practicing command decision making without troops and for probing into the changing character of war without bloodshed. The Prussian and later the German general staffs refined the science of gaming and made it an essential instrument for translating and evaluating national security policies into a military context. Preparations for the 1918 spring offensive, for the invasion of France in 1940, and for Hitler's operations against the Soviet Union in 1941 were tested and refined by the General Staff in a series of increasingly complex and insightful strategic games.

121

The United States military continues the wargaming tradition as a means of anticipating the military implications of political and technological changes in the strategic environment. Games conducted at the U.S. Army War College (and elsewhere) during the last decade have sought to look well into the distant future in an effort to gain insights into how the United States will fight its wars. The games were played in the year 2020 and beyond in regions bordering on the "periphery of Eurasia," perceived as including Europe, the Balkans, the Middle East, Central Asia, and South Asia.

The Army After Next series of games, conducted over three years from 1996 to 1999 at the War College, were among the most complex and participative of any ever conducted in the United States. These games proved particularly successful because gaming directors adhered scrupulously to the tenets of gaming that for centuries have proven necessary to ensure fidelity, integrity, and objectivity. All were force-on-force (blue versus red), free-play exercises in which either side was free to make decisions limited only by the resources, policies, and military doctrine of their respective militaries. In order to create a world-class opposing force, the red commander and his staff were chosen for their familiarity with the contested region and their skill in the art of war. The red commanders always fought to win—and often did. Gaming facilities at the War College were technologically the most sophisticated and digitized of any in the world. The synthetic battlefield created within the facility was remarkably real and the collection schemes fully capable of capturing an electronic version of what soldiers call "ground truth."

Insights gathered from the games were remarkably consistent over many iterations. A joint force possessed with strategic speed, precision, aerial maneuver, and information dominance proved to be optimally suited to succeed on the future battlefield regardless of variations in region, level of war, enemy, climate, and geopolitical circumstances. All the more striking was the realization that practical insights gained from the study of recent campaigns reinforced the efficacy of these same capabilities with remarkable fidelity. This fortunate confluence of practical and theoretical circumstances gave the Army's leadership a degree of confidence unprecedented in recent history that the U.S. military is on the right path to formulating a concept of warfighting that will meet the demands of the future.

The following vignette is a composite of several wargaming scenarios played out at the War College. It is a synthesis of those games told in the form of a "history of the future." Kosovo was chosen as a venue for depicting the major findings only because it was both familiar and easy to portray realistically without treading too close to existing classified war plans. The Carlisle games are designed to create a series of likely strategic environments that will stress the capabilities of American military power over the next two decades. The setting and the geopolitical and diplomatic road to war depicted here is not as important as the opportunity that the scenario presents to provide a clear and graphic depiction of how the new American way of war will evolve in the years ahead as new structures and technologies are integrated into the force. The scene of conflict could just as well have been Afghanistan, Iran, Iraq, or North Korea. The only difference between fighting in each of these prospective areas of operations would be in the numbers of forces employed and the time and relative difficulty inherent in executing the operations. In practice, the strategic, operational, and tactical principles involved would be virtually identical.

THE "SERBIAN" PLAN

In 2020, the Serbian leader, driven by blind ambition for regional hegemony, seeks to capture the neighboring independent state of Kosovo through a lightning-fast strategic *coup de main*. Aware that he is playing in a region of the world considered vital to U.S. interests, he has prepared carefully for the coming campaign. He uses state-controlled media to inflame centuries-old racial, ethnic, or cultural animosities in a calculated effort to incite just enough popular outrage to make his aggressions, both regional and international, palatable to the country's population. His army and police guarantee that those who are reluctant to support his plans for international aggression are silenced through exile, arrest, or execution. Many decades of social kleptomania have impoverished the people and threatened the elevated standard of living that has sustained the loyalty of his political and military cronies. Yet the Serbs, while not necessarily fond of the ruling regime, are a proud, nationalistic, industrious, and stoic people with a long history of defending their homeland against foreign invasion.

The army brought the leader to power. Driven by a combination of gratitude and a desire to maintain the army's loyalty, the leader has kept a small, militia-like ground force well equipped and reasonably well trained. The Serbian Army exists to serve the personal ambitions of the leader. It is a heterogeneous force consisting of a few mobile heavy brigades to provide the offensive mobility needed to overcome a neighbor quickly. But most of the army is light. Legions of infantry gain mobility from their feet or from commercial rough-terrain vehicles. The infantry has considerable experience fighting in the crowded cities and barren mountains of the region. Firepower comes in the form of light artillery and anti-tank missiles, with a particularly ubiquitous assortment of heavy, medium, and light mortars. The country is laced with minefields put down over decades. The leader has spared no expense in money and labor to construct fortifications suitable for sheltering and shielding his army. Command centers are underground and connected by a redundant system of fiber-optic cable and secure cyber-cellular networks. The logistics system is dispersed and nonnodal in that all commodities necessary for a protracted campaign are hidden, dug in, and placed forward as close to the fighting forces as possible.

But even tyrants must deal with fiscal realities. No leader who derives his military strength from the resources of a less-developed economy will be able to complement a substantial ground force with conventional air, sea, and strategic forces. Yet this leader has learned that a successful war against the United States can be conducted only if he is able to create enough of a surrogate threat in the air to ensure that the United States is denied absolute freedom to attack his forces from above. He has no combat aviation to speak of—just a few light helicopters and obsolete fighter aircraft left behind by Soviet occupiers many years before. He seeks to restrict U.S. access to the air by constructing an air defense network consisting of a cheap but relatively sophisticated and dispersed system of guns and shoulder-fired missiles linked together by fiber-optic cable and secure radio. Most of the missiles use passive seekers or very mobile tracking and search radars and are effective from low to relatively high altitudes just above 20,000 feet.

Although unable to defeat the U.S. air campaign, the leader hopes his air defense network will be just robust and effective enough to rob the Americans of total dominance in the air. His objective is both modest and reasonable: to keep intruding aircraft as high and far away as possible in order to lessen their effectiveness. He will attempt to shoot down an occasional aircraft in the hope that a few dead or captured airmen displayed on international television will induce the Americans to slacken or end the aerial assault before it causes too much damage to the country. His only aerial offensive strike force consists of a crude assortment of cheap ballistic and cruise missiles. By the standards of the era, they are not terribly modern. But he has many of them—each capable of delivering a warhead out to distances of several hundred miles. Missiles are the jewels in his deterrent crown, so he has taken every precaution to hide and disperse them across a wide expanse of his homeland.

If given a choice, the leader would of course prefer to achieve his ambition without having to confront an invasion from the United States and its regional and extra-regional NATO allies. His hope is to confine the conflict—to conquer quickly before any outside power has had time to coalesce against him. He seeks to browbeat and intimidate his Slav neighbors—those with strong ethnic-cultural ties, into supporting his aggression, or at least into denying any support to the United States. He portrays himself to the West as reasonable, moderate, and willing to compromise—even as he pushes callously to the border with the full intent to invade Kosovo. He will flex his military muscle and demonstrate in an attempt to make his army appear both fully capable and willing to fight. He uses the foreign and domestic media to blur the moral distinctions between his own cause and that of his intended victim.

The leader uses his country's sovereignty to make it a sanctuary for exporting terrorism, but terrorism in a subtler, sophisticated form than that exercised by the failed efforts of al-Qaeda. He commits acts of terror with a signature sufficiently distinct to be recognized by the disaffected masses in the region that blame the United States and the "evils of liberal democracy" for despoiling their culture and religion. Yet the leader takes great care to leave no "smoking gun" at the scene sufficient to give the United States the moral capital necessary to justify an invasion of his territory. The strategic end of his terrorism campaign in this instance is both logical and traditional: to humiliate, wear down, and deflect the attention of the United States so that he will have the freedom to gain regional dominance without interference from outside.

The leader intends to have the Serbian Army advance very quickly into Kosovo in order to present the West with a strategic *fait accompli*. His military strategy depends for success on a rapid infusion of forces to neutralize the small Kosovar militia, followed by a push inland with the objective of first capturing the urban areas that represent the political and economic centers of gravity. Once the cities are secure, the army will rapidly disperse across the countryside to quell resistance. The leader's long-term strategy is to absorb Kosovo quickly and efficiently into the social, economic, and political polity of Serbia. If the United States intervenes, then control of the countryside will become even more critical. Holding the countryside will allow the Serbian Army to subsist off the land and give them the ability to disperse and hide ground and missile forces and vulnerable facilities underground. As long as the Americans do not threaten a ground invasion, the Serbian leadership gambles on the assumption that an army so scattered will be invulnerable to systematic destruction from the air.

The Serbian Army's operational approach is focused on the doctrinal principle of area control. Taking a page from the experience of others who have opposed the United States successfully in the past, the Serbian leader plans to disperse his forces in scattered autonomous groups, each of which is capable of operating independently without substantial resupply. Each small unit will be responsible for controlling critical points to include cities and key routes of entry. To protect sites from destruction, enemy commanders will distribute artillery and anti-aircraft batteries within enclaves created and protected by ground units. Mobile ground reserves are small and local, perhaps no larger than companies of tanks, infantry carriers, and civilian vehicles centered within each major enclave and dispersed to remain hidden from aerial eyes. Likewise, logistical support and local transport is broken up and allocated among forward units. All of these expansive complexes are linked together via fiber-optic cable and secure cellular networks.

Fighting doctrine centers on the principle of trading men, equipment, and territory for time. Each major ground unit is expected, first of all, to endure and survive the air campaign relatively intact. Should intervening U.S. and allied forces invade and a ground campaign ensue, Serbian ground units will fight from fixed locations seeking to destroy as many invading forces as possible. The object of the Serbian defense is to delay and disrupt in order to retain the time advantage. The Serbian forces must create sufficient confusion and cause enough casualties to force the invading allies to shift from a preemptive strategy to one of attrition—to effect a transition from an operation like Just Cause in Panama to one like Task Force Smith, which characterized early U.S. efforts in Korea.

THE CAMPAIGN

Early on the morning of March 24, 2020, Serbian special forces begin to infiltrate Kosovo with the mission of selecting, verifying, and marking farm trails, back roads, and rural pathways for the use of the armored columns soon to follow. With the help of indigenous Serbian collaborators, the soldiers hastily fall to the task of turning shallow points across the Sitnica and Ibar rivers into hidden underwater highways, using hastily constructed steel and wooden beams laid just below the surface of the stream. Detachments of Serbian special forces crammed aboard farm tractors, buses, and vans rush into the northern towns to occupy town halls, schools, hospitals, and factories. With brutal efficiency, they push occupants out at gunpoint. As the rightful owners depart, Serbian staff officers and advance parties arrive and begin to prepare the vacant structures for occupancy by the main force armored units now lined up along roads across the border and waiting for the signal from the high command to invade.

Particular care is taken by the Serbian intelligence services, in collaboration with the state-controlled media, to ensure that all appears normal within the confines of Belgrade and other major Serbian cities. Operatives have managed over time and with the help of collaborators in Western regimes to tap into the codes of French, American, and British diplomatic communications. The Serbs know just enough from these intercepts to predict how long NATO leaders will take to collect the resolve and political will necessary to begin a military intervention against them. NATO watches with alarm as the Serbs begin to move against Kosovo. The imperative to gain the support of nineteen member nations delays NATO's ability to respond at the critical strategic juncture and gives the initiative momentarily to the Serbs.

While committed to interceding only under the auspices of NATO, the U.S. administration nonetheless exercises as much unilateral authority as it thinks prudent to prepare for the eventual military action sure to come should the Serbs match their threats with action. Air and ground rapid-reaction forces are steadily displaced overseas by air and fast sealift from bases in Texas, Kentucky, Georgia, and New York into staging bases in Germany, Hungary, Austria, and Italy. The movements overseas are executed with the intention to ensure: first, that as large an early-intervention force would be positioned on the ground as near the potential theater of conflict as political and diplomatic circumstances would permit; and second, that the movements are made publicly, as an unambiguous statement of America's sincere commitment to fight the Serbs if necessary—should they be foolish enough to violate Kosovo.

Contrary to the Serbs' best hopes, the NATO command is not entirely unaware of the Serbian intent to become the aggressor against Kosovo. An experienced cadre of U.S. Special Forces operatives planted into Serbia many years before has been watching and reporting continuously on the deteriorating situation in Serbia. By 2020, many of these operatives have established themselves as respected participants in academia, business, as well as in several sensitive political and administrative positions very close to the seat of Serbian power. Consequently, the U.S. supreme commander in NATO can rely on the eyes and firsthand judgments of trusted agents to verify the reports from satellite images flooding into NATO Headquarters in Mons, Belgium. Those in special positions within the Serbian hierarchy are also able to provide compelling insights into the minds and impulses of those who are ordering and controlling the invasion.

By the time NATO responds, the Serbian invasion is under way, but by no means complete. Armored columns and supply convoys still clog the major roads that lead south from the Serbian border into the heart of Kosovo. Leposavic, Podujevo, Mitrovica, and Pristina in the north are quickly coming under Serbian military control. Gestapo-like squads of state police follow closely behind the military phalanxes carefully rounding up civic and political leaders. It immediately becomes evident to NATO planners that the Serbs also were putting into motion a diabolical plan to evict all Albanian Kosovars, regardless of age or circumstances, out of Kosovo and into any neighboring state willing to accept them. Two major railroads—from Zvecan to Obilic and from Podujevo to Pristina—are virtually clogged with rail traffic sent south in the hopes of cramming as much bulk fuel, food, ammunition, and equipment into Kosovo as possible before NATO air attacks begin in earnest.

Fully aware of the strength of NATO once stirred into action, the Serbs move very quickly to inject their main force units into Kosovo. Within a matter of twenty-four hours, seven Serbian divisions have rushed across the breadth of Kosovo to occupy all of the major cities. By the time the NATO military council finalizes orders to launch a counter-offensive, the Serbian high command begins to establish an intricate and redundant communications network that links together all of the major headquarters within the newly conquered territory. Air defenses in the form of autonomous, small firing units scatter quickly across northern Kosovo, seeking to find secure firing sites within a few kilometers of major headquarters and munitions storage sites. The few aircraft remaining to the practically defunct Serbian Air Force create a diversion by flying sorties provocatively against the Hungarian, Montenegrin, Albanian, and Bulgarian borders. Shielded from the prying eyes of Western media, the Serbian Army begins to spread out and break apart into small platoon-size units, each with the mission of "pacifying" a specified segment of Kosovo territory. The citizens of Belgrade are prepared for the aerial onslaught that they know will be unleashed against them once NATO regains its balance and gathers the will and focuses the strength to respond.

The intervention to preempt the Serbs from overwhelming Kosovo begins with a public address by the NATO commander to announce that a combined air and ground campaign began just after nightfall on March 27. Using live video from the scene, reinforced with numerous topographical charts and statistical graphs, the general takes his time to explain in great detail when and how the attacks will progress. Television images of fighter and transport aircraft taking off from bases surrounding the Balkans fill the screens of viewers in Europe and the United States.

The immediate effect of the NATO announcements is to halt the horrific persecution of the Albanian Kosovars by the Serbs. The need to seek cover and disperse away from urban centers suddenly takes precedence over the eviction, herding, and slaughter of innocent civilians. The Serbian political elite and the Serbian Army react to the NATO assault with the fury of a state prepared to fight tenaciously. The skies fill with bright red and green tracers from light, medium, and heavy anti-aircraft guns and the bright arcs of surface-to-air missiles are capped with the unmistakably vivid and fiery patterns of aircraft caught in the missiles' deadly, explosive grasp.

With the dawn, however, both the Serbs and the reporters and camera crews of the world news media discover that the aerial onslaught was in fact an enormously complex strategic hoax. Not a single manned aircraft violated Serbian airspace. Instead, thousands of unmanned aerial vehicles launched from land, air, and sea platforms streaked across Serbian territory, destroying fixed missile sites and knocking out power in the entire country. Serbian soldiers manning air defense sites had frantically fired off thousands of missiles, some of which struck lumbering unmanned aircraft that appeared on Serbian radar screens as transports filled with American troops and equipment. U.S. strategic sensors take in all of this. Satellites in geosynchronous orbit as well as ground stations and aerial collection platforms flying continually around the periphery of Serbian territory meticulously scoop up, catalog, and collate volumes of information as the NATO deception operation succeeds in lighting up and revealing the locations of most of the Serbian anti-aircraft and some of the most sensitive Serbian command and control sites. Special operations teams—some disguised in "plain sight" within cities, others hidden along the slopes of the mountain chain that rings the southern perimeter of Kosovo—watch the Serbian "sound and light show" firsthand and carefully mark and confirm the data collected by electronic sources.

Once the Serbs realize the extent of the allied deception operation, they counter by initiating one of their own. Immediately, the high command orders the elaborate shell game of "hide the launchers" to begin. NATO special operations teams watch carefully as the roads fill with mobile radars and missile launchers. Each movement is carefully monitored as the teams work hurriedly to ascertain which of the newly created Serbian positions are real and which are fake.

The NATO command and the Serbs know the obvious: that the Serbian ground-based air defense network is the most critical center of gravity in the campaign. Should the allies succeed in opening aerial pathways into the Kosovo Plain, they will have succeeded in flanking the ring of encircling mountain ranges that for centuries has protected Kosovo from invasion by land. This time, with no public fanfare, the allied incursion into Kosovo begins just after dark on the next evening with the culminating fight for control of the aerial entry points into the Kosovo Plain.

A second wave of unmanned aerial vehicles flies into the dark, dispatched in a manner intended to appear to the Serbs to be exactly like the phony invasion of the previous evening. Fooled once already, the Serbs are more cautious now, and their reaction is measured and circumspect. Only a few new useful targets reveal themselves to the attention of the allied command. About midnight, the "real business" of precision strikes begins. Waves of cruise missiles, each targeted against a vital and protected fixed facility, continue to reduce the Serbian civilian and military infrastructure. Serbian radars go blank as the full effect of the allied electronic warfare campaign begins to become apparent.

Waves of manned fighter and bomber aircraft follow closely behind the electronic "whiteout" to launch precision weaponry from standoff positions well away from the deadly reach of enemy surface-to-air missiles. Air force and naval strike fighters concentrate the effort along the shoulders of the major mountain passes leading into Kosovo from Albania, Montenegro, Hungary, and Bulgaria. Special Forces "hunter-killer" teams begin methodically to order the dispatch of hundreds of precision missiles contained in the bellies of huge loitering unmanned air vehicles above them. Without warning, air defense radars and missiles carefully hidden in caves and farm buildings by the Serbs evaporate in showers of flaming metal. Special Forces direct-action teams inserted with the first attacking wave now join with their comrades engaged in long-term strategic surveillance to form dozens of strike teams with the mission of taking out every missile position, however small, sited along the periphery of the mountain passes. Moving cautiously and guided by sophisticated night vision and navigation devices, the teams approach just close enough to the target areas to determine which are still active and occupied. With the aid of positional designators, the teams methodically laze each critical launcher, gun, command center, and radar capable of causing the aerial invasion harm. One by one, the anti-aircraft positions along the course of four aerial routes into Kosovo no longer respond to calls from Serbian regional command centers.

Two days of direct action and focused air strikes against Serbian antiaircraft positions along the invasion corridors are needed before the allied command is convinced that the aerial highways are secure enough to sustain a ground presence in Kosovo. Some argue that more time is needed to fly additional strike sorties, but the NATO commander-in-chief demurs when intercepts begin to indicate that the Serbian high command is waking up to the allied plan. A third concentrated wave of unmanned vehicles both armed and unarmed now fans out over the Kosovo Plain. Some take position in leisure orbits high above the planned aerial flight routes. Others slam into the few remaining Serbian missile sites only recently uncovered by electronic and direct reconnaissance. A final allied effort at deception begins with a wave of unmanned vehicles flying in geometrically precise formations and at low altitude to replicate the image of a fleet of invading transport aircraft and helicopters. Confusion among the Serbs intensifies as they discover that this new invading force is approaching the heart of Kosovo from seemingly every direction and in no discernible pattern. Each sacrificial drone gives off an electronic signal precisely matched to the radar and electronic profiles of allied transport aircraft.

By now, the enemy response to each succeeding wave of unmanned assault and electronic deception is becoming increasingly tepid and more cautious. And thanks to the global media, the NATO allies are discovering that the Serbs are becoming increasingly more difficult to fool. After a few days of well-publicized outrage over efforts to exploit them as unwitting co-conspirators in NATO's deception campaign, the media recover quickly and begin diligently to fill in the strategic missing pieces for the Serbs by transmitting images of the conflict directly from the battle zone.

From their intelligence sources, the enemy immediately concludes what the allies already know: Once the air bridges are secure, the NATO allies will quickly be able to occupy Kosovo and put the strategic cork in the bottle by blocking routes of retreat back into Serbia. While the allies' strategic intent is now clear to the Serbian high command, their operational method for executing their strategy is only just coming into focus. One thing is certain: So far, the allied operation is adhering closely to U.S. military doctrine. The allies are methodically clearing away all anti-aircraft positions along a series of routes—each generally following existing mountain passes into Serbian territory. With the stakes so high, the ensuing battle for control of the aerial corridors is fought ferociously in plain sight—with the Serbs uncharacteristically willing to risk massing in daylight to move men and materiel into the corridors. The price of the Serbian sacrifices is extraordinarily high. In an effort to mass, the Serbs momentarily discard their trump card, the ability to hide from the prying aerial eyes of the allies. The Serbian rush to close the corridors creates a new and very lucrative hunting ground for allied air strikes. Roads formally devoid of traffic are now thick with towed anti-aircraft guns and missile-carrying vehicles rushing to reinforce the air defenses along the corridors. Tactical fighters flying high and attack helicopters flying low and in mass succeed in creating a twenty-first century version of the "highway of death." Within only a few hours, most of the sophisticated Serbian anti-aircraft guns, missiles, and radars are destroyed from the air.

Realizing that they can no longer close the corridors, the Serbs attempt to put into place a tactic reminiscent of the age of guerilla warfare. They begin to replace the destroyed missile and gun batteries along the air corridors with less sophisticated machine guns and the few remaining shoulder-fired, anti-aircraft weapons still in working order. The object now is not to close down the corridors so much as to create aerial ambush points from which they hope to down a few of the vulnerable transports. But the price for the Serbs is the nearly total destruction of their once impenetrable low-level air defense system.

On the third day of the campaign, as the battle of the corridors rages, the allies begin the actual aerial incursions into Serbian territory. The armada consists of hundreds of C-130 transports from the U.S. Air Force, two squadrons of U.S. Marine V-22 Osprey vertical-lift aircraft dispatched from amphibious ships cruising in the Adriatic Sea, and several dozen medium-lift, long-range helicopters lifting off from Albanian and Macedonian bases near the battle area. Still wary of Serbian air defense ambushes, the U.S. commander dispatches only special operations aircraft and flight crews on the first wave into Kosovo. Superbly trained crewmen flying aircraft specially equipped for low-level solo navigation are able to approach the objective areas along hundreds of random paths and appear suddenly and in mass over the objective areas. The special operations command chooses the most unlikely routes—some passing directly over Serbian cities, others sweeping high over the highest mountain ranges surrounding Kosovo. The result is total surprise with no loss of aircraft.

The mission of the special operations phase of the Kosovo intervention is to create confusion inside the enemy's operational area by destroying his ground command and control links, seizing and securing as many C-130–capable landing sites as possible, and continuing to infiltrate direct-action teams into the flanks of the aerial corridors with the intention of making these safely traversable. Three battalions of U.S. Rangers drop out of the night sky by parachute and quickly capture stretches of road and unused airstrips near the cities of Podujevo, Stimlje, and Decani—all strategically located in the central plain of Kosovo astride the main road and rail links connecting Kosovo with Serbia. Though primitive, each of these landing areas has been determined by previous reconnaissance to be capable of receiving the first C-130s soon to land burdened with the weight of armored vehicles and other heavy equipment.

The most difficult and dangerous seizure mission of the ground campaign is the assault against the international airport on the outskirts of Pristina, the Kosovo capital. Pristina airport has to be captured if the allied aerial buildup is to be sustained over time. The Serbs are of course fully aware of the importance of the airport, and the defenses there, particularly the ground defenses, are substantial. Nevertheless, the overwhelming firepower assault brought down on the airfield by U.S. Special Forces hunter-killer teams calling in precision strikes from loitering UAVs keeps Ranger casualties low.

While the fight for Pristina airport rages, U.S. Marine reconnaissance elements take advantage of the superb vertical landing capabilities of their Ospreys to seize a series of unoccupied low-lying areas in the vicinity of the southern cities of Suva Reka and Prizren. Special operations direct-action teams emerge from hiding to locate and cut or destroy fiber-optic and satellite-transmission stations linking Kosovo to the high command in

Belgrade. The NATO allied command is sensitive to the presence of any extant Serbian surface-to-surface ballistic or cruise missile sites. A considerable proportion of the available direct-action teams, to include U.S. Delta and SEAL counter-terrorism task forces, are dispatched deep into Serbian territory to find and destroy any weapon or delivery system even suspected of causing serious harm outside Serbian territory.

The success of the allied campaign depends on the bloodless insertion of one British and four U.S. brigade battle groups as well as a single U.S. Marine brigade amphibious force. The tactical mission of each battle group is to establish an initial security zone by aerial assault and then to expand the area quickly outward to secure the terminus of the brigade's aerial lifeline. Once the air bridge closes, the brigades will maneuver aggressively to surround and cut off Serbian ground forces across an ever-increasing expanse of Kosovo territory. Since the Serbian army has gone to ground and dispersed to avoid destruction from allied precision assault, the allies, despite all their sophisticated aerial and ground sensors, are finding it difficult to locate each enemy ground element exactly. By the third day of the campaign, ground reconnaissance has become reliable and pervasive enough to find virtually any enemy formation that might foolishly seek to move or mass. The allied picture from firsthand sources is sufficiently clear to find and track generally where the enemy is concentrated in groups of about platoon size, which is about as large an aggregation as the enemy is willing to risk at this point in the campaign. More important, the NATO allied command knows the location of operationally significant empty spaces that may be suitable as initial landing points for the air-delivered battle groups.

Enough transport is available to lift all of the battle groups' assault elements simultaneously. Enough airstrips have been identified to accommodate the mass of assaulting elements without risking serious interruption due to congestion or delay during unloading and turnaround. The main body, consisting of the first group of each battle group's fighting vehicles, is sequenced to land an hour behind the U.S. Rangers and other Special Forces elements. The schedule is intentionally tight to allow the more vulnerable battle group echelons to exploit the confusion wrought by their special operations comrades. In sum, the first assault is intended to insert air-landed forces into more than twenty landing sites scattered from the Serbian to the Albanian border.

Despite the wealth of navigation aids, radars, and beacons available to them, the less skillful transport pilots have difficulty finding some of the more remote and difficult landing areas—particularly those hastily laid out along roads and open fields. Consequently, by daylight, only four of the six battle elements are securely in place and ready to receive large volumes of traffic. But by then the skies around Pristina are sufficiently safe from Serbian anti-aircraft to allow the first sorties of C-17 airlifters to arrive. Each carries a single forty-ton multiple-launch rocket system capable of ranging the entire expanse of Kosovo from positions near the airport. Later in the day, C-17s begin to arrive with a few Apache and Comanche attack helicopters on board. Not all the attack helicopters are flown into Kosovo. Limited space on the ground and limited lift for fuel and other necessities for these fuel-voracious "war birds" makes their presence inside the brigade control zone a luxury. But each brigade commander fears the consequences of isolation should the notoriously fickle Balkan weather close down aerial routes over the mountains, and a few of these long-ranging "birds" will be essential if the brigade is to extend its reach well beyond the security zone.

By the end of the first day of ground combat, a steady stream of C-130s continues to disgorge light-armored fighting vehicles throughout each of the six brigade security zones. While flying toward the target, the vehicle crewmen stay in immediate contact with their commanders, receiving continuous tactical updates through video linkages piped directly from the turrets of their comrades' vehicles already in action. From inside the aircraft, each vehicle commander follows the action and listens to the planning sequence, so that immediately upon landing he needs to do nothing more than disconnect from his aerial transport and roar away in the direction of his first assault position. Like spokes spreading outward from the hub of a wheel, pairs of fighting vehicles extend the perimeter of the security zone until sensors aboard the vehicles collectively can see and command all of the territory previously assessed to be devoid of enemy troops.

As soon as the troop commander arrives on the scene, his first order of business is to expand the vision of the troop into unknown enemy terrain by gaining the information advantage throughout the control zone. From the confines of his command vehicle, the young troop commander logs on to his real-time information net and begins to form an increasingly clear image of the territory outside the immediate confines of his security perimeter.

On the troop commander's signal, a pair of small, unmanned, aerial vehicles lifts off from the turrets of two vehicles and speeds away to orbit over sites most likely to contain a hidden enemy. The commander punches in his "distribute" button on the downlink to the drones so that he can share images with soldiers mounted in vehicles closest to the suspicious area. At a range of about five kilometers from his most distant vehicle, the commander is alerted by the infrared and millimeter-wave sensors aboard the drone to a series of randomly dispersed foxholes and fighting positions around a static Serbian tank carefully hidden in a barn and camouflaged to resemble a farm tractor. Nearby, the troop's sensors spot what appears to be a two-gun mortar section, and, most sinister of all, a light anti-aircraft gun equipped with what appears to be a small radar dish. Considering the tank not to be an immediate threat, another troop member, the commander of a fighting vehicle nearest the enemy, touches his screen to designate the exact location of each individual target.

The rest of the response is automatic. Fire-support computers at brigade receive the target data and immediately select the most suitable weapons to destroy the enemy mortars and anti-aircraft gun. A group of metal boxes (each about the size of a kitchen wastebasket) laid haphazardly beside the landing strip suddenly comes to life as lights sitting atop them begin to blink rhythmically. Seven lids suddenly spring open and, with a muted rush, seven small silver rockets rush vertically upward into the atmosphere. A minute later, the trooper locks on the targets through his uplink to the missile's television camera and watches as seven images of the target crowd his screen and grow rapidly larger and larger and then turn ominously to static as the deadly missiles slam unerringly into seven individual targets. As the images go blank, the trooper switches back to the drone's image in time to witness the carnage emerge from the fading smoke and dust of the explosions.

Sensing the beginnings of a really bad day, the enemy tank suddenly coughs to life and the American trooper watches on his screen as the color of the machine turns from dull gray to bright silver, indicating that the heat of the enemy tank's engine is increasing. Like some prehistoric beast suddenly awakened and brought to life by the unexpected appearance of a predator, the tank crashes through the wall of the barn and claws an embankment in a frantic attempt to reach the road to Podujevo and safety. Intent now upon his tracking, the trooper turns the selector of his main gun to "indirect." The onboard sensors continually feed direction and velocity data into the computer. The trooper realizes the importance of keeping the enemy tank inside the range of his sensor's vision, since the range to target is long, almost ten kilometers. Once all his lights turn green, the main gun on his vehicle fires, and the precision-guided projectile disappears into the dark. Quickly, the trooper turns back to the aerial feed from the drone. He sees in his screen that the Serbian tank glows an iridescent white just a few seconds before the color turns to bright red as the trooper's round finds its target.

In the heat of the action, the troop commander is comforted by his realization that the engagement unfolding around him tracks very closely with live-action battles that he and his troopers fought repeatedly in the brigade's simulation facility. The simulated enemy was far more of a challenge than this one—at least so far. Also comforting is the realization that all of the assumptions made in planning for this engagement are being confirmed with remarkable fidelity. As advertised in the simulation, the road to Podujevo is the decisive point within the brigade control zone and must be first priority for the attention of his troop. His sensors tell him that while enemy forces are positioned on both sides of the road, a connecting route along an undefended path is open for exploitation. His computer tells him that the route along the path is for the moment out of the enemy's observation. Quickly, he designates two pairs of fighting vehicles to move along the path, keeping all sensors active. He activates another drone and dispatches it to a position overhead for added protection. Within a few moments, all four machines arrive in over watch positions from which they can observe a stretch of twenty kilometers or more with on-board sensors. They now command the route all the way to the border with remote sensors and long-range, on-board precision weapons. As an added precaution, the platoon commander in charge of the vehicles dispatches two motorized robotic sensors to cover approaches north and south of the road. The troop commander informs brigade of his actions and gains permission to dedicate more brigade sensors to cover the route. As a bonus, he receives first priority for use of the big rockets and attack helicopters. The length of the road to Podujevo is firmly under allied control. The first cork in the bottle is firmly in place, and it called for only four fighting vehicles.

From the point of view of the soldiers responsible for securing the cork, the surrounding area seems strangely empty and menacingly surreal. While secure in the knowledge that nothing can approach them, the soldiers mounted aboard these isolated fighting vehicles must be able to fight an enemy they can see only vicariously, through instruments. They must be able to fight as a team with teammates whose closest approximation to physical contact may be nothing more than icons on a computer screen.

A platoon leader's challenge in circumstances such as these is both physical and intellectual. He must possess the indirect leadership skills to allay the trepidations of men who are even more remote from their leader than from each other. Likewise, he must possess the intuition and ability to visualize and anticipate the course of the battle and order movement across the length of a battlefield visible only as an abstraction. His challenge is to fight aggressively, to anticipate the enemy's actions, and to counter the enemy with great agility and speed without becoming decisively engaged in a direct firefight that would risk unnecessary losses among his lightly protected troops.

By the end of the second day of ground combat, the allied command has wrapped all of Kosovo and most of Serbia in layers of multiple and overlapping ground and air sensors. The presence of ground reconnaissance, dispersed throughout all brigade control zones, effectively eliminates any chance that the enemy will be able to deceive the allied forces. Eyes on the ground, supplemented by layers of aerial sensors, literally prevent the enemy within the control zones from massing at any level. Within a few minutes of touchdown, combat vehicles emerge from their carriers and immediately rush across secure terrain to the outskirts of the security zone and eventually deeper into the control zone to ferret out and destroy enemy forces now so dispersed and beaten down by unrelenting precision fires that they have begun to lose the will to fight. The march to an allied victory is accelerated, thanks to a rather inept, frustrated, and overzealous Serbian commander who, seeing his unit slowly disintegrate around him, foolishly orders his few remaining elements to mass within the protection of the city of Suva Reka. He intends to make a dash for the Montenegrin border, where safety might be found. Caught road-bound on the outskirts and within the narrow confines of the city's streets, the armored formations are mercilessly picked apart by manned and unmanned vehicles.

The Suva Reka incident proves to be the catalyst that sparks the Serbian high command to change its plan. They cannot miss the fact that the allies have established a pattern of sticking to the countryside—of refusing to venture into cities even if the cities are devoid of Serbian troops. Even Pristina contains only a token allied presence—mainly the cadres and advanced parties of civil affairs units and humanitarian relief liaison personnel. On the evening of the fifth day, the Serbian high command dispatches couriers with instructions for all units to abandon their heavy equipment and move in an orderly fashion, with fight still left in them, to occupy and defend to the death three so-called "citadels": Pristina, Prizren, and Srbica. Wounded soldiers, or those deemed by their commanders to be non-essential to the defense of these citadels, are instructed to attempt to escape to a bordering country. While on the way, they are instructed to cause as much confusion and destruction as possible in an effort to mask the movement of Serbian units into the citadels.

Perhaps the overconfidence derived from the totality of their success—or perhaps the distraction caused by the task of returning the Albanian Kosovar refugees to their homes—makes the allies miss the Serbian change of mission. Unmanned sensors and the operators who command them are watching for the movement of missile and tank units. An occasional sighting of Serbian soldiers roaming about the countryside is considered nothing more than one more piece of corroborating evidence to confirm the already formed perception that the Serbian Army has disintegrated.

In any event, as soon as it becomes evident that the Serbs have changed strategy, the NATO high command is obliged to change strategy in turn. The task is not an easy one. The media is beginning to highlight the plight of Serbian soldiers wandering pitifully toward sanctuary. International capitals, particularly those with Slav sympathies or with no stake in the conflict, are demanding an accommodation that might lead to negotiated settlement. Friends and sympathizers of the Serbs in Europe and in Asia lobby global opinion to accept the prospect that the conflict can be ended and the suffering stopped by allowing the Serbs to forfeit control of Kosovo in exchange for continuing keeping the Serbian elite in power.

The Serbian elite realizes that a successful defense of the citadels represents their last hope for continuing in power. They have known all along that casualties represent the ultimate weakness of the allied coalition. Perhaps they might salvage some success if they could lure allied ground forces into their cities, where the fight would be close, bloody, and even. Or perhaps they might simply seek to outwait the allies in the hope that impatience and growing global revulsion at the continuing violence and destruction and casualties on both sides might allow them to achieve at the peace table what they failed to achieve on the battlefield.

Common sense and a growing political resolve to end the conflict decisively on the part of the NATO allies win the day. The allied command tightens the noose around each citadel, but refuses to take the bait and challenge the Serbs in urban combat. The first order of business for the allies is to eliminate remnants of Serbian resistance in the countryside to enable the establishment of humanitarian relief centers with the help of the United Nations and other independent relief organizations. This strategy meets the desperate needs of the urban refugees. But the humanitarian effort also solidifies the image of the allies as peacemakers and substantially quells opposition to the continuance of the conflict from overseas capitals. The prospects of finding food, clothing, and shelter also serve to lure Albanian and Serbian citizens away from the urban enclaves, robbing Serbs in the citadels of helping hands and useful propaganda.

Allied patience allows for the arrival of heavier fighting materiel essential for finishing the conflict against an enemy determined to fight on at any cost. Light, air-transportable fighting vehicles might be best suited for winning wars of intervention, but close combat in cities might be better fought using old-fashioned, industrial-age implements of overwhelming firepower and heavily armored protection. The intervention phase of the conflict has bought the allies precious time to consolidate control of the countryside and to close the land and sea lines of communication in sufficient time to allow the delivery of mass and numbers in the form of heavily armored forces to the battlefield. If the enemy's will is not broken by preemption, the allies have no choice but to end the campaign by attacking the last remaining hard points with mass and concentrated killing effects. Time purchased during the intervention phase of the campaign was also spent prudently to open land communications with neighboring Hungary.

Within two weeks of the beginning of the land campaign, rail cars begin to disgorge battalions of Abrams tanks and Bradley Fighting Vehicles. Heavy conventional artillery ferried across the Atlantic from the United States arrives by fast sealift and immediately begins to shell known enemy locations within the citadels. Patiently and cautiously, the armored noose closes around the citadels. Soon, the last of the resupply routes to the outside are closed. The Serbian defenders, facing the prospects of a season spent alone and isolated, eventually convince their leaders that the military situation is both futile and hopeless. After less than a month of resistance, the last of the Serbian defenders surrenders. Without popular support at home, now an anathema in the global court of public opinion, and, most important, with the source of all power, their army, locked away in Kosovo and unable to protect them, the Serbian ruling elite are left with no alternative but complete and unconditional capitulation.

· 9 ·

Strengthening U.S. Land Forces
Ten Principles for the Future

$\mathcal{T}$he recent campaigns in Kosovo and Afghanistan provide the latest evidence to confirm that the American military has over time developed a unique method of fighting that suits its own geostrategic, political, and technological circumstances. U.S. success in Afghanistan in particular demonstrates that, with some creative modification, the American method can be successfully applied across a wide spectrum of conflicts ranging from combat with a significant military power to a campaign against a distant terrorist state. The American method is, in virtually every aspect, conceptually unique. No other military today has the technological expertise or the operational skill to duplicate it even in part.

The concepts behind this American style of war are influenced most by a commitment to trade firepower for manpower. Three technologies—stealth, precision, and information—have allowed the United States to perfect a system for delivering extremely effective killing power against a wide variety of enemies. The most efficient means for delivering this killing power is from manned and unmanned aerial vehicles. Success is most assured when the United States can control the variable of time. Americans fight long, attrition wars poorly and short, preemptive wars well.

From Korea to Afghanistan, U.S. strategic planners and operational commanders have learned from their mistakes how best to capitalize on the firepower advantage to shorten the duration and lower the casualty cost of success on the battlefield. For over thirty years, technological and doctrinal refinements of the American method of fighting limited wars have kept ahead of attempts by enemies to devise ways to defeat it. The task of transformation will be particularly demanding for land forces. This is because in the decades ahead, war on land will undergo far more complex and thorough changes than

141

war in the air or at sea. The open and uncluttered nature of the skies and the seas offers no sanctuary for smaller, technologically inferior air forces and navies. The overwhelming quantitative and qualitative superiority of the U.S. air and sea services will guarantee that they will not have to contend with serious opposition within their respective domains for several decades. For the future, the essential tasks for air and sea services will remain the same as in past limited wars: the delivery of materiel to sustain ground operations and the delivery of munitions to destroy ground targets within the battle area. Whether the target is Osama bin Laden's lair in Afghanistan, the Serbian Army headquarters in Belgrade, or a dispersed enemy ground force, the routine for striking a land target from benign air and ocean environments will be essentially the same regardless of the period, the nature, or the location of the conflict.

The infinite variations of the earth's surface create a form of friction unique to ground warfare. A smaller, technologically less sophisticated enemy can exploit folds of ground, thick foliage, and the complexities of man-made structures to ambush and slow a more modern and powerful opponent. Tenacity and the will to win are catalysts that amplify the advantages afforded by terrain. For these reasons, the course of land conflict, even with an overwhelming qualitative advantage, is always the most difficult to manage and its outcome too elusive to predict. If wars on land are to be won with certainty and at minimum cost in life, the differential in combat power between opposing forces must be made far greater for ground forces than for air or naval forces. In past limited wars, the relative disparities have been the reverse: U.S. air and naval forces have far outnumbered and outclassed their opponents, while land forces have fought on a much more level playing field—and suffered for it disproportionately in the price paid in death and suffering. The arithmetic, as shown earlier, is compelling: In recent wars, over four-fifths of American combat deaths have been suffered by infantrymen, who comprise less than 4 percent of the total force.

Therefore, it should be a matter of national priority to gather the resolve and the resources necessary to break with tradition and support the creation of a land force capable of fighting and winning a campaign against a serious competitor and winning it quickly at minimum casualty cost. This goal is achievable but, if a fully capable landpower force is to be available for serious war within a generation, reform must begin in earnest very soon.

The U.S. Army and the U.S. Marine Corps are far too complex to be transformed completely. A future land force commander will find much in a 2020 motor park, flight line, or training area to remind him of his days as a lieutenant. Transformations always seem to proceed with agonizing slowness because, as General DePuy discovered during the U.S. Army's last major transformation effort, the process cannot begin in earnest before the culture and attitudes among the officer corps have changed. Moreover, while the Army leadership may know what needs to be done in general, the "devil" is always in the programmatic details.

Set out here are ten "guidelines" for future land warfare. They offer to those who will make the key decisions in the years ahead a "short list" of what needs to be done conceptually if the U.S. Army and the U.S. Marine Corps are to address the three great challenges of ground warfare—time versus risk, maneuver versus firepower, ends versus means—and remain focused and on the right path to reform.

1. INCREASE THE SPEED OF OPERATIONAL FORCES AS A NATIONAL PRIORITY

If future wars are to be won at minimum cost, they must be won quickly. The strategic speed of an early arriving force is best achieved by lightening the force sufficiently to allow it to be projected principally by air.

A perceptive football coach shifts from a running to a passing offense when he realizes that every team in his conference has a very weak secondary. He knows how hard the task will be. He may have to break with a long-standing "three yards and a cloud of dust" tradition to create a faster and more agile team. To be successful, he will have to lighten and quicken all of his players—not just the running backs and receivers. The strategic challenges are similar for a landpower force that seeks to increase strategic speed by lifting its early arriving force into the third dimension. An aerial versus a ground attack demands that the velocity of the entire team, even those arriving by sea and ground, be accelerated in order to complement the quickened pace of the forces first to arrive. Doing otherwise risks creating a dangerous strategic deployment gap and increases the prospect of an operational pause in the tempo of the campaign that an aggressive enemy could exploit to his advantage. Thus the task of transforming the army from a running to a passing team involves lightening and trimming the entire player roster. There is an immutable relationship on the battlefield between mass and velocity. The latter increases as the former is reduced. Every soldier, shell, or gallon of fuel left behind or kept out of the area of operations incrementally increases the strategic velocity of the total force.

Experience in recent strategic wargames, as well as recent experience in Kosovo and Afghanistan, reinforces the lesson that no amount of strategic lifting power can substitute for the advantage of having forces present within or near the threatened theater of operations before the conflict begins. Effective forward presence can take many forms and does not necessarily demand that soldiers be stationed permanently in the region. Allies such as Great Britain and France, which have a history of long-standing relationships with many countries, often can act as strategic placeholders—particularly in regions on the periphery of the Eurasian landmass that are most likely to be of importance to the strategic interests of the United States. Regional states known to possess reliable, effective, and modern military forces can also be called upon to join a warfighting coalition in the early stages—to dissuade an aggressor, or to fight the opening campaign in order to buy time until U.S. reinforcements arrive to take up the burden.

The bulk of materiel needed within most theaters of war will in the future still consist principally of non-military items such as fuel, water, food, medical supplies, and construction materials. Strategic velocity can be accelerated enormously if these commodities can be purchased or supplied locally by the vendors of friendly nations or coalition partners. Although precision weapons will in the future lessen reliance on bulk munitions, a large proportion of the lifting weight needed by U.S. forces in a war of preemption can be saved by pre-positioning much of this bulk near the theater of war in secure and mobile sites, preferably at sea. Ships loaded with supplies and materiel can be kept close to the conflict yet safe from terrorists and missile strikes.

A direct relationship exists between strategic speed and electronic bandwidth available to an intervening force. The more securely and completely the fighting forces are connected to their support, the fewer support units will be needed to accompany the fighting forces into the operational area. With robust electronic connectivity between the United States and the combat zone, most non-combat units and functions can be left behind. Administration, finance, higher-order intelligence, logistics management, to name only a few such units, could remain securely in place as long as the information connection is sufficiently robust to guarantee that support functions maintain a virtual presence in the battle area.

In the Gulf War, anticipating high casualties from Saddam's chemical weapons, the U.S. command took far too much medical infrastructure into Saudi Arabia. Four hospitals, with more than 14,000 beds and 24,000 medical soldiers, comprised more than 5 percent of the total deployed force.[1] In future wars, the size of the medical "footprint" will decrease by at least an order of magnitude as modern medical science begins to influence how combat casualties are identified, processed, and treated. Fewer and more competent close-combat soldiers inside the combat area will ensure that psychological and physical casualties will be significantly lower. A wealth of airlift available inside the operational area will allow rapid evacuation of even the most seriously injured soldiers to first-rate hospitals—often within hours of being wounded. Medical technologies newly developed in the civilian sector will be available to treat emergency trauma cases. Operating facilities will be fitted aboard aircraft returning from the combat area, so that surgeons will be able to perform even the most sophisticated procedures while outbound from the battle zone. Modern tele-medicine technologies will allow medics, nurses, and doctors inside the battle area to perform major surgery and other complicated medical procedures under the direction of specialists seated in major medical facilities in the United States.

In the latter days of the Vietnam War, each enemy casualty came at a cost of over a thousand rounds of artillery. Thanks to the appearance of cheap precision, ground combat platforms will need only one round to kill each target. Precision munitions in the hands of maneuver and artillery units will reduce the size and bulk of early arriving forces by a factor of perhaps a hundred or more. Today, the weight of artillery and the equipment to transport and shoot it comprises approximately 60 percent of the total weight of a division. By 2020, that percentage will diminish to perhaps less than 20 percent.

In 2020, however, armies will still be reliant on fossil fuels for locomotion. The fuel efficiency of ground and aerial vehicles will therefore become a factor of considerable strategic importance, since the largest contributor to strategic drag on the future battlefield will shift from artillery ammunition to fuel. As future fighting vehicles begin to rely more on superior situational awareness for self-protection, the need for armored protection will diminish, and thus the weight, bulk, and need for fuel will diminish in proportion.

In the Gulf War, the U.S. Army transported many times the materiel it needed—in large measure because of the traditional American propensity to "worst-case" and "safe-side" every battlefield contingency. To some extent, the habit, while wasteful, is understandable. If an automobile plant runs out of fenders, the production line idles, and the company loses money. If a commander cuts a demand for ammunition too close in the interest of economy, soldiers die. Thus, in the machine-age era of total war, taking too much into battle was considered as much a virtue as a vice. But in information-age warfare, the time needed to deploy may well be a greater contributor to the accumulation of casualties than any potential scarcity of weapons or ammunition.

The surest way to guarantee the welfare of soldiers in future limited wars may well be to assume some risk in the amount of materiel taken into battle in order to reduce the time necessary to deploy. Industry has shown the value of "just-in-time" inventory control as a means of reducing stockpiles; by improving the ability to track demand and decrease the time needed to deliver materials to the shop floor, commercial enterprises are able to reduce cost and improve the quality of service. The same principles apply on the battlefield. A "just-in-time" system would greatly reduce the tonnage necessary to sustain the battle while ensuring that only what is needed is delivered just when it is needed. The key variable in the supply equation will be *trust*. Combat commanders charged with preserving the lives of their soldiers will be asked to trust that, in the heat of battle, some precious commodity will be there just when it is needed—a tall order, given the chaotic and unpredictable nature of battle.

Industrial research offers another possibility for decreasing mass to increase strategic speed. The reliability of aerial and ground vehicles has improved considerably thanks to the microchip and to the superior quality control now being built into the machines of war. Breakdowns are becoming a rarity, and modern diagnostic equipment often can anticipate a material failure before it occurs. Building greater reliability into future fighting vehicles will diminish the need for spare parts and maintenance units forward on the battlefield with the fighting forces. More reliable weapons can fight longer. Perhaps in the future a vehicle's operational cycle will outlast the physical stamina of its crew.

If the U.S. Army is able to undertake such initiatives to reduce mass in order to increase strategic speed, the tip of the operational spear will become a very lean and lethal instrument. An early arriving battle force projected from the United States, or perhaps from a neighboring theater, might consist solely of combat units optimized to deliver fire, maneuver, sense and track the enemy, and perform only the most essential support tasks inside the battle area.

But reducing mass resolves only a part of the challenge of balancing time and risk. Even a leaner and compact land force cannot be accelerated to the necessary strategic velocity unless the strategic lift capacity of the United States is increased substantially. The solution to fixing the deficit in strategic lift should not be limited to airlift alone. In all of the U.S. Army's most recent strategic wargames, the most efficient accelerator of an expeditionary force overseas proved to be fast sealift rather than airlift. In the near future, advances in hull design and ship propulsion technologies will offer the capability for a fast ship to move a battalion's worth of heavy equipment transcontinental distances at speeds well above forty knots—perhaps as high as sixty knots. Even assuming the more conservative speed, a single fast ship could put a lighter and leaner ground combat force ashore in less than half the time that it took to deliver a much less potent force during the early days of the Gulf War. Fast sealift has its drawbacks for delivering early arriving forces, however. No matter how rapid the transit, a fast ship will still have to disgorge its cargo across a beachhead, or through a vulnerable and perhaps primitive seaport. The cargo will then have to be trans shipped to ground transport to finish the journey to the battle area.

Most likely the urgency of the situation on the ground will demand that early-entry ground forces, certainly the operational maneuver component of the invading force, will have to arrive by air. As exemplified by the Afghanistan experience, such a force would most likely stage through an intermediate strategic sanctuary close enough to the battle area to be reached in one operational bound, yet far enough away to be safe from missile and terrorist attack. Success will depend on the ability of the intervening force to push combat power quickly through these intermediate jump off points. Any delay here caused by transit bottlenecks at airfields, or by a shortage of available lift, will serve to stretch out the deployment time, increase risk to soldiers in the close-combat area, and perhaps even threaten the success of the operation. Despite concern to the contrary, the campaign in Afghanistan offers considerable comfort to those who fret over the availability of access to intermediate staging bases to support access to the operational area by air. Even the most pessimistic U.S. Department of Defense policy maker or diplomat could not possibly have postulated a more difficult strategic set of circumstances to impede entry into a theater than that presented by Afghanistan. Yet competent diplomacy and the strength of American will served to convince some of the most unlikely strategic partners to grant the United States access to bases within striking distance of the enemy.

Even a lean and lethal early-entry force will not compensate completely for a shortage of strategic lift. During operations such as Just Cause, Desert Storm, Kosovo, and Afghanistan, the appetite for airlift was never satisfied. Simply stated, the United States will never "transition" to a new level of war unless its air fleet is increased dramatically over the next two decades. The Air Force is no more likely to favor the purchase of airlifters over fighters than the Army is to favor trucks over tanks. But the imperative for more airlift must go beyond service prerogatives. Airlift is a *national* requirement, not a service-specific one. The purchase of transport aircraft must become a serious national priority.

2. PROJECT AND MANEUVER LAND FORCES BY BRIGADES

Land forces will best be able to achieve the necessary balance between strategic speed and sustainable fighting power if all early arriving, close-combat forces are dispatched and fight as autonomous, self-contained brigades of about 5,000 soldiers each.

Every army in every age has been built around signature units of uniform size and composition. As a matter of principle, this base unit is generally considered to be the smallest operational formation possessing all the essential components of battle to make it capable of sustained combat without reinforcement. Over the centuries, the size and shape of the base unit has expanded or contracted in response to the dynamic tension that has always existed between the imperative to keep the unit small, agile, and quick, yet large and massive enough to withstand the stresses of sustained combat. For the Romans, the base unit was the legion of about 5,000 men; for Napoleon and the armies of the American Civil War, it was a corps of about 15,000 to 25,000 men. Machine-age armies in wars of this century formed around the division—varying in strength generally between 12,000 and 18,000 men. The division remains the basic building block of the U.S. Army today.

Experience in recent limited wars seems to support the conclusion that a *brigade* of some 5,000 soldiers rather than the division is the proper base operational unit for the U.S. Army in the future. In every limited war fought since the end of the Second World War, all maneuver forces have been dispatched into the theater by brigades. From Korea to Afghanistan (with the occasional exception of some major armored formations in Desert Storm), brigades of one sort or another—armored, infantry, aviation, and cavalry—have fought autonomously. In Korea and Vietnam, division operations, common in the early phases, soon gave way to combat controlled at a lower level; this was done to match the tactical mobility and agility of an enemy who fought a dispersed non-linear style of war at levels rarely above platoon level (about forty soldiers) and equipped with nothing more than what each soldier could carry on his back. Similarly, in Grenada, Panama, the Falklands, Bosnia, Lebanon, and Afghanistan—and in Chechnya, and for that matter in practically every serious conflict of the past half century—the basic element of maneuver has been the brigade or a brigade-like entity.

This trend toward a downward shift in the unit of basic maneuver among modern armies is due in part to the increase in the lethality and range of modern weapons. As the battlefield becomes more lethal and expanded, fewer soldiers are required to ensure dominance of a given piece of territory. A brigade today can command about twice the territory that a division did in the Second World War. Also, this new era of "expeditionary" warfare increases the requirement for Western armies to organize into lighter, more flexible, and more projectable entities. Experience in recent deployments clearly confirms that a "package" of about 5,000 soldiers is the optimum size for force projection. Anything less becomes unsustainable or leaves out important combat functions, and anything much larger becomes too cumbersome and inflexible for rapid projection. Brigades therefore are the most projectable entities. They also comprise the most efficient formation for tiered readiness—a scheme essential if the Army is to create a force optimized for rapid, no-notice deployments overseas. Brigades are both small enough to be placed in a continuous rotational cycle and sufficiently self-contained to project immediately—without the need for last-minute additions and augmentation that in the past have proven to be debilitating to unit readiness and cohesion. A self-contained force ready for deployment also lessens the temptation for last-minute structural tampering, or the impulse to dispatch command and control overhead to a theater at the expense of combat power. A rotational set of discrete, clearly defined, and properly prepared brigades that are designated and certified in advance for immediate deployment will allow the national leadership to know exactly what ground forces are available globally for dispatch in a time of crisis. Finally, the first rule of warfighting is always to organize as you intend to fight. As the preceding discussion has shown, the trend away from linear to non-linear warfare will continue to favor the shift to maneuver by brigades rather than by divisions.

The same forces of war that are compelling a shift from a division-based to a brigade-based army will have a similar influence on the composition and functions of echelons of command above the division level. As brigades begin to act more like divisions, divisions will act more like corps. Evidence of this phenomenon can be seen in recent deployments to Somalia, Haiti, Panama, Bosnia, and Kosovo. In these conflicts, division commanders and staffs spent most of their time not conducting battlefield operations, but interacting with other services, allies, non-governmental organizations, and U.S. diplomatic and political agencies.

The Afghanistan campaign also highlighted the trend toward command and control of large forces from a distance. As the quality of the battlefield picture available to higher-level commanders improves, and as the bandwidth to transmit that picture to distant places widens, the need to place operational- and strategic-level commanders and their staffs close to the fight will decrease in proportion. Some traditionalists decry this trend as harmful, suggesting that the presence of commanders at echelons above division is necessary to permit commanders to see, and be seen by the troops. The changing nature of war argues against this position. The campaign in Afghanistan anticipates a future when close-combat soldiers will be so widely distributed across a vast and thinly held battlefront that they will be lucky to be in direct contact with their platoon leaders—much less their corps or theater commanders. The operations conducted by Special Forces soldiers in Afghanistan reinforce the age-old tenet that, the fewer the echelons of command, the faster will the forces arrive, and the faster will decisions be made by commanders operating at the tip of the spear.

Because of these changing dynamics, the future function of the corps level of command is uncertain. In the unlikely circumstances of another major regional conflict such as Desert Storm, the corps would be the most likely level for the land-component commander and his staff to reside. As a theater matures and follow-on forces arrive to take up the task of consolidating the advantage gained through early entry, some form of long-term presence will be necessary to control Army and Marine forces on the ground. However, echelons of this size should be reserved for later entry. Certainly the transport of additional layers of command should not take precedence over the arrival of decisive combat power.

3. MANEUVER BY AIR AT THE OPERATIONAL AND TACTICAL LEVELS

Increasing the strategic speed of a force is of little value unless the momentum generated by global projection can be sustained by aerial maneuver at the operational and tactical levels as well.

The need to accelerate the velocity of maneuver at all levels of war becomes more important when an adaptive enemy begins to level the firepower playing field by acquiring his own precision weapons. Without the speed of maneuver to complement an advantage in firepower, the U.S. military runs the risk of forfeiting the time advantage and being forced into an attrition style of war that will inevitably play to the advantage of the enemy.

The surest means for commanding the time advantage is to create an operational and tactical maneuver force capable of approaching the enemy's centers of gravity indirectly. Such a force, maneuvering principally by air, would be able to bypass the enemy's concentrations of combat power and strike directly at his brain. The technology necessary to achieve these capabilities is expensive. Therefore, in most modern armies, the operational-maneuver component makes up only a small part of a total land force. The German mechanized operational-maneuver force that succeeded in collapsing the French Army in 1940 comprised less than 10 percent of the total strength of the Wehrmacht. German success in that campaign highlights the conclusion that, if employed with audacity and imagination, a relatively small operational "tip of the spear" will still be large enough to achieve dramatic and decisive effects.

Velocity differentials necessary to maintain the ability to maneuver on a battlefield dominated by firepower cannot be achieved, at least not at the operational level, without exploiting the third dimension. But with the exception of the recent campaign in Afghanistan, U.S. experience with aerial maneuver has been disappointing and, more often than not, tactically inconclusive. The problem is one of weight versus lifting capacity. The physics of the problem is fairly easy to explain. Modern aircraft such as the Air Force C-5 and the newer C-17 can lift most of the Army's tanks, infantry fighting vehicles, and artillery. But they cannot deliver these loads onto short, unimproved airstrips such as those of most of the areas where American soldiers are most likely to fight. Helicopters can land in virtually any terrain, but their upper limit (given today's rotor technology) is about ten tons—a weight capable of transporting, at best, only small, unarmored wheeled vehicles.

The lift versus weight gap can be closed only through the adoption of technologies that permit a substantial weight compromise for both air and ground maneuver vehicles. Tactical vehicles must be designed to be lighter while retaining all of the essential fighting characteristics of heavier, machine-age fighting vehicles. Aerial-lift vehicles must gain greater lifting capacity while retaining the ability to operate from short and austere airfields. Today, the practical limit for aircraft delivering cargo into primitive airfields is about twenty tons. Aircraft carrying anything heavier than twenty tons are too large and vulnerable to survive and function in a forward area. At present, only the venerable C-130 is capable of delivering twenty tons into a forward area such as the brigade security zone described in chapter seven. The success of the C-130 in performing this mission in the past gives hope that either a modernized, fixed-wing aircraft like the C-130, or a vertical-lift vehicle such as an enlarged version of the V-22 tilt rotor—or perhaps even a very large conventional helicopter, might be an ideal operational maneuver vehicle for early-entry ground forces in the future.

True aerial maneuver will not be possible until a ground fighting vehicle capable of extraordinary lethality, protection, and maneuverability, and packaged into a twenty-ton (or less) platform can be mated to a compatible vertical-lift machine. The most challenging technological problem in designing such a vehicle is to provide some measure of self-protection while remaining within the twenty-ton weight limit. Heavy steel or aluminum armor remains the only reliable means for protecting combat crews from direct enemy fire, and a great deal of armor is needed to protect vehicles from larger anti-tank weapons. Perhaps the only way to achieve the desired degree of self-protection for lightly armored vehicles will be to replace reliance on heavy armor with an indirect form of protection, achieved through superior situational awareness. If the enemy vehicle can be identified, tracked, and destroyed well outside the enemy's lethal range, then substantial self-protection from heavy armor might no longer be necessary. There is of course risk involved in substituting information for armor. To provide the necessary degree of assurance that no enemy can get too close or achieve surprise in the tactical fight, multiple, redundant, and overlapping levels and layers of information gathering will be required—beginning with on-board sensors and expanding outward and away to include an impenetrable protective shield of information enveloping the entire maneuver force.

Ground vehicles alone will never provide the tactical speed and agility necessary to adequately support the maneuver concepts inherent in this new style of war. The complexities and frictions inherent in moving across the earth's surface will never allow even the most sophisticated ground vehicle to gain much of a maneuver advantage over the most primitive enemy vehicle. Some part of the tactical force must be able to maneuver much faster in order to intercept an enemy ground force at a distance and surround and defeat it very quickly. Such a differential in tactical agility and speed can only be achieved by maneuvering through the air. Successful sweeps by formations of Apache helicopters against massed formations of retreating Iraqi armor as well as the dramatic success achieved by heli-borne raids by special operations forces in Afghanistan clearly reinforce the truism that significant advantage in velocity over the enemy offered by aerial maneuver can achieve decisive results. Attack helicopters today remain the surest means for destroying masses of hardened vehicles on the move. Experience in Afghanistan likewise demonstrated the value of attack helicopters for getting in close enough to the tactical fight to find even the most carefully concealed terrorists. The austere environment in Afghanistan also highlighted the truth that a voracious appetite for fuel, missiles, and maintenance will limit the number of attack helicopters that can be airlifted into the brigade security zone, particularly early in a preemptive operation.

While the tip of the operational spear should be transported into battle aboard Air Force and Army aircraft, the shaft of the maneuver spear should be constructed from more massive and pedestrian materials. Even in the most successful and overpowering preemptive campaign, the pace of battle often slows as the enemy runs out of maneuver room and tactical options and hunkers down to fight a last-ditch slugging match on terrain of his choosing. The advantage of information dominance diminishes considerably in tight tactical encounters, when fighting against an enemy collapses into hardened points of resistance. In such circumstances, old-fashioned firepower delivered in mass, and traditional armored protection in the form of heavily protected tanks and armored fighting vehicles and self-propelled artillery, become essential ingredients in the success of the close fight. But by this phase in a preemptive campaign, with the enemy in retreat and the countryside secure, a more deliberate pace of battle will be permitted and necessary if the battle is to be won at limited casualty cost. With the initiative on the side of the intervening force,

time will be available to bring heavier equipment into the theater by fast
sealift or perhaps by rail over land approaches.

4. ESTABLISH AN "UNBLINKING EYE"
OVER THE BATTLEFIELD

**Lighter and smaller early arriving forces can win against a more numerous
and heavier enemy only if they are protected by an "unblinking eye"—a
constant, reliable, ubiquitous, and overwhelmingly dominant sphere of information.**

Maneuver forces cannot hope to win quickly at minimum cost in life
unless soldiers on the ground are guaranteed absolute command of information. The terms "guaranteed" and "absolute" are important, because on a future battlefield, information dominance must compensate for what will be
forfeited in weight, mass, and numbers in order to achieve speed, agility, and
lethality. A land force of the future must possess the ability to protect itself
with a shield of information from the moment it touches the ground. Think
of this protective "info-sphere" as both an invisible barrier to blind the enemy and an "unblinking eye" that shifts, moves, and hovers over the formation to watch and track the enemy with great clarity, reliability, and precision. Experience in Kosovo and in Afghanistan has shown dramatically that,
to a great extent, today's technologies now permit air and naval forces to create a fairly impervious shield of information to protect them in their relatively uncluttered mediums of war. The complexities of *terra firma* make the
task far more challenging for maneuver forces.

An info-sphere that is robust, layered with redundant capabilities, and
reliable enough to accommodate the rich calculus of ground warfare will
require an enormous amount of bandwidth. Even the global Internet and
satellite communications of 2020 will not be sufficient to provide the connectivity necessary to construct the info-sphere. Therefore maneuver forces
in all probability will have to take their bandwidth with them into the battle area. Most of the maneuver unit's information systems and capabilities
will be self-contained. Reliability and security will be ensured by a robust,
layered system of sensors and communications that begin in space and descend down through the atmosphere to systems on the ground.

Dedicated tactical satellites in high earth orbit will tie the force to its
support base in the United States. High-altitude, long-endurance, unmanned
aerial vehicles (UAVs) flying in the stratosphere above the formation will provide continuous observation of the battle area and will be linked into the com-

mand centers of the battle force. Lower-flying tactical vehicles will be dispatched when needed to focus a spotlight on a particular segment of the battlefield whenever a contact with the enemy is imminent. A local Internet established on arrival over the battle force will tie together all of the information-gathering systems and link them to external sources of information, so that the commander and his staff get as clear a picture of the battle as possible in real time. Equally important, all soldiers mounted aboard fighting systems in the tactical constellation will have much the same access to the combat Internet as higher commanders. They will be able to witness decisions being made and will understand the "why" of the mission as well as the "how." Each soldier will also know exactly where each of his buddies is located and will be able to gain moral strength by participating in continuous "team chatter" as the battle heats up.

Each soldier in contact with the enemy will receive as complete a picture of the enemy as technology will allow. He or she probably will be able to exploit on-board sensors to identify enemy vehicles and dismounted soldiers in the immediate proximity, perhaps out to the limits of direct observation day or night and without regard to weather conditions. More distant vision and knowledge will become less distinct and less timely as sources become more distant and remote.

A word of caution: A determined enemy who understands the American style of war will see the American information advantage as both its greatest battlefield advantage and its most assailable weakness. If the enemy is able to collapse the combat Internet communications system through the use of clever tactics or ingenious homegrown technologies, the battlefield advantage will shift very quickly to his heavier and less sophisticated machine-age opponent. Too much reliance on and confidence in mechanical means of intelligence as sources of *knowledge* rather than *information* can have a similarly debilitating effect on the quality of battlefield decision making.

The ability to maintain an unblinking eye over the enemy is of course entirely dependent on the ability of the United States to maintain absolute dominance in information technology over all potential enemies in the decades ahead. But information dominance can by no means be guaranteed. In many ways, the benefits of the information revolution in the future may well favor enemies who are able to tailor new technologies to their particular style of war without becoming information-dependent. Future opponents, given their expectations and aims, will require much less information to strike effectively—particularly since their aim is not to win a decisive victory. Moreover, they will be less dependent on the microchip to conduct their method of warfare. A resourceful opponent will quickly realize that American intensive reliance on information-age technologies becomes a weakness that can become an asymmetric target.

Asian armies in particular are placing extraordinary emphasis on information operations and information warfare. Recent writers and some field commanders in China contend that Internet and wireless non-nodal communications will allow armies to continue to disperse yet retain the ability to mass rapidly. As information becomes more secure, and as information centers become more dispersed and less vulnerable, potential opponents will wield more flexible and agile land forces. Moreover, they will be able to divide their forces into smaller, and thus less detectable, increments. In perhaps one of the strangest potential ironies of the future, Western information technology may well provide non-Western armies solutions to two vexing problems. First, cellular technology and the Internet may allow them to maintain concerted action for long periods among widely dispersed units. Second, these same technologies will allow them to orchestrate the rapid massing of dispersed units when opportunities arise to "transition" to the offensive.

The result may well be a technological foot race that either side could win. As the United States develops the technologies to sense, track, and kill an enemy, potential opponents will develop the technologies to become more difficult to find. The prospect grows even more sobering when one considers the fact that the commercial sector is now providing future competitors with the tools they need as U.S. research centers continue to perfect non-nodal, distributed, and net-centric global information technologies for paying customers on a worldwide basis. Moreover, potential U.S. opponents do not have to spend a dime for the development of any of these systems.

5. PROLIFERATE PRECISION
AND DISTRIBUTE IT DOWNWARD

Maneuver forces must be provided with the tools to adequately support an offensive strategy dominated by precision firepower on a distributed battlefield. To do this, ground forces at the lowest tactical level must be given the same relative advantage in precision firepower as that possessed by the air services today.

Modern precision technologies permit air platforms to kill very deep targets with great precision by employing weapons launched from positions well away from the enemy's defenses. But unlike their aerial partners, ground soldiers lack their own means for applying precision killing power. Whether employing their own weapons or calling the fires from aerial platforms, soldiers must expose themselves to either designate the target with a laser or physically guide the missile to the target over direct sights. With a few exceptions, precision weapons cannot be fired easily from positions in close proximity to the enemy.

Close-combat soldiers still lack the ability to kill with precision at precisely the point on the battlefield where they are most exposed to enemy fire. Today, in a surreal twist of technological irony, a planner in the Pentagon can locate a target in Belgrade, Baghdad, or Kabul and dispatch a bomber to strike it with near-certainty of a direct hit. Yet a platoon leader still has no means at his disposal to take out a mortar killing his soldiers from over the next hill without exposing them to the dangers of a firefight at small-arms range.

At present, precision weapons are both precious and expensive, and most are optimized for destroying fixed structures such as buildings and bridges. An enemy who disperses and goes to ground may win simply because he will offer more targets than there are precision weapons to engage them. The development of very cheap yet precise projectiles fired from artillery, mortars, and rockets offers the best prospect for meeting the future challenge posed by a dispersed enemy ground force. Such fires must be delivered from well inside the brigade security area, since time of flight becomes a very important consideration when engaging fleeting tactical targets. Fires must also be capable of delivery immediately in front of friendly troops, so that an enemy will not be able to find relief from precision fires by hugging close in a firefight.

Precision munitions must be distributed in great profusion to every firing platform inside the brigade security zone. A maneuver soldier must have nearly instantaneous access to precision without having to go through the bureaucratic friction inherent in a stack of decision-making intermediaries. The often frustrating experience of Special Forces soldiers in Afghanistan with cumbersome, inaccurate, and unreliable targeting devices highlights the importance of developing more effective devices for locating targets and guiding projectiles. These devices must be small, cheap, and mobile enough to be placed in the hands of every close-combat soldier. The soldier's individual weapon should be used only as a means of last resort. The first choice in a close fight should be a precision weapon that is lethal to the enemy, but as simple and safe to employ as science can make it.

6. ADOPT AN OPERATIONAL MANEUVER DOCTRINE BASED ON FIREPOWER DOMINANCE AND AREA CONTROL

On a vastly more expanded and lethal battlefield, where maneuver supports fire, a force will succeed only if freed from the traditional constrictions of linear maneuver and direct control.

Until the end of the machine age, the relationship between the two primary variables of warfare, firepower and maneuver, remained essentially unchanged. The role of firepower was to support the movement of ground forces. The delivery of fires was a function subordinate to ground maneuver. Fires killed very few. The shock and paralyzing effects of explosive munitions were essential to freeze the enemy in place and incapacitate him long enough for maneuver forces to cross the deadly zone and close with and destroy the enemy with hand-held weapons such as rifles and machine guns. Weapons technology generally determined how difficult and costly the crossing would be. The more technology favored firepower over maneuver, the more costly the crossing. The simultaneous appearance and eventual dominance of information and precision technologies on the battlefield has effectively shattered the conventions of the past five centuries to such an extent that the relationship between firepower and maneuver has been reversed. Precision fires now kill with an efficiency at least two magnitudes greater than "dumb" machine-age munitions. Superior knowledge of the enemy gained through a dominant advantage in information technologies now permits close-combat soldiers to avoid being drawn within range of the enemy's most lethal weapons. The task of destroying the enemy now belongs to firepower, not maneuver, systems. Close-combat forces today perform the paralyzing function formerly reserved for firepower systems. Instead of closing with and destroying the enemy with fire and maneuver, close-combat soldiers will exploit superior maneuverability to first find and then fix the enemy long enough for precision to do the killing.

The actions of close-combat soldiers in Afghanistan demonstrate the power inherent in the reversal of roles between firepower and maneuver and serve as a model for how this function will be performed in the future. Small, discrete maneuver elements cautiously move in to just outside the lethal range of the enemy's weapons and begin the deadly and methodical process of directing precision fires. Each position, no matter how small, is carefully identified and taken out one at a time until the enemy's morale begins to slowly disintegrate under the precision onslaught. Even the bravest enemy soldier becomes terrified and gripped by a sensation of helplessness if he witnesses his comrades obliterated in a seemingly random and catastrophic series of very precise strikes. He cannot see his attacker. He only hears the occasional drone and chatter of aircraft overhead. He feels as if he were in a fish bowl as every attempt to move to a safer position is met with another deadly strike. Paralyzed and unable to attack or withdraw, he is left with no alternatives but surrender or death.

The same technologies that today give firepower extraordinary precision will in the future allow units to maneuver with an equal degree of precision. At the operational level, the challenge of delivering soldiers by air deep inside enemy territory without suffering serious losses will depend in large measure on the ability to anticipate where the enemy points of concentration are located and, equally important, where they are absent. Precision maneuver at the operational level pits the rapier against the mace. It substitutes speed, agility, and flexibility for weight, numbers, and mass. When enemy movements are tracked with precision, small maneuver units will be able to occupy discrete, out-of-the-way ground that is valuable not because of its dominating position, but only because it is momentarily devoid of enemy troops. These small units will be able to substitute a precise knowledge of the enemy for mass. They will be able to remain dispersed, yet they will retain the ability to take out larger enemy units by maneuvering just close enough to spot and engage the enemy just before the enemy can react in time to bring his own weapons to bear. A precise knowledge of everything around him gives the small-unit commander the confidence to anticipate the enemy's every action and to engage him, secure in the knowledge that every contact with the enemy will be an ambush and every firefight will be executed from positions of relative safety.

Since the days of the Romans, armies have fought and maneuvered in lines. A linear formation maximizes frontal firepower, whereas close alignment in lines allows leaders to maintain control and reduce the friction inherent in maneuvering across open ground. The perpendicular geometry of warfare is also linear. Even the most primitive armies must crowd soldiers together along road networks in order to approach the battlefield quickly and to sustain the battle once there. The growing pressure imposed on traditional forms of battle by the lethality of modern weaponry has steadily forced linear formations to open up, even while improved communications have made possible the orderly and disciplined maneuver of more open formations. Yet both the perpendicular and the parallel linear geometry of battle remained relatively unchanged until the hazards of the precision age and the opportunities of the information age conspired to stretch out and diffuse the geometry of war to the extent that linear warfare is fast becoming an anachronism. Both technology and the continued prevalence of limited wars will accelerate the evolution toward non-linear warfare into the future. As the Iraqis learned at the Battle of Khafji and along the "highway of death," convoys can no longer crowd vehicles together along roads close to the battle area without risking annihilation from precision strikes. Similarly, the need to escape destruction by fire has continually forced armies to disperse, making the battle area more diffuse and porous.

This trend toward dispersal has continued to the point where traditional linear constructs no longer are suitable for controlling ground maneuver. Wars of the future will be fought to capture and control expanses of territory rather than to approach and penetrate or envelop the lines of fighting formations. There will be no front or rear area, only an expanse that both sides will seek to control in order to isolate, fragment, and disintegrate the opposition. As armies break apart, decisive points—such as headquarters and logistical nodes—will disappear into the clutter. Critical points of ground, or "key terrain," will no longer be easily identified or easily assailed.

In past wars, the decisive advantage went to the side occupying the high ground. Command of observation ensured command of territory. Thus, from Little Round Top, to Monte Cassino, to Pork Chop Hill, the infantryman's bloody obligation has been to take the hill. But in the future, the side that controls the high ground of the atmosphere and space will no longer have to capture the terrestrial high ground. In a battle for area control, the side with the information advantage will be able to nest on almost any piece of ground. It will be able to exploit the open and porous nature of the battlefield to approach the enemy indirectly by occupying those empty spaces that offer a key advantage of position. A future battle force commander viewing his video display will see his force spread about the enemy's territory like a patterned blanket of small, discrete units, each moving with deliberation to isolate and destroy a similarly discrete enemy unit within its respective zone of control. A successful area-control maneuver cannot be accomplished without an exceptionally sophisticated command and control structure capable of maintaining cohesion and unity of effort among forces scattered across a huge mass of territory. A commander with such a capability will have the means to orchestrate the movement of many small units at once and in harmony until every corner of the enemy's area of operations comes under the direct control of the attacking force. With the intruder in his midst, the enemy can no longer exploit time to his advantage. The object of area control is not to destroy the enemy as much as to paralyze his movements, disintegrate the cohesion of his units, and collapse his will to resist.

7. SUPPLEMENT MANNED
WITH UNMANNED RECONNAISSANCE

Information- and precision-age technologies offer considerable promise as a means for producing unmanned aerial and ground vehicles capable of performing effectively as surrogates for manned tactical reconnaissance.

Finding the enemy traditionally has been the most dangerous and costly close-combat task for a maneuver unit to accomplish. In limited wars, fully 70 percent of all close-combat engagements were precipitated in an effort to find the enemy or to discern the outline or composition of his force. If a way could be found to find and fix the enemy at lower cost, then surely the overall casualty rate of U.S. forces would diminish considerably.

In the near future, unmanned aerial vehicles (UAVs) will be prolific and sensitive enough to give the lowest-level tactical commanders a clear and immediate view of their surroundings. Infrared and radar sensors mounted aboard low-flying drones will be able to spot individual soldiers—even those hidden in deep foliage. Direct control, robust bandwidth, and prolific distribution give virtually every soldier a bird's-eye view of what is in front of him. To see and track the enemy with the necessary degree of certainty and precision, aerial vehicles must be proliferated profusely at every level of command. On a future battlefield, the sky will virtually be thick with layers of drones ranging from those loitering just above the treetops to some cruising on the edge of space.

Perhaps within a decade, developments in artificial intelligence technologies will allow tactical commanders to deploy remote, mobile, ground sensors in the form of wheel- or track-driven "robots" to precede the scouts as they move closer to the enemy. Robots might well be capable of verifying the exact location of an enemy ground force. These robots might even possess the ability to engage the enemy with on-board weapons. As in the case of manned systems, however, the complexities of the ground versus the aerial dimension will not allow sensor technologies to be as effective from the ground as from the air.

Given the enemy's penchant and skill at deception on his own turf, no commander will be able to rely exclusively on "remote eyes" to find and fix the enemy with the certainty necessary to allow his troops to close to within lethal range of the enemy's weapons. But armed with the refined knowledge of his surrogate eyes, the commander will be able to send his mounted ground scouts closer to the enemy with greater assurance and confidence that they will be relatively safe from surprise. The scout's mission will be substantially complete once the enemy force is found and fixed in place. Taking care to stay well away from the enemy's direct-fire weapons, the scouts will begin to bring down remote precision fires on the enemy elements that they can observe both directly with their eyes and indirectly by using sensors.

8. MANEUVER WITH ALL ARMS AT THE LOWEST PRACTICAL LEVEL

To fight on a dispersed battlefield, all of the essential ingredients of fighting power—including the ability to see, sense, move, shoot, and

communicate—must be delegated to the lowest level of command (most likely the company) consistent with the ability to fight autonomously for the duration of the tactical battle.

The tactical level at which maneuver units will have to operate autonomously will continue to shift lower as the battlefield expands and empties. Eventually, this process of tactical division will reach a point of diminishing returns, where the need to disperse is balanced by an equally compelling need to maintain robustness and redundancy of capabilities as well as cohesiveness within the unit.

Given the probable course of improvements in materiel and communications technologies over the next two decades, it seems prudent to conclude that a small company of all arms—infantry, armor, artillery, engineers, and combat support—restricted to a strength of a hundred or less, is about the proper point of balance between "divisibility" (the smallest possible collection of any single arm capable of collective action) and sustainability (the smallest collection of all arms capable of prolonged combat without reinforcement). Such "all-arms" companies will be self-contained and capable of operating for limited periods autonomously, much as a maneuver battalion does today. With the right mix of precision weapons and situational awareness on hand, such a company should be able to control an expanse of territory of about a contemporary brigade with the lethality and mobility to mass against and destroy an enemy formation at least three times its size. The company's endurance will be determined largely by the conditions of battle, such as the nature of the terrain and the skill and tenacity of the enemy. With replacement crewing on hand for fighting vehicles, abundant precision weapons, and the ability to refuel on the battlefield, a company should reasonably be expected to remain effective in the field for at least two weeks—and perhaps more, if the tempo of operations remains moderate.

As maneuver units divide into smaller fighting increments, the arms that habitually support them will follow suit. Artillery support in the form of rockets, mortars, and cannon units will divide into firing units of about section size, perhaps no larger than pairs of systems for larger-caliber weapons. Such a degree of dispersal is necessary in order to be able to cover with firepower all the territory controlled by the maneuver force. In theory, the enormous ranges of today's precision weapons will allow supporting fires to be delivered from outside the immediate battle area. But too great a separation from the supporting to the supported units in combat takes away both the immediacy and the closeness of the system—characteristics that will be as important to success on a future battlefield as they are today.

The proportion of shooting to supply systems within a firepower unit will be reduced dramatically as precision projectiles replace the "dumb" munitions of today's artillery, rocket, and mortar systems. A firing section of two indirect firing systems armed with perhaps 500 precision projectiles will have the killing power of a contemporary artillery brigade. Armed with killing power as concentrated as this, a brigade battle force will be able to escalate its lethality geometrically without hindering its mobility. Support activities in strategic sanctuaries, protected by distance and a shield of ballistic defense, can be made as large and efficient as necessary to deliver essential support to combat units inside the battle area just in time and in precisely the right quantities. The few tactical logistical units still essential inside the brigade area will divide and scatter across the battlefield—both to provide the necessary support and to avoid becoming a target for the enemy's precision weapons. Once precision weapons have been distributed widely across the battlefield, the greatest challenge for forward logistics will be fuel. To extend his direct vision as far as possible into the enemy's territory, the battle-force commander will rely heavily on aerial vehicles, both manned and unmanned. Aircraft, particularly attack helicopters, demand enormous amounts of fuel, and nothing on the technological horizon promises to reduce this need. Until a land bridge can be extended into the battle area, a period of perhaps weeks, all fuel will have to be lifted in by air.

To add to the challenge, tactical logistics units will have to be smaller and at least as mobile and self-sufficient as the units they support. Fuel, water, spare parts, and ammunition will have to be maintained off the ground and ready for movement or distribution at a moment's notice. Medical support will be a particularly difficult challenge in a combat area where the nearest hospital is hundreds of miles away. To save soldiers' lives in combat so far from treatment facilities, doctors may have to be assigned down to company level and sent well forward into the close-combat zone. Modern medical treatment and monitoring technologies will help in the treatment of combat casualties. The medical condition of soldiers in combat will be monitored remotely—using devices attached to the body. Commanders will learn immediately when a soldier is in trouble and exactly where he is located. Miniaturized stabilization kits will be used to place wounded soldiers into a climate-controlled sterile cocoon with all the necessities for maintaining their vital functions for long periods.

9. ESTABLISH A "BAND OF BROTHERS" APPROACH TO SELECTION, TRAINING, AND READINESS

The surest way to reduce casualties among close-combat units is to place in harm's way only soldiers trained through a "band of brothers" approach—

those who, over a period of years, have worked collectively to achieve physical fitness, emotional maturity, technical competence, and confidence in their leaders.

Close combat may in the future become less deadly, but it will certainly remain enormously stressful and physically exhausting—particularly for those soldiers inside the battle area. Isolation, both from the outside world and from comrades, will require that soldiers be psychologically hardened. Leaders will have to make very critical and often very visible decisions alone—often without the personal collaboration and reinforcement of their immediate superiors. Every soldier must carry more than his load in an environment where the "bench" of experience will be only one soldier deep, and a single misstep by a soldier may jeopardize the entire battle. Finally, the challenge of ends versus means will require that all of the complex, demanding and dangerous tasks of the close-combat soldier be accomplished with a minimum loss of life.

The traditional machine-age methods for training, selecting, and educating the combat soldiers of today simply will not suffice to produce the exceptional level of personal and collective performance necessary for warfare under these conditions. In the future, every close-combat soldier must be selected with the same care and discrimination used today for special operations soldiers. Close-combat soldiers should pass stringent and objective evaluations for intelligence, flexibility, emotional balance, and physical strength. The process of bonding and coalescence should begin immediately after selection by grouping soldiers together into permanent close-combat platoons with the intent that they stay together for a period of several years. Peacetime training and acculturation should be patient and thorough; a year or more may be necessary to bond these units together and to teach them all they need to know about the complex task of close combat.

Combat leaders should be selected to perform at least at the psychological and physical levels of their subordinates—with the added requirement that they demonstrate the ability to lead indirectly, think independently, and act with initiative and courage. Assessments for these qualities must be made objectively and often. The leadership of the U.S. Army should not have to wait until an officer has had the opportunity to perform at the National Training Center to discover whether or not he has "the right stuff." This would not be fair either to the officer or to the soldiers he leads. At every level from lieutenant to colonel, close-combat officers should be given an opportunity to be assessed in an instrumented, live-fire, force-on-force engagement simulating as closely as possible the actual stresses of combat. Failure to make the grade at each level must not be construed as professional failure. The U.S. Army needs talented officers with a wide variety of skills. But the skill to lead in the heat of battle is a rare one, and only a very few possess it in abundance.

The Army must possess the ability and, most important, resolve to find those few and nurture, train, and educate them to perfection.

10. MOVE BEYOND JOINTNESS
TO TRUE INTERDEPENDENCE OF SERVICES

Combat functions such as operational maneuver and precision firepower—functions provided principally by one service yet vital to the warfighting effectiveness of another—must be removed from the constrictive rules of joint warfare and elevated to a new dimension of interdependent command and control.

An unexpected curiosity in the U.S. Army's most recent series of strategic wargames was the discovery that operational failure in many of the engagements occurred not as a result of enemy action, but because of slowness and lack of strategic flexibility within U.S. commands. On several occasions, forces designated as early arriving were in fact late because of bureaucratic, regulatory, or procedural frictions caused by the interventions of other regional commanders-in-chief or individual services. It was discovered that even "joint forces" were not at all joint when it came to the task of separating them from service-specific missions and integrating them effectively into true joint commands.

The issue of "jointness" is a complicated one, fraught with all the vitriol inherent in the prerogatives of the individual services. No single command or service can be completely "joint." At best, only a small portion of each service's capabilities needs to be subordinated to the collective will of a joint command. The principal mission of an Aegis cruiser is to defend the fleet from air and submarine attack. A bomber's task will most likely be to strike strategic targets. Neither system is optimized to participate very closely with the combined operations of the several other services—nor would it be the best use of these very specialized weapons to do so. However, recent experience with joint operations in Grenada, Desert Storm, and particularly (and most recently) in Afghanistan, suggests that some combat functions—such as fire support, communications, intelligence, and aerial lift—should, by their nature, habitually be associated with joint warfare. The success of a joint expedition might in fact depend on the ability to integrate these functions seamlessly into the campaign plan. But joint operations are, also by their nature, too linear and sequential, and they are characterized by methodical plans, delivery schedules, and broad arrows on a map. Strategic speed and operational acceleration of the magnitude described in the previous chapters can be achieved only by moving beyond joint and toward interdependent operations.

Interdependence implies the need for a level of interoperability between land, sea, and aerospace mediums that will allow a nearly simultaneous application of precision fires and maneuver applied in broad patterns of effects that strike and check the enemy everywhere he can be seen and engaged. Operational control of four specific combat functions deserves to be elevated from jointness to interdependence: operational fires, operational maneuver, intelligence, and command and control. Operational fires are those delivered against enemy ground forces from platforms outside the battle area. Experience in recent campaigns tells us that, as fires against enemy troops have become more precise, their delivery times have slowed to the extent that they are relatively ineffective against *moving* ground targets. Most of the slowness in delivery is caused by slow decision making. The full value of firepower systems will never be realized until a method for delivering them is devised that cuts out the many layers in decision making between the soldier on the ground who requests them and the platform at sea or in the air that delivers them. But there is hope. Perhaps no single event provides more reason for optimism that a degree of interdependence can be created on the battlefield than experience in Afghanistan with the delivery of precision fires by strategic platforms to support a tactical-level ground operation. That operation demonstrated that, given sufficient justification and pressure, it is possible to break down long-held barriers to interdependence of this sort very quickly and to achieve dramatic, decisive results.

In twentieth-century warfare, wheels and tracks gave operational maneuver formations the velocity advantage essential to strike deep and destroy an enemy's centers of gravity. Operational formations in this century will depend on aerial vehicles to achieve the same proportionate velocity advantage over enemy mechanized forces. In campaigns against dispersed enemies in distant theaters, Army forces must rely almost exclusively on Air Force aircraft to gain the operational advantage. A branch of the Air Force more accustomed to operating as a transcontinental air carrier rather than as a carrier for close-combat forces will require an exceptional degree of training and cultural readjustment to fulfill the demand of this complex and often dangerous mission adequately.

Shifting to yet another facet of interdependence versus jointness, if information is to be "the shield of battle," there must be as little friction as possible in the passing of orders and the collection and dissemination of intelligence. The technology to achieve near-perfect connectivity for these functions is with us today. Unfortunately, bureaucracy and functional stovepipes inherited from the Cold War inhibit the ability of today's joint commands to capitalize fully on the opportunities provided by U.S. telecommunications dominance. Problems experienced in Afghanistan with passing tactical information from national intelligence services to soldiers on the ground reinforce again the lesson that much of the authority to alter the priorities of intelligence from a strategic to a battlefield focus resides outside the immediate purview of the military services.

The Cold War is over. America dominates the air, sea, and space mediums. Only the ground will be seriously contested in a future limited war. Therefore it stands to reason that perfecting and safeguarding the maneuver soldier's info-sphere by focusing on the soldier's communications and intelligence needs should be the first order of business.

NOTE

1. Robert H. Scales Jr., *Certain Victory* (Washington, D.C.: Brassey's, 1994), p. 80.

• *10* •

A Cautionary Conclusion

*C*lausewitz's most significant contribution to an understanding of the immutable nature of war was the concept of "friction." He realized that "everything in war is very simple, but the simplest thing is very difficult. The difficulties accumulate and end by producing a kind of friction that is inconceivable unless one has experienced war."[1] Clausewitz thus warns us from the distant past that technology alone will never eliminate the fear, confusion, ambiguity, fog, and friction of battle.

In tomorrow's information-rich environment, U.S. military combat leaders will have considerable advantages over the military leaders of Clausewitz's time. Future combat leaders will certainly be able to see friendly and enemy forces with greater clarity. Nevertheless, they will still confront the problem of determining the enemy's intent. No technology will be able to determine intent until the battle begins, and even then, the enemy will deliberately conceal his designs. Commanders may be able to increase the quality and quantity of information available to them by more efficiently processing data into knowledge. But information is most certainly not wisdom. The challenge in combat has never been a lack of data about what is occurring or is about to occur on the battlefield. What matters most is what the data means.

The translation of information into knowledge has in fact represented an intractable and almost unsolvable problem that has not significantly improved over the past half-century. Masses of information tend to obscure what commanders need to know. In the spring and early summer of 1990, there were plenty of indications that Saddam Hussein was preparing to move against Kuwait. But since so few in the intelligence community understood the implications of Ba'thist ideology and Saddam's megalomaniac aims, virtually no one in Washington predicted what was going to happen *despite* the flow of information coming out of Baghdad and the Middle East.

A world in which friction dominates is a world in which more and more information tends to drown the users. Commanders tend to see what they want to see and the enemy figures out how to disrupt the system sufficiently to make its predictions unreliable. To be sure, technology will improve the quality and timeliness of intelligence over time. Sensors and observation devices, particularly as they become increasingly "internetted" together into a vast system of devices, will provide a symbiosis that will remove some friction, uncertainty, and ambiguity from the operational equation—or at least reduce the frictions of war to manageable and controllable proportions. Yet as technology serves to clarify the picture of the battlefield, the nature of the battlefield may well reduce the advantage of clarity. The changing battlefield will become a lonelier place. Those who fight in the future may well have even less psychological support from their comrades as the space between individual soldiers increases in order to lessen the killing effects of precision weapons. Danger and the corroding fear of violent death that grips every soldier in combat will always accompany acts of war.

Soldiers fear most the enemy they cannot see. Therefore, while total casualties may be fewer in the future, the psychological intimidation of dying suddenly and unexpectedly at the hands of some distant, invisible enemy may well heighten the anxiety and apprehension of facing death. Long, uninterrupted periods of fighting in particularly distant and primitive parts of the world will continue to be accompanied by sleep deprivation, fatigue, hunger, miserable conditions, and the sight of the dead and the wounded. Despite the best situational awareness, conditions such as these inevitably lead to mistakes in judgment, miscalculations, and reluctance to act.

If this terrifying environment will challenge soldiers, surely those who command them will face even greater psychological stress as they confront the prospects of making decisions on which the lives of tens, if not hundreds and thousands, of those in their charge depend. This drumbeat of psychic trauma will only be heightened by the presence of the public media—ever ready to amplify and distort the consequences of those decisions and then broadcast them to the world.

Not every future enemy will offer the gifts of ineptitude and lack of will. The United States may well face a *skilled* enemy who is convinced that he can win. Americans have a tendency to fight the opening battles of a campaign poorly—in part because they are at first reluctant to realize how much an enemy hates them or how proficient the enemy is in combat. Experience in recent limited wars teaches the lesson that an adaptive enemy with a will to win will find a way to surprise. Likewise, a campaign that lasts too long gives an adaptive enemy time to discover his opponent's weaknesses and to learn how best to minimize his own.

War will always be unpredictable; it is not an orderly phenomenon. More than any other human activity, it melds order and chaos into unpredictable variations so numerous that no machine can ever gather enough data to predict the course of combat once "the dogs of war" are set loose. Technology scarcely diminishes this unpredictability; in fact, in many ways it magnifies it. Before technology amplified the variations of war, battles were fought among like combatants armed very similarly and led by officers raised in the same cultural milieu. Since then, thanks to the foment induced into civilization by the information age, wars have become increasingly variegated in terms of the number and diverse types of contestants, their relationships with the polities for which they fight, and the organizational, technological, and social context of the encounters.

Consequently, in the decades ahead, the United States must be prepared to confront potential adversaries ranging from major competitors with the will and the means to fight a very destructive style of war to extranational organizations with access to many of the more primitive modern war making technologies but restrained by few of the political, territorial, or moral inhibitions of national governments. In such a future environment, strategic success will place a huge premium on military versatility. Even the United States cannot afford to maintain military capabilities uniquely tailored to every possible challenge that the nation may confront—nor is any single military instrument likely to prove suitable for dealing with all such challenges. Instead, U.S. military capabilities must be designed from the outset to facilitate rapid adaptation to accommodate the full range of strategic tasks and conditions with which they may be confronted.

All revolutions play out in evolutionary steps. Revolutionary change in the nature and character of war—like other forms of change in collective, complex behavior—follows patterns and cycles whose course can be traced and anticipated. Cycles of change in warfare, particularly revolutionary change, are particularly difficult to comprehend and even more difficult to anticipate because, unlike endeavors in finance, medicine, or law, active experience in war is, fortunately, infrequent. Soldiers must gather most of their empirical evidence vicariously—by observing the course of war through the laboratory of contemporary conflicts.

Thus the process of observation is much like viewing a kaleidoscope in which the scenes are sequential but appear to be only tangentially related in form and pattern. Fifty years of firsthand and vicarious experience offer just enough of the images we need to see patterns beginning to emerge. In this book, the experience with limited wars fought since the end of the Second

World War constitutes a body of evidence that points very clearly to the conclusion that, like all great powers in the past, the United States has evolved a method of fighting its wars that is distinctly its own. It is a method of war that accepts and accommodates into its scheme the imperative that the limited ends expected of its fighting forces must be balanced with a proportionate limit on the means expended to achieve those ends. Chief among these limitations is the expectation that national objectives will be met and success in combat achieved with a minimum loss of life.

Major wars in which the stakes are high and killing is involved will be of two varieties. The first will be wars of preemption similar in pattern to Grenada, the Falklands, Panama, Kosovo, and Afghanistan. These strategic takedowns will succeed when the enemy can be isolated and frozen in place long enough for the overwhelming power of the intervening force to arrive and secure the decision. The second will be wars of attrition, such as those in Korea, Vietnam, Lebanon, and Somalia. These conflicts will be far more difficult to conclude successfully, and success will depend on intangibles that the United States cannot control, such as geography, the collective will of the people, and the resolve and skill of the opposing army.

The one factor that will control the shape and character of a prospective conflict is *time*. Resolving the strategic time-risk challenge in favor of early intervention will be the essential ingredient to ensure that the intervening force will be able to fight and win quickly. Early arrival alone cannot guarantee that the time advantage will remain on the side of the intervening forces. Resolving the operational challenge of firepower versus maneuver—by finding the proper doctrinal and materiel mix between the ability to kill with precision and the ability to move about the battlefield with speed and agility— will allow a balanced air and ground force to take down an enemy by severing the connection between the brain and the sinews and muscles of his army.

As experience in Afghanistan illustrates, a *balance* between firepower and maneuver robs the enemy of the luxury of countering in only a single dimension. An enemy who, like the Taliban, arrays his forces to absorb a firepower assault makes his force vulnerable to systematic defeat in detail by maneuver. The converse, of course, is also true. Like the Iraqis at Khafji, a force that masses to facilitate maneuver makes itself vulnerable to massed effects of firepower. But in the American style of war, the two variables of firepower and maneuver are not equal. Firepower will dominate.

Once the enemy is isolated and the close battle is joined, the conflict will be up to the United States and its allies to win. The enemy's last-chance alternative to snatch victory from the jaws of defeat will be to make the cost of the tactical fight too high in human life. Resolving the ends-means challenge favorably demands that, once the shooting starts, the United States and allied armed forces keep casualties low. Fighting and winning at the least cost in life demands the exploitation of the advantage in precision and information to keep the close fight outside the effective radius of the enemy's most lethal weapons. Maneuver forces must change the way they fight to be able to exploit fully their overwhelming advantage in precision firepower. Neither superior precision nor information dominance will guarantee that a shooting war will be short and relatively painless unless the United States and its allies can get their forces to the theater of war quickly. Strategic or operational speed does not come cheap. But unless the U.S. military possesses the ability to move great distances swiftly, it will never be able to take away the enemy's inherent advantages of proximity, presence, and mass.

Practical experience in past limited wars teaches the painful lesson that even a preeminent power cannot expect to solve every international conflict successfully by applying military force. Not all wars are winnable. Even a great power must continue to choose its wars very carefully. The Duke of Wellington once observed that, to a great power, there is no such thing as a small war. Every time the United States ventures into foreign territory to advance its interests—with broad international approbation—the prospect will always be present that the effort will escalate into a serious shooting war. Every time the United States executes a campaign plan, the enemy gains invaluable experience and insights on how to win the next conflict. Thus, to preserve preeminence in world affairs, the United States must never expend military capacity needlessly nor allow the perception to grow that its will to fight and win will diminish with each occasional disappointment. Finally, because the course of human conflict is so difficult to predict or moderate once begun, the U.S. dispatch of military forces into an exploding region of the world for any purpose must be accompanied by the resolve to fight and win at a cost acceptable to the American people.

NOTE

1. Carl von Clausewitz, *On War*, edited and translated by Michael Howard and Peter Peret (Princeton: Princeton University Press, 1976), p. 119.

Index

About the Author

In 2000, **Dr. Robert Scales** was appointed president and CEO of Walden University after serving over thirty years in the Army, retiring as a Major General. He commanded two units in Vietnam, winning the Silver Star for action during the battles around Dong Ap Bia during the summer of 1969. Subsequently, he served in command and staff positions in the United States, Germany, and Korea and ended his military career as Commandant of the United States Army War College. He has written and lectured on future warfare to academic, government, military, and business groups in the United States, Australia, Asia, the Middle East, Europe, and South America. He is the author of several books including *Certain Victory*, the official account of the Army in the Gulf War; *Firepower in Limited War*, a history of the evolution of firepower doctrine since the end of the Korean War; and *Future Warfare*, a strategic anthology on America's wars to come. He is a graduate of West Point and earned his PhD in history from Duke University. He has appeared on many major media networks as an authority on military history and contemporary warfare.